The Crossover that Won the Game

Jamell Ponder and Joseph Ponder

Copyright © 2017 **Jamell Ponder and Joseph Ponder**
All rights reserved.

ISBN: 0990021513
ISBN 13: 9780990021513

Book 1

Prologue

Shay was born amidst chaos and conflict among those closest to him. His parents quarreled often, and the nature of the relationship eventually caused Shay's father to walk out of his life at a very young age. Shay longed for his dad to be in his life, but he found another source of happiness. Basketball was a way of escape for Shay. He found so much joy when playing basketball. However, he did struggle when one, sometimes two, of his nine siblings would tease him, thus causing him to have prolonged self-esteem issues. Shay lacked family support but even as a young child, he knew he needed a role model and continued support. Every day of his life, he missed his father, but he continued to look forward to the joy he discovered when engaging in sporting activities, basketball especially.

Shay was looking forward to the start of the school year. He surely did have a love for education. He was doing well in school, getting As and a couple of Bs. His only C was in math, the subject in which he struggled most. Shay continued working hard in school, but he was looking forward to his first day of basketball practice and working with the new coach. He lacked confidence, but the gym teacher, who was also the basketball coach, Mr. Crossover took an interest in Shay and encouraged him to try out for the team this year.

Here we go, Shay thought to himself as he walked into the gymnasium and took a seat on the Oakwood floor.

The Beginning

"All righty children, as you all know I am Coach Crossover and I coach the fifth and sixth graders. I coach at Confidence Elementary for so many great reasons," the coach said with pride in his voice and a sparkle in his eyes.

"Sir, why is this school called Confidence Elementary? And did your parents name you Crossover or did you give yourself that name?" Little Shay asked.

Coach smiled at these questions. He remembered how naive, brutally honest, and pure little children were. His mind took a trip down memory lane when he was playing freshman basketball at St. Caramel College. There were ten seconds left in the fourth quarter. It was the final game of the season and he himself was handling the ball. Yes, he had the opportunity to be the star of the school. He turned his back to his defender while handling the ball with his right hand. This was his opportunity. Certainly it could be his big moment. Many people were there to support him, but it was his dad he wanted to impress most of all.

Crossover spun quickly to the right and switched the ball to his left hand.

"Back up," he said to his opponent as his defender put his left forearm on the right side of Crossover's upper body.

While using his right hand to push his defender's forearm off his oblique, he heard his dad yelling from the bleachers, "Son, son...hey, son, do the famous CS we worked on."

Crossover created space between him and his defender as he quickly stepped back and slightly to his left, switching the ball to his strong hand, his right hand.

He smiled. He knew his dad abbreviated the word so no one would understand. Instantly, his defender lunged with his right leg and reached to steal the ball using his right hand. Crossover stared his defender straight in the eye, stepped outward to his right side, crouched slightly, and crossed the ball from his right hand to his le—

"Hey, Coach, are you going to answer me?" Shay asked, bringing Coach Crossover out of his daydream about his moment of fame.

Gee whiz, how he wished the kid would have waited before he interrupted his daydream.

"Yes, Crossover is really my last name. Well, just so you know, before any of my students depart from Confidence Elementary, they will all have a beautiful crossover that will destroy any defender. The school is called Confidence Elementary because we aim to help all of our children to have confidence in themselves. Not only while they are here, but long after they depart."

"Thanks, Coach Crossover," Little Shay said with excitement in his voice. He wants a nice crossover like the great Iverson.

"Now let's go, we have a lot of work to do," Coach Crossover said.

Over the next two months, Shay thought often about wanting to improve in basketball. Even before basketball came Shay's schoolwork. Shay kept his grades up. Shay's mom would not allow him to practice before all of his homework was complete. However, as soon as all of his homework was finished, Shay was back to pounding the pavement. Shay tried and tried and tried some more, but he had difficulty learning how to do a crossover. Shay was overly critical of himself and he frequently wished someone was there to encourage him.

Two Months Later

Coach Crossover kept a sharp eye on Shay during practices. He was short but quick as lightning and had a quick release on his jump shot. But for some reason, he just couldn't perfect the crossover move. Every time he attempted the crossover, someone seemed to strip the ball away from him. Shay would lower his eyes and hang his head downward, but Coach Crossover never let Shay be too hard on himself.

"Never give up, Shay. If you work hard enough, you will learn how to do a crossover very well," Coach Crossover would always say.

Game 1

Shay looked up into the bleachers and became nervous by the stream of incomers and observers.

"Confidence, confidence," Shay told himself.

"Shay, you're starting," the coach said.

"Ok-k-k-kay th-th-thanks, Coach Crossover," Shay said with a slight stutter, showing that he was nervous and truly afraid.

"Go out there and give it your best, Shay," Coach Crossover said.

"All right, team, put your hands in here, Confidence on 3. 1…2…3!"

"Confidence," the team yelled in unison.

The first three quarters went by so quickly. At least it felt that way to Shay. He played hard but couldn't shake the words his brothers, Jeremiah and

James, had spoken about him for so many years. Things like "You're nothing but a loser! You're best at quitting! You will always be a failure!"

The team struggled overall, but the score was still close. He kind of thought Coach Crossover believed in him, but he wasn't convinced.

Fourth Quarter of Game 1

"We're down 2. Rick, you will inbound. Shay, you have to take the three-pointer," Coach Crossover instructed during a timeout.

Looking around the flailing hands of the player guarding the inbound pass, Rick passed the ball to Shay at the three-point line. There were twenty-two seconds left on the clock. Confidence low, but no time to waste, Shay knew he had no choice but to try.

Ball in hand at the three-point line! The opponent trades stares between Shay's eyes and his waist! Shay faked as if he was going to move to the right! The opponent didn't flinch. The opponent was slowly inching closer. Shay did a pump fake with the ball, as if to trick his opponent into thinking he was going to shoot the ball. The opponent still didn't flinch. Instead, he moved forward, attempting to get body-to-body with Shay so he could steal the ball or cause him to shoot a shot that was almost impossible to make.

Now only twelve seconds remained.

What am I going to do now? Shay thought to himself.

"Whatever I am going to do, I must do it soon," Shay reasoned within himself.

Shay turned his back to his opponent. With the ball in his right hand, he dribbled. His opponent had his right elbow on Shay's back. Shay looked up in the bleachers at the older brother who always put him down.

I will show him, Shay thought to himself.

Shay quickly, and rather beautifully, spun to the right and smiled.

"He cannot guard me," Shay told himself, using positive self-talk.

Just as he went to switch the ball to his left hand, the opponent stripped the ball with his right hand, then moved quickly around Shay's body, grabbing the ball with his left hand.

"No!" the coach yelled as the opponent took the ball down the court, watching the buzzer as time ticked away.

6...5...4...3...2.

The opponent squared his feet, bringing both evenly under his shoulders.

1, the opponent released the ball.

0, the players from Confidence Elementary watched and waited, hoping he would miss. The players from the other team watched with great expectation. Wait no more!

The suspense for all players ended when the ball swished through net, making a snapping sound that crushed the hearts and spirits of the players from Confidence Elementary.

Little Shay listened to the uproar of screams and cheers coming from the opponents' bench and fans. As he buried his head in his hands, he sat on the bench and cried. The strong hand on his right shoulder did not faze him.

"Shay, it's okay. You played a great game. I think you got a little arrogant, but in life, there are always lessons to learn. Never get overconfident, but likewise, never stop believing in yourself. Now, wipe those tears from your eyes and cheeks and walk with me to the locker room. This is only the first game, we have a long road ahead of us," Coach Crossover said with a huge smile.

Shay held the words of Coach Crossover close to heart. Secretly, he wished that it was his dad encouraging him. Nonetheless, he carried Coach Crossover's words with him everywhere he went over the next month. Shay's confidence increased a little with each game and practice. When Shay felt like giving up, he remembered the words of Coach Crossover. For the first time in his life, Shay was learning to believe in himself. He remembered Coach Crossover saying, "Simply keep bettering yourself in every area of life because you never know when your big moment will come!"

Shay continued working hard in school and equally as hard on the court. He had no idea that his big moment would be approaching so soon, but he was sure of one thing: he had to believe in himself and never give up. Confidence Elementary won the games that mattered most and would be playing in the championship. Shay received a rush of adrenaline when he realized that he and Rick would meet again.

The Championship Game

The first three quarters and what little had been played of the fourth were hard for Confidence Elementary. Shay and the other players refused to give up, though. Shay had an opportunity to face the player that once embarrassed him. Rick looked just as fierce as he did before, but things were different now. Shay had a newfound confidence and sense of determination. He had waited for this moment. Coach Crossover noticed his team struggling late in the game and knew he had to do something...

Fourth Quarter of the Championship Game

"Timeout," Coach Crossover yelled, after the rebound that followed Chip's poor shot. "You're doing a great job, Chip, but don't rush, pal. I want you to drive to the hoop."

"No, Coach, I can't."

"Why not?" Coach asked.

"I twisted my ankle because I stepped on my opponent's foot while trying to drive past him. That is why I shot the bad shot. Sorry, Coach," Chip apologized.

Coach Crossover hadn't noticed Chip limping off the court because he was talking to the other players and conversing with the referee, sharing his frustration about there not being a foul called on the last play, as it appeared the opponent pushed Chip.

"There are no bad shots. You tried and that is what matters most. You made the decision that you thought was best in that moment. Chip, what counts right now is that you did what you thought was the best thing to do. Again, there are no bad shots. Some shots are not just good as others, but that is normal. Take a seat, Chip, and I will get you some ice and an Ace bandage for your ankle."

The Coach patted Chip on the back and smiled. "You did well, Chip. Don't you worry, we still have time to win this game," Coach Crossover said.

"Shay, it's all on you. You are the one. Everything happens for a reason. Chip is a great player, but he is hurt now. That makes you the chosen one for this moment. Stay confident, believe in yourself, because guess what?" Coach Crossover asked.

"What?" Shay replied.

"I believe in you," Coach Crossover uttered the words that meant so much to Shay.

Shay smiled, as all he wanted was someone to believe in him.

"I'm ready, Coach," Shay spoke with excitement and a reignited confidence.

The ball was passed to Shay. With his tongue sticking out like a young Michael Jordan, Shay dribbled the ball from left to right and right to left at varying speed.

There were eighteen seconds left in the fourth quarter.

"Off me," Shay said as his opponent grabbed his jersey and hand-checked him. Shay never flinched. He never looked at the ref to alert him that his opponent was playing defense illegally.

"You remember how I stripped you in the first game? I'll do it again," Shay's opponent said.

Shay looked his opponent directly in the eyes, scanned his body up, down, and side to side. He laughed. "I lacked confidence then. Not today, buddy," he said with that MJ confidence. Shay smiled as he told his opponent, "You won't be stripping me this time."

"Watch me," the opponent said.

Ball being dribbled from left to right, right to left, Shay watched the time clock. Shay turned his back to his opponent. 12…11…10…Shay spun… now facing his opponent again with a grin that communicated "I am confident and I do not fear you at all."

"Ready?" Shay questioned his opponent.

"I was born ready. Are you ready?" his opponent questioned.

9...ball switched from right to left.

8...Shay faked as if he was going to drive past his opponent. His opponent flinched.

7...

"Where you going?" Shay laughed as he asked the question.

6...ball dribbled twice quickly between both of Shay's legs.

5...ball switched from left to right hand.

His opponent made the biggest mistake of his career; he reached.

"CS now, CS now!" Coach Crossover yelled.

4...Shay flinched. His opponent reached.

3...Shay flinched again. His opponent reached. Now crossing the ball over to his left hand, his opponent reached and fell.

With two seconds remaining on the clock, Shay took off to the basket.

1...Shay laid the ball in the basket using the famous finger roll. As the clock went down to zero, the basketball went through the rim and net, causing the uproar of cheers from fans and teammates. Shay, the once-ridiculed kid who lacked confidence, made the winning shot.

"Yes!" the crowd yelled. "Good move, man! We loved that crossover," the crowd continued to praise.

Shay laughed and wore a smile no one would ever forget, as his teammates and Coach hugged him.

"Hey, Coach?"

"Yes, Shay?"

"Because of my teammates' and your belief, your confidence in me and my crossover, we won."

"No, Shay," Coach Crossover said. "Because of the perfection of your crossover, your ability to listen and learn..." Coach Crossover paused. This silence seemed to last forever, but Shay waited patiently. "Because of your confidence in you...we won!"

"Remember that no matter your obstacle or opponent, your success or failure is ultimately in your hands," Coach Crossover ended his conversation of encouragement.

The End

"Hey, hey…Shay," the coach from Wilson Middle School called out as he was very briskly walking over to Shay. Shay quickly turned around to find out who was calling him.

"Oh hey there, Mr. Scott, you wanted to talk to me?" Shay asked with great enthusiasm.

"I loved the crossover that won the game, and great job sinking that layup in the final seconds!"

Shay smiled. "Thanks, Mr. Scott."

"No, thank you for putting on such an awesome performance! You must play for my school next year, okay?"

Shay turned his head and looked at Coach Crossover, then back at Coach Scott, looked at Coach Crossover once more, and again at Coach Scott.

Staring right in Coach Scott's eyes, Shay replied, "Well…"

Seventh Grade

Swish! That was the sound the ball made as it fell through the net.

"Yes!" the crowd roared as Little Shay sunk the three-pointer with two seconds left in the fourth quarter.

"Boy, when did you start shooting threes?" a teammate asked.

Shay shrugged his shoulders, letting his hands fall to his sides like the great Michael Jordan and said, "Hey, I was feeling it, so I took the three."

"Shay, Shay, he's our man. If he can't make it, no one can!" the cheerleaders chanted.

Shay only smiled. "These cheerleaders sure know how to boost a person's morale."

"Shay, have you ever thought that perhaps you don't know how good you are? Maybe you don't have enough confide—"

"Hey guys, let's wrap it up. We're headed for pizza and wings," Coach said. "And let's give a round of applause to Shay for hitting the winning three-pointer."

"Wait! Wait," someone shouted as the team stopped. "I'm Grace Better, and I'm with Channel 3 News. We'd like to have a word with your player Shay. Would that be all right, Coach Scott?"

Coach Scott smiled. "Now that's up to Shay. But I'm not used to seeing the media at a junior high school," he said.

"Yes, Shay, yes," his family yelled from the bleachers above.

Shay smiled and heard a compliment that almost made him cry. Never before had that person given him a compliment. It was his brother Jeremiah.

"Great shot, Shay. They can't stop you," Jeremiah yelled words of encouragement from the bleachers.

Well, Shay thought. *All the years you've put me down...*

♦ ♦ ♦

"Hello there. Can you tell us where you learned to shoot a three-pointer? And where did you get the confidence to take the winning shot?" Grace asked.

"Well, I practiced three-pointers a lot over the summer. As for the confidence, I accredit that to my coach and teammates and Coach Crossover from Confidence Elementary. Coach Crossover taught me to be patient and that if I work hard, I have no choice but to improve. And I can't forget Jesus Christ. I have learned that if I believe in myself, anything is possible. My dad taught me that through Jesus, all...yes, all things are possible!"

"So there you have it, young seventh grader Shay hits the game-winning shot with an amazing three-pointer. And at the end of all the people he recognized, he did not forget to thank God. This is Grace Better for Channel 3 News, have an awesome night."

"Wow, Shay, I'm impressed," the coach said and then turned to the sound of footsteps.

The Crossover that Won the Game

"Hey, Shay," Christopher said. "I made a rap for you, you want to hear it?"

Everyone gathered around because they knew Christopher was the best rapper in the school.

"Yeah, sure," Shay said, though he was not used to the all the publicity.

> "Hey there, Shay,
> You're the man.
> If you can't do it,
> No one can.
>
> You have the perfect jumper
> Like the great MJ,
> But then there's more...
> You have his fadeaway.
>
> Never let anyone
> Get in the way.
> You're the best on the team,
> You're Crossover Shay."

"Yes, yes!" the group shouted.

"I like the way you rap," the coach said.

"You know, Coach" Christopher said. "One thing my dad always told me was to always let a person know how much you appreciate them. Shay and I are great friends, and I know what he's been through. For example, I know how his two of his five brothers always put him down. Well, I made that rap from the heart. I believe in my friend, and we all need someone to believe in us."

Shay held his head down and closed his eyes to try hiding his tears. He had never encountered such a selfless group of people than the group he was surrounded with.

"Any words for us, Champ?" the coach asked through a smile.

"Yeah," he sniffled. "I want to say, I'm not the champ." He then hugged the crew. "As one man, I'm weak. But as a team, I'm strong. Nothing is impossible if you have confidence and faith!

I have learned how important it is to be determined. You guys have no idea how much it means to me to have your support."

The car ride home was peaceful. Shay and his brother Jeremiah listened to random music, but Shay wasn't really listening. He had so many thoughts going through his mind. He was thinking mostly about getting to the basketball court to practice his ball control, jump shot, and especially his crossover. Deep inside, he wondered when his brothers would put him down again. One thing he had learned is that he had to have confidence and he had to stay determined.

Practicing with Brother Jeremiah

Shay sat on the hard metal bench with his head down.

"Shay, you can work harder. I can do that move with my eyes closed," Jeremiah said.

Shay remained silent. Frustrated, he did not know how to respond.

"If you do not want to practice, then I am just going to leave," Jeremiah said.

Shay stared at Jeremiah. He really did want him to stay and continue helping improve his between-the-legs crossover. Jeremiah walked away.

The Crossover that Won the Game

He did not notice Shay's tears as he watched Jeremiah walk away. Oh, the mixed messages of support, success, and failure Shay received. When Jeremiah was out of sight, Shay began practicing again.

Shay bounced the ball with his right hand. He counted to three, then switched the ball into his left hand.

What if I switch the ball back into my right hand really quickly? Shay thought. *I will work on the between-the-legs crossover some other time.* Shay smiled as he developed faith and confidence in the new move he had just thought of.

Bouncing the ball again in his right hand, 1…2…3, Shay counted. He then switched the ball into his left hand.

1…Shay counted as he quickly switched the basketball back into his right hand.

"Oh yes!" Shay yelled in excitement. "Coach Scott and the team are going to really like this new move."

Shay was so happy about this new move that he practiced it over and over and over and over again. He put trash cans on the basketball court. He put construction cones on the basketball court. Shay even put broken chairs on the basketball court and used all of the items as makeshift defenders.

"You want to see this new move?" Shay asked the makeshift defenders. "I know you think you can take this ball from me, but guess what?"

In Shay's imaginary world the items would answer back, "What?"

"Last year, I got the ball taken away from me. I was disappointed, but I just kept practicing. Then the moment came when I had to face the person that had once defeated me. The last guy thought he was going to take the ball away from me after I developed faith in myself and..." Shay paused as he remembered the highlight of the championship game.

♦ ♦ ♦

Shay looked his opponent directly in the eyes, scanned his body up, down, and side to side. He laughed. "I lacked confidence then. Not today, buddy," he said with that MJ confidence. Shay smiled as he told his opponent, "You won't be stripping me this time."

"Watch me," the opponent said.

Ball being dribbled from left to right, right to left, Shay watched the time clock. Shay turned his back to his opponent.

12...11...10...Shay spun, now facing his opponent again, with a grin that communicated "I am confident and I do not fear you at all."

"Ready?" Shay questioned his opponent.

"I was born ready. Are you ready?" his opponent questioned.

9...ball switched from right to left.

8...Shay faked as if he was going to drive the past his opponent. His opponent flinched.

7... "Where you going?" Shay laughed as he asked the question.

6...ball dribbled twice quickly between both of Shay's legs.

5...ball switched from left to right hand.

The Crossover that Won the Game

His opponent made the biggest mistake of his career, he reached.

"CS now. CS now," Coach Crossover yelled.

4...Shay flinched. His opponent reached.

3...Shay flinched again. His opponent reached. Now crossing the ball over to his left hand, his opponent reached and fell.

♦ ♦ ♦

Shay ended his memory. He stared his imaginary opponent in the eye. "If you really think you can take this ball from me, then try. I will make you fall just like—"

"Shay, it's time to go home," Jeremiah yelled from far across the park. Shay was glad Jeremiah interrupted him because he starting to feel overconfident. He walked toward his house as he remembered what Coach Crossover said about being overconfident:

"Shay, it's okay. You played a great game. I think you got a little arrogant, but in life, there are always lessons to learn. Never get overconfident, but likewise, never stop believing in yourself. Now wipe those tears from your eyes and cheeks and walk with me to the locker room. This is only the first game. We have a long road ahead of us," Coach Crossover said with a huge smile.

Shay was careful not to get overconfident, but he remembered how important it was to believe in himself. Shay knew he had improved. He knew he had played some great games, but like Coach Crossover said, there would be a long road ahead. Shay thought often about the big game the team would have in one week. He knew if the team were to make it to the playoffs, they would absolutely have to win their last game.

Shay couldn't wait to show Coach Scott and all of his teammates his new crossover move.

"Hey, guys!" Shay yelled with excitement.

"Yes, Shay?" the coach answered. Shay's teammates answered shortly after.

"I learned this new move. I have been practicing a lot," Shay told Coach Scott and his teammates.

"Oh, we cannot wait to see this new move, Shay," different players told Shay with excitement.

"Maybe I can practice it on some of you, guys," Shay said with a smile, joking with his teammates as he often did.

"Shay, that is really great. I like to see players working hard," Coach Scott told Shay.

"Thank you, Coach Scott!"

"You're welcome! Oh hey, Shay!"

"Yes, Coach?"

"I almost forgot. We are going to need your three-pointers in Friday's game."

"Okay, Coach, I am going to make sure to practice my three-point shot," Shay replied.

"That's great, Shay! Remember the importance of hard work. You get out of life what you put into it!" Coach Scott told Shay.

The Crossover that Won the Game

"Okay, Coach!" Shay replied while thinking that he really just wanted to show these guys his new move.

"All right, you five put on the red practice jerseys and you five put on the yellow practice jerseys," Coach Scott directed the players. "Shay, you're playing on the yellow team today."

"All right, Coach, I'm ready," Shay said while skipping toward the other four guys he was teaming up with.

"I want to see this new move, Shay!" one of the players said with a smile.

"Yeah, man! Make sure you show us what you have been working on!" another player said with excitement.

"Hey, team?"

"What's up, Shay?" the other four teammates responded.

"Let's show these guys how to play some basketball!" Shay responded with a smile that told his team he was really confident. Perhaps even overconfident!

"All right, here we are. Red versus yellow. Come to the center of the court guys. Listen!" Coach said with a serious tone. "Play hard, but be fair. I will call all fouls. If you miss a layup without a defender around you, you will have to run a lap around the gym."

"All right, Coach!" the players yelled out together, showing their excitement to play ball.

"Another thing, team!"

"Yeah, Coach?" the team once again spoke in unison.

"If you do not get back down the court to play defense after a missed shot, I am going to sit you down and put one of the reserves in the game. Ready?"

"Coach, you know we have been ready!" Shay spoke for the team. Shay's response was echoed by various players.

Coach Scott laughed at his team's sense of humor. "Yel—" Coach tried to speak through his laughter. Composing himself Coach Scott continued. "Yellow starts with the ball."

Shay brought the ball up the court. He only had one thought in mind. However, Coach Scott had another plan for Shay.

"Shay, I want you to visualize the entire basketball court. Make sure you know where all of your teammates and defenders are."

Shay listened but didn't pay much attention to what Coach Scott was saying.

"Pass to the open man," Coach Scott told Shay.

Shay reluctantly passed the ball. He really wanted to practice his new move. *Boing* was the sound heard when Shay's teammate missed his jump shot.

"Get back on defense, Shay. It is your job to defend the fast break," Coach Scott yelled out to Shay.

"I'm on it, Coach," Shay replied. Shay ran as fast as he could, caught up to his opponent.

"You aren't the only one with a crossover," Shay's opponent began taunting Shay as he did a quick behind-the-back crossover from his left to his right hand.

The Crossover that Won the Game

"Oh yeah?" Shay replied.

"Yeah! I am going to embarr—"

Shay stripped the ball using his left hand. "Looks like I just embarrassed you," Shay said as he dribbled the basketball with his right hand. Shay crossed the ball into his left hand and then rather quickly behind his back.

"I think you better back up," Shay warned his opponent.

"I'm not worried about you, Shay," his opponent answered the challenge.

"All right then," Shay said in a deep voice.

"What? What are you going to do, Shay?" the opponent questioned.

Shay put the ball behind his back again into his left hand. "I am going to treat you like you are from another school."

Ball now past the half-court line.

"Oh, I am so afra—" the opponent began speaking back as Shay crossed the ball quickly through his legs into his right hand. His opponent backed up, then charged forward with aggression as Shay bounced the ball twice in his right hand. He then switched the ball into his left hand, then quickly switched the basketball back into his right hand. His opponent hopped to the left, stumbled, and fell over his own feet before even finishing his word. Shay just smiled. Shay taunted back.

"You should have been afraid," Shay said as he was about to shoot a three-pointer. But before he could shoot, he heard a sound that distracted him.

Thweeeet! The whistle sounded very loudly and Coach Scott did not blow for very long as he called Shay. "Come here, Shay!"

"Yes, Coach?"

"Sit down!" Coach Scott said in a very stern voice.

"What did I do wrong?" Shay asked using a tone of voice that let the coach know that he was really confused.

"This practice is not about showing off. Fancy moves do not win ball games!"

"But, Coach, I was just—" Shay's sentence was cut short as Coach Scott interrupted him.

"Let me start by saying I know it is rude to interrupt people when they are talking, but I know you wanted to show off your new move. Basketball is a team sport. I do not need you to show off. I need you and the team needs you to play hard, play wise, play fair. Shay stay confident, stay determined. Never stop believing in yourself and having faith in your ability to succeed. But, Shay, I need you to realize that you do not have to prove yourself to others."

"I am sorry, Coach. Thank you very much."

"Hey, kiddo, no one is perfect. As long as you are willing to learn, you can be taught!"

"All right, Coach! Can I go back into play?"

"Shay, I want you to sit and listen to me coach your teammates so you can understand what I want in a leader."

Shay sat and listened. This was sure a lesson in learning how to be patient. Shay really wanted to play, but oh, how excited he was to learning what it meant to be a leader. This was also a lesson in how to be a follower. Shay knew if he could learn to follow the instructions of others, he could become a great leader.

Final Game of the Season

"All right, team," Coach Scott began his pregame speech. "We really need this game in order to make it to the playoffs. Even more important than winning, I want you guys to play hard, play wise, and play fair."

"Coach, we can do this!" Shay said. "Right, team?"

The team yelled yes altogether.

"Shay! Team! I appreciate your confidence. We do have a tough game ahead of us, guys," Coach Scott told the team. "Bring it in...Confidence on three."

"One, two, three, Confidence!" the team and Coach Scott yelled.

The teams battled for three quarters. Shay was forced to withstand double- and triple-teams. New Perspectives Junior High School were losing for most of the game but fought hard to rally back to get back in the game. Coach Scott poured out the positive words on his team and refused to let them give up.

4th Quarter of Final Game

"Team listen you have played a great game out there. You guys have almost tied the game after losing by 15." Coach Scott began encouraging his team as they were approaching the final seconds of this game.

The Crossover that Won the Game

"Shay it's been a hard game huh?"

"Yeah Coach it really has," Shay replied while shaking his head in frustration.

"Shay, they have only played so hard against you because they respect your skills." Coach Scott comforted Shay.

"I know, but double- and triple-teams Coach?"

"Yes, Shay! Double- and, yes, triple -teams."

Shay just shook his head in disbelief. "So what now, Coach?"

"Well, we are down by two points. I believe they expect you to shoot and will put a lot of pressure on you."

"Oh really?" Shay asked rhetorically. "I just do not believe they will put pressure on me. They wouldn't dare put a double- and triple-team on—"

"Shay!" Coach Scott interrupted Shay's sarcasm. "Focus! I need you to run the play that I design. Remember before you can be a great leader, you have to learn how to be a great follower."

"Okay, Coach."

"I want you to inbound the ball. Then run behind James and get the ball. Your defender will try to stop you from getting the ball, so run toward James as if you are going to hit his body, then step slightly beside him to create space between you and your defender. I want you to dribble past your defender. If they double-team you, I want you to pass it back to

James for the shot. Shay, we are going for the tie, not the win. I believe we can beat these guys in overtime."

The team was anxious and afraid. "Guys, remember, whether you win or lose, you gave it your all out there. And your best is all anyone can ask for. Hands in here, determination on three."

"One, two, three, Determination!" the team yelled.

"Hey, Shay!"

"Yes, Coach Scott?"

"As you prepare for this final play of the game, remember this, sometimes it's not about whether you win or lose, but about how you play the game!"

The clock had eight seconds left on it.

"Here is the ball, Shay," the referee said as he handed Shay the ball. It was hard to pass the ball to James with the defender jumping and swinging his arms in front of Shay. Shay finally passed the ball under the defenders legs to James.

8…Shay ran toward James and got the ball even though he and his defender were almost touching bodies. Shay got the ball and began dribbling in front of his defender.

With not much time left, Shay knew he had to act fast and he had to act now.

This is my moment, Shay thought to himself. With a defender in front of him, Shay dribbled the ball in his right hand.

7...The defender grabbed his jersey and Shay quickly smacked his hand off the jersey.

"Don't grab me if you can't guard me," Shay told his defender.

6...Shay dribbled the ball three times in his right hand. Crossed the ball into his left hand. With the clock now reading 5, Shay crossed the ball quickly back into his right hand. His defender hopped left, but just as Shay thought he was free of a defender, he heard a voice.

"I got him, Coach," James's defender yelled as he came to guard Shay.

4...Shay faked right then quickly crossed the ball into his left hand. Shay's original defender had stepped over to double-team Shay.

"Shay, I'm open," James yelled.

"Shay, look to your right," Coach Scott screamed with desperation.

With the clock reading 3 and two defenders guarding Shay, he stepped back behind the three-point line after crossing the ball into his left hand.

This is enough space, he thought.

2...Shay released the ball and all hopes extending the team's season lay within that basketball. Shay watched with great anticipation and anxiety as the ball flew through the air toward the basket.

Book 3

Summer Practice and the Lessons Learned

"Lord, please!"

Sweating profusely, Little Shay prayed out loud. "Please, God. Please let that shot go in," he pleaded as he clenched his fists, raising both arms into the air. Beads of sweat rolled down his forehead before dropping onto the shiny hardwood floor.

He kept his brown eyes on the game clock as the ball hit the rim and rolled. It continued to roll and roll and roll and roll around the rim. Shay was not the only one clenching his fists in anticipation.

0…time expired as, shortly thereafter, the ball fell off of the rim and the season for New Perspective Junior High School was over. Shay held his head down as his sweat now mixed with his tears of sadness. He did not see all of the stares of hatred from his teammates and fans. So distraught, Shay became deaf to boos from fans of New Perspective Junior High School and the hoorays from the opposing team and their fans.

♦ ♦ ♦

Shay walked over near the exit and sat on the bench. Feeling defeated, he sat on the bench and cried. Sadly, none of his teammates came to sit with him. Shay thought hard about a solution this problem, and not making it to the playoffs was a problem, at least to him. But trying to find a solution was like the Americans trying to find Osama Bin Laden.

"God, I'll never take the final—"

His thoughts were interrupted by a reassuring arm, no resting around his puny shoulder by the man Shay admired, his ex-coach and friend, Coach Crossover...

"You miss a hundred percent of the shots you do not take." Coach Crossover surprised Shay. Shay had no idea that Coach Crossover had come to support him.

Shay just looked and waited for Coach Crossover to say more.

"Coach Crossover, I'm sorry that I let you down! I am such a disappointment!" Shay said as he choked on his words a little.

Coach Crossover cleared his throat. "Shay, do you know what I really liked about the last shot that you took?"

"What did you like about that last shot, Coach Crossover?" Shay asked sarcastically. "I missed and we lost the game because of me!" Coach Scott overheard Shay's frustration while he was talking to parents and the other coach.

Coach Crossover touched Shay's upper arm. "You believed in yourself and that will never be a disappointment."

"I agree!" a voice was heard from behind Shay. It was Coach Scott. Coach Scott and Coach Crossover shook hands and greeted each other.

"Hello, Coach Crossover."

"Hello, Coach Scott," Coach Crossover replied.

"Thanks for coming out to support us," Coach Scott said.

The Crossover that Won the Game

"It was my pleasure! And I plan to be a positive role model for my buddy Shay here for as long as I can," Coach Crossover said with a smile.

"Shay, I'm here for you as well," Coach Scott followed Coach Crossover's statement.

Shay had a smile on his face. "Thank you so much, guys. You have no idea how much that means to me."

Coach Scott and Coach Crossover looked at each other and smiled.

"You're welcome, Shay," they said in unison.

"This is New Perspective Junior High School, Shay!" Coach Scott said as if to remind Shay. "I am going to give you the good along with the bad here, Shay. I believe that someone should not only be told about what they did to fail but also what they can do differently in order to succeed."

"Okay, Coach," Shay said with a voice of uncertainty.

"First, Shay, let me address something else. I noticed that when I used the word *fail*, you lowered your eyes and began looking discouraged. By no means are you a failure but everyone has moment of success and failure. What is important is that you figure out what needs to be done differently in order to be successful whether it takes you one, two, or fifty tries!"

Shay smiled and, with a more confident voice, said, "All righty, Coach, I am all ears."

Both coaches laughed at Shay's sarcasm.

"I was talking to the other coach and telling him how both teams really played a great game. The parents were upset, but I told them and now I am telling you: sometimes, it is not about whether you win or lose, but how you play the game. Was I unhappy at first?"

"I bet you—" Shay began interrupting Coach Scott.

"That was a rhetorical question," Coach Scott said as he laughed.

"What in the world does that mean?" Shay asked in a very animated voice.

"It means that the question was not meant to be answered. A rhetorical question is asked in order to make the listener think," Coach Scott explained.

"Oh, now I understand," Shay replied. "So were you unhappy, Coach Scott?"

"Well..." Coach Scott began to speak.

"And by the way, that question was not rhetorical," Shay said as he laughed.

"Yes, Shay, I was unhappy. At first, I felt like perhaps if Shay had followed the instructions that I gave him, we could have had a better chance at winning the game. Everyone likes to win right?" Coach Scott asked.

"Yes! I sure wanted to win that game, Coach," Shay said in a sad voice.

"There is value in learning how to follow. Shay, you have the potential to be a great leader, but guess what?"

"What?" Shay replied.

The Crossover that Won the Game

"Every great leader was a great follower first!"

"Wow! I never thought about that!" Shay said.

"If you made the shot, of course, me, Coach Crossover, and your team, your and their families would have been excited. But the lesson I want you to learn is that this game was not about whether you made or missed the shot or whether we won or lost. The lesson was about following instructions and being able to learn from the results. I believe you were doing what you thought was best."

"I was definitely making the decision that I thought was best, Coach," Shay replied.

"And, Shay, I would never discourage individuality and the ability to think for yourself. Do not stop developing your decision-making skills but understand that sometimes other people make decisions that you have to follow whether you agree with them or not. Please understand, Shay, that I value your feelings and thoughts, so if you do not agree with something that I say or think that a different plan may work, tell me so we can both sit down together and take a look at an alternate plan."

"Thank you for respecting my perspectives and giving me a stronger voice, Coach," Shay said.

"You're welcome!" Coach Scott replied.

"More importantly, thank you for teaching me new perspectives."

"Well...this is New Perspectives Junior High School." Coach Scott and Coach Crossover laughed and patted Shay's back.

Shay laughed as well. "You guys are so silly!" Shay spoke through his laughter.

"Shay, you showed belief and confidence in yourself. You demonstrated determination to win. Faith can never be disputed as anything less than positive."

"Thank you for being positive, Coach Scott. You and Coach Crossover have taught me the importance of believing in myself but also the importance of believing in and trusting others. Coach Scott, I apologize because I believed that my plan was better and would be more effective than yours."

"Apology accepted but, Shay?"

"Yes, Coach Scott."

"You miss one hundred percent of the shots you do not take!" Coach Scott said a familiar phrase. "Learn to follow in order to know how to lead, and never ever stop believing in you!"

"All right, Coach, well, I will practice very hard this summer."

"Shay, we will have a great year together for the eighth grade season."

"Hey, Coach Scott, perhaps we can join Shay in his practices this summer in order to help him learn and improve this summer." Coach Crossover shared his idea.

"That would be a great," Coach Scott began to speak.

"Oh! Oh! Oh! I would love that," Shay interrupted.

Both coaches chuckled. "Shay, one day, you will learn the value in hearing what others has to say. You will learn that it is respectful to not interrupt others when they are speaking."

The Crossover that Won the Game

"Okay!" Shay, Coach Scott, and Coach Crossover laughed uncontrollably. A situation that seemed negative was turned into something positive. What Shay learned was that success was sometimes connected with small victories and step-by-step growth.

"All right, guys, let's get together at New Perspectives Junior High School one month before the school year starts," Coach Crossover said.

Coach Scott and Shay quickly agreed and good-byes rang out as the three parted ways.

Summer Practice

"Son, stop bouncing that ball in this house. Who do you think you are, Michael Jordan? I wouldn't let him bounce a ball in my house either."

"Sorry, Mom," Shay said.

Momma walked over to her baby son and wrapped her arms around his shoulders. She looked into his brown eyes and spoke, "Have I ever told you how much I love and admire you?"

"Mom, how could you admire me? I suck! I missed the final shot of the last game of the season. I could have been a sta—"

His words were silenced by the index finger of Mom's right hand upon his lips. "Son, you're not the only basketball player to miss the final shot."

"But, Momm…"

"Shay, I asked you before not interrupt people when they are talking."

"Sorry, Mommy."

"Your apology is accepted. Basketball is not the only sport where a player missed the last shot of the game. But I have watched you grow. It took courage to take the final shot. Don't ever forget that I..." were her last words as she turned, noticing the black Lamborghini convertible with a dark-skinned bald man wearing shades and a huge diamond earring reflecting off the rays of sun.

"But who is he?" she questioned inquisitively. She was so sure she had seen him before. "He really reminds me of this 6'6" basketball player from—"

"Mom!" Shay called out. No answer! "Mom!" Shay called again. She turned with a baffled look on her face.

"Mom, you look like you saw a ghost," he said, concerned.

"I'm fine! Now that the rain has stopped and the sun is out, get your diligent self out there and practice so you can make it to the NBA and buy your mommy a new home and van."

"Sure, Mommy," he said as he rushed out the door. In such a hurry to get out of the door, he did not even hear the giggling from his older brothers, Jeremiah and James.

◆ ◆ ◆

The reddish-hot sun beamed on the black asphalt, causing steam to rise. Shay smiled.

"I'm about to cross y'all over," Shay said as he placed his imaginary opponents—garbage cans, chairs, and construction cones—on the court right across the street from his house.

The Crossover that Won the Game

As the sweat poured off his head, Little Shay bounced the ball twice in his right hand. "Listen...back up!" Little Shay said to his opponents as he switched the ball quickly to his left hand. He then bounced it two more times as he taunted his opponents, "You know you can't guard me, right?" Little Shay wasn't known for waiting for answers. He crossed the ball between his legs to his right hand, smiled, then put the ball swiftly behind his back to his left hand. With great anticipation, Jeremiah and James watched and waited as Little Shay pulled up for the three-pointer.

"Swish!" Little Shay yelled in his opponents' face as he waved his index finger on his right hand from side to side, smiling like the great MJ.

Mouths wide open, eyes enlarged and glassy, Jeremiah and James stared in disbelief.

"Wow!" they said to each other as they stared from the second-floor patio. This was all they could utter, but they could not and would not ever let their baby brother know how much they truly respected his determination, courage, newfound confidence, and skills.

"Oh man, I really wish Jeremiah and James could have seen that shot," Little Shay said as tears began to form in both of his eyes. Little Shay wiped a tear from his left and right eye as he thought, *Why is that my big brothers who are supposed to be role models are always putting me down?* Little Shay began his long walk home.

♦ ♦ ♦

"We're losing him...we're losing him," the paramedics said as his mother sat in the back of the ambulance with tears streaming from her eyes.

Jamell Ponder and Joseph Ponder

Why would his brothers push him in front of that truck? she thought. *Were they that jealous of their little brother to try to ruin his chances at a basketball career?*

This young man's long walk home became his last walk home, one paramedic thought.

"I'm sorry, ma'am, he's gone…"

Book 4

Eighth Grade

"Ahhh," Coach Crossover screamed as he sat straight up in bed, clenching the sheets as the tears poured down his face.

"Thank you, Lord, that it was only a dream!" Coach Crossover said, frightened out of his midday nap. Putting on his shoes, grabbing his car keys, he darted out of the home, heading quickly to Shay's house.

♦ ♦ ♦

Baffled, Little Shay opened the door and stared into the watery eyes of Coach Crossover, who placed his arms around Shay's neck and declared, "I will always be a part of your life." His tears soaked Shay's back.

1 Week Before Beginning of Eighth Grade Season

"Let it roll off your fingertips, Shay," Coach Crossover said.

"Okay, Coach. This is too hard though!" Shay said out of discouragement.

"Shay!"

"Yes, Coach Crossover?" Shay said.

"Nothing is too difficult. Do you remember what I told you during the sixth grade season?"

"Please remind me, Coach!" Shay said in desperation.

"Never give up, Shay. If you work hard enough, you will learn how to do a crossover very well."

"Oh yea, Coach, I remember now," Shay said with a little more joy in his voice.

"The same thing is true about learning to shoot a jump shot well."

"Thanks, Coach Crossover."

"Pass me the ball, Shay."

"Okay," Shay said as he passed Coach Crossover the ball with a bewildered look on his face.

"Here is a brief explanation of how you shoot an efficient jump shot: First, position your aiming hand to catch the ball. This will be your recessive hand. Second, position your right/dominant hand near the left hand with fingers spread wide. Your thumb will grip the lower part of the ball as it rests comfortably on the palm of your hand. Third, square your feet beneath your shoulders. The fourth step may seem silly, Shay, but…jump. Fifth, you extend your right arm high above your head with a quick release and a snap of the wrist."

"Thank you, Coach. You are awesome."

"You're welcome, Shay. You are too little, buddy. Are you ready for a drill?"

"Of course I am, Coach!" Shay said excitedly.

"All right, Coach Scott, I want you to guard Shay as he tries to create space in order to get the ball and shoot the final shot."

The Crossover that Won the Game

"Shay, I want you to make Coach Scott think you are running to the basket and then quickly step back out to the three-point line and follow steps 1 through 5 and shoot the best jump shot you can."

"Okay, Coach Crossover."

"All right, Shay, you know you are not about to score right?" Coach Scott said as he chuckled.

Coach Crossover laughed. "On three, guys! 1…2…3 go!"

Shay sprinted toward the basket. "I'm about to take you to school, Coach Scott!" Shay said as he smiled and quickly turned and ran back toward the three-point line. Shay positioned his aiming hand, positioned his shooting hand. "You're going to be calling me Coach Shay pretty soon!"

Coach Scott just smiled as he caught his bearings to chase Shay toward the three-point line.

Shay forgot to square his feet. He caught the ball, jumped, then extended his shooting arm, and quickly released. Shay anxiously watched with wavering expectations as Coach Crossover and Coach Scott just stared at each other.

Honk! The horn distracted the guys, causing them to take their attention away from the ball.

"Oh, guys, I have to go! Thank you so much," Shay said as he ran toward the door of the gymnasium.

"Wait a second, Shay," Coach Crossover called out.

"Yes, Coach?"

"You did well today. Keep practicing and just as you learned to do a crossover really well so will you develop a great jump shot!" Coach Crossover put some finishing touches on the practice.

"Yeah, Shay, I really admire your honesty, diligence, and determination."

"Thanks, guys," Shay said.

"You know what else, Shay?" Coach Scott asked.

"What, Coach?" Shay replied impatiently as his mother was waiting in the car.

"The first step to growth is knowing your weaknesses as well as where you excel. And of course, my friend, the second step is working to improve the areas in which you lack. But..."

"You certainly have learned the value of hard work!" Coach Scott and Coach Crossover said in unison as they smiled and patted Shay on each side of his back.

"See you next week," Coach Scott said.

"Okay, but, Coach Crossover, when will I see you again?" Shay asked.

"Well, Shay, you are certainly in great hands with Coach Scott. But you know I am only a phone call away."

"Thanks, Coach Crossover."

"I will make sure to come to your games when I am not volunteering at various recreational centers."

The Crossover that Won the Game

"I'd love that a lot," Shay said as he smiled. "Bye-bye." Shay headed out of the gym and hopped into the car. "Hey, Mom!"

"Hey, son, how was practice?"

"Oh, Mom, oh, Mom, it was a lot of fun. It was hard, but Coach Crossover and Coach Scott are so patient and positive. I struggled with my form on my jump shot but…"

"Excuse me, son!"

"Yes, Mom?"

"What is a jump shot?"

"Um…well…well…I'll just explain later!" Shay said quickly as he wanted to talk more about practice.

"All right, son," Momma said as she smiled. "So tell me more!"

"So, Mom, listen! Coach Crossover is so nice. He always encourages me. It makes me so very happy that he believes in me. He never lets me stay discouraged. He always tells me in his semi-deep voice: Never give up, Shay. If you work hard enough, you will learn how to do…whatever…very well!"

"That is so great, Shay. I really wish your dad was more invested in your life. But it is great that you have positive role models."

"Mom," Shay called out.

"Yes, son!"

"Where is Daddy anyway?"

Momma never answered. The two of them rode in silence as Shay stared out the window, wondering what type of father abandons their child. The phone began to ring.

"Hello, John!"

"Hey, Ruby!"

"How is Shay?"

"John, you should ask him yourself!"

"I will! I am also going to try to make it to his game."

"He would like that. He would really like you to attend!" Ruby said in a frustrated tone.

"It's not necessary for you to…"

"I said I'll try to attend," John yelled at his wife, whom he had abandoned.

"I am not the one who walked off from the family," the wife said with tears of love and hurt in her eyes.

"Well, I will do my best to be at this game," John said as he exited the car and slammed the door so hard that the small basketball statue that sat on the dashboard fell onto the floor.

♦ ♦ ♦

"Thank you, Daddy. I am so glad you called, I have not heard from you in a while. Well, the first game is this Friday and I will look for you then," Shay said with joy. Just the sound of his father's voice made him forget

The Crossover that Won the Game

how angry he was with his dad. "I will look up in the bleachers for you." HE hung up the phone and ran downstairs to his mother. "Guess what? Guess what?" Shay said.

"What, son?" his mother replied.

"Dad will be at my first basketball game," he said with excitement in his voice and a sparkle in his eyes.

♦ ♦ ♦

New Perspectives Junior High School fans held their gold, blue, and green banner high up in the air with enthusiasm. They were so loud that they were the only voices being heard. But Shay was cooler than the breeze coming off the ocean on a hot summer day. He was not fazed at all, not even a little. His dad would be at his first game ever, and that meant it was showtime.

Ball in hand, Shay dribbled slightly beyond the half-court mark. There were fifteen seconds left in the first half. This next shot was for his dad. With two defenders on him he pump faked as if he was going to shoot the ball, he then passed it to a teammate. The teammate was double-teamed so he then passed the ball back to Shay. Shay had a look in his eyes that not many had seen before. More confident than he had ever been, Shay crossed the ball between his legs from his left to right hand, then behind his back with his right hand, then back to the front of him, now holding the ball in his left hand. Oh, how Shay really hoped his dad was watching. Bouncing it twice with the left hand, he switched the ball quickly to his right hand. His opponent was confused as Shay hopped to the right and then crossed the ball back to the left.

"Coach Crossover taught me that," Shay said with a smirk as his defender reached into to steal the ball. After crossing the ball quickly to his left hand, Shay stepped back behind the three-point line. With his opponent a far enough distance away, feet squared beneath his shoulders, Shay pulled up for the three. As Shay released the ball, the crowd watched in awe and wonder. As the ball going through the net made a whipping sound, the fans from New Perspective Junior High School cheered loudly. The other team was now silent while some of the others yelled boos. Shay did not react. He just looked up in the stands. As the hardwood floor emptied for halftime, Shay just stood there staring into the bleachers in awe, disbelief, and wonder.

Shay continued to look up into the bleachers. He was in awe of all the unfamiliar faces cheering for him. He held his head low as he thought to himself, *I cannot believe that Dad is not here like he promised. I wonder why he's not here!* Shay's thoughts were interrupted by Coach Scott calling out to him.

"All right, Shay, let's go, buddy. We have a lot to talk about in the locker room."

The second half, he played as a young man with a lot on his mind.

"Why, why?" he yelled as he sat on the bench in the locker room, causing everyone to stare.

Coach Scott laid his hand on Shay's shoulder. He asked Shay if he wanted to talk about what was on his mind. Shay kind of wanted to talk but, even more, he felt like going home and writing.

♦ ♦ ♦

The ride home was akin to two people sitting in the funeral home for a wake. Mom could tell he was hurt and disappointed so she gave him his space. She could not fully understand how he felt, but she knew he was not a happy camper. As they pulled into their driveway, she exited the

The Crossover that Won the Game

vehicle and went straight to his bedroom and pulled out his notepad that he used as a diary.

The sun was still out and it was rather bright, which was a great time for little Shay to write.

With pen and pad, it was now time that he wrote his dad.

Today
Daddy, Daddy
can you and I play?
"I'm sorry Shay,
Daddy works today."

"Okay, Daddy,
I understand
you need money,
you're a working man."

Daddy just smiled
what could he say?
He didn't have time
no, not today.

The next day came
but it was really cold
Shay didn't care
he was young and bold.

"Hey, Daddy, Daddy,
the working man
Please tell me
of your plan?"

"I'm so sorry, son,
I hate to say
once again,
I cannot play because
I have to work today."

Again, Shay smiled,
He was both mild-mannered and meek
I still love you, Daddy,
perhaps next week.

Dad looked at Shay
while he walked away
Oh, how he wished
He was free today.

The weekend came
and went again
Shay went to his tree house
with his imaginary friend.

"Hey, little buddy,
what do you say
how would you like
to come out and play today?"

Shay laughed and joked
with his imaginary friend
oh, how he wish
Dad would attend.

Then from a distance,
late in the day,

The Crossover that Won the Game

Shay smiled when he heard
his daddy say,

"Hey, Little Shay,
What do you want to play?

Daddy has time
to play with you today."

Shay wiped the tears from his eyes after rereading the poem and said, "I know you will come when you can and with that being said, I will forgive." Shay lay on his bed and wished Daddy could understand his pain. *"If Daddy understands my pain, then he would certainly make time for me,* Shay thought. Shay knew these thoughts would not subside easily, but he had to try to get some sleep so he could be well rested for school and the game tomorrow. Shay tossed and turned and tossed and turned some more for what felt like hours.

Shay's alarm rang loudly. He did not wake up due to only sleeping a few hours the night before. Shay was abruptly woken up to his mother's hands, shaking him. "Shay, wake up. You are about to be late for school, son."

"Okay, Mom, I am getting up," Shay responded slowly as he was not fully awake yet. Pillow wet from the tears he had unknowingly cried while asleep. Shay figured it was time to roll out of bed, put his best face on and his best foot forward. He would try really, really hard to put his game face on for their challenge tonight versus Win, Lose, No Draw Middle School. The name of the opponent's school snapped Shay into reality. As Shay was going through his morning routines, he thought endlessly about how Win, Lose, No Draw related to life. "You either win or you lose. In life, there are no draws. But there is forgiveness, and as long as someone is breathing, there is opportunity to love better, to live better, and to right your wrongs. I will give Daddy a chance," Shay said as he hopped out of the shower, now almost ready to go for the day.

This day felt like the longest day of Shay's life. Certainly, he could think of a few longer days. The classes felt a little longer for some reason. Shay was really anxious for classes to be dismissed so he could borrow Coach Scott's cell phone to call his dad. He wanted to invite his dad to his game tonight versus Win, Lose, No Draw Middle School.

Pit-pat, pit-pat! The sound gradually increased as Shay bolted down the hallway toward the athletic center.

"Hey!" Shay was abruptly stopped in his tracks.

"Yes?" Shay replied.

"There is no running in the hallway," the middle-aged African-American man said.

"I'm sorry, sir!" Shay apologized.

"I will let it go this time, but next time, I will give you an in-school suspension."

"Thank you!" Shay said as he turned to walk away.

"Hey, Shay!" Shay quickly turned around.

"Yes?"

"It seems like you have a lot on your mind."

"I do, sir." Shay was surprised that he could tell.

The Crossover that Won the Game

"If you need to talk, just stop by my office anytime."

"Thank you, Mr. Principal," Shay said as he turned to walk away.

"You're welcome, Shay."

"Shay, there's one more thing."

"What's that, Mr. Principal?"

The principal smiled. "Have a great game tonight. I and many others will be watching you!"

"I am going to try, Mr. Principal."

"All you can do, Shay, is give your best effort."

"Thank you, Mr. Principal. I will see you later."

"See you later, son."

Shay knew that the principal was always calling the students "son," but this time, it angered Shay. *I really hope my real dad sees me later*, Shay thought to himself. *If he doesn't answer...* Shay stopped himself as he did not know what to think or feel. He just knew he had to hurry to the athletic center so he could have a few minutes before practice to call his dad.

Ring! Ring! Ring! The phone sounded in Shay's ear. Shay's heart pounded with great anticipation. The phone rang and rang and rang until Daddy's voice message began playing. Shay had heard this so many times he could now recite it. Shay begrudgingly mumbled this message as it was playing in his ear.

"Hello, you have reached the voice mail of John W. Ponder. I am sorry that I cannot take your call at this very moment. However, I assure you that your call is very important to me. So please do not hesitate to record your name, number, and reason for this call. I am quite busy, but you can be sure of one thing…I will call you back at my earliest convenience!" Shay finished reciting the message.

"Hi, Dad, this is Shay. You have been promising to come to one of my games and well…well…" Shay began to stutter. "Well, tonight, we have a game against Win, Lose, No Draw Middle School. The game will be right here at my school, New Perspective Junior High School. Dad, I really hope you can come. If you can't, Dad, please call Mom and let her know because I do not want to expect you or wonder if you are going to come or if you are too busy to watch me play tonight. Well, that's all I have to say Dad. I hope to see you tonight. Bye." Shay hung up the phone.

Shay just shook his head and lowered his eyes in sadness.

Tap! Tap! One of Shay's teammates hit him on the shoulder. "Why are you looking so sad? You played really good last game."

"Thanks," Shay said as he half smiled.

"Man, what is wrong with you, Shay? You are not acting like the Shay I know!"

"Chris, thanks for your concern, but I'd rather not talk about certain things."

"Hey, no problem, Shay, I understand."

The two of them firmly gripped each other's right hand.

The Crossover that Won the Game

"What you need to be worrying about is how I am about to cross you over in practice! Ha! Ha," Shay laughed.

"Ha! Ha!" Chris chuckled. "I don't think so, buddy."

"Come on now, Chris, you know what is going to happen if Coach Scott asks you to guard me during practice."

"What's going to happen?" Chris asked.

"You'll just have to wait and see!" Shay replied.

"Ha! Ha! Ha! Conversation over, man." Chris continued to chuckle.

"Ha! Ha! Good idea," Shay replied through his laughter.

The two shook hands and continued walking toward the gymnasium. "Hey, guys, how's everything going today? Are you ready for practice?" Chris answered, but Shay did not. Shay just thought to himself for what seemed to be a really long time.

"I guess Dad was honest about him being a busy person. He wasn't so honest about calling back, unless my call really isn't important to him at all. I do not think he is sorry that he could not take my call…"

"Shay! Shay! Hey, Shay! Snap out of it, buddy," Coach Scott said as he was waving his hand in front of what appeared to be daydreaming Shay.

"Yes, Coach?"

"Are you all right?"

"Yes, I am fine," Shay replied.

"You seem a little upset today!"

"Don't you worry, Coach, I am fine and I am ready for a great practice and a great game," Shay said with a smile. He simply wasn't ready to reveal the things that were on his mind.

"Well, all right, Shay. I will not pressure you. I am going to keep my eye on you though to make sure you are all right," Coach Scott said.

"Thanks, Coach," Shay said as he tried really hard not to show any emotion.

Practice

Shay struggled through practice. He didn't joke as much as usual.

"Hey! Hey, Shay," Chris called out.

"What, Chris?" Shay responded.

"Remember all that crap you were talking earlier?"

Shay just ignored him. Shay dribbled the ball twice really quickly in between his legs. He faked left and then quickly went right. Chris hopped over to guard Shay. Just as Chris moved over, Shay quickly spun toward his left side using his right hand. Shay waited for Chris to come back to guard him. Shay thought to himself, *Where are you going, Chris? I'm over here so why are you way over there if you are supposed to be guarding me, defending your basket, you know?*

Shay smiled but didn't say a word. Chris came back and squared his feet to defend Shay. Shay quickly faked left, then put the ball under Chris's legs and did an impressive finger roll layup. Shay just stared at Chris like he was his rival from another team. Chris didn't know that the fire in Shay's eyes was for him at all.

The Crossover that Won the Game

"All right, Shay, that was a nice strong move to the basket. Be direct and efficient. No need to taunt and tease, just make your move and either shoot or make the necessary pass. Good job! I like your patience and ability to score," Coach Scott said.

"Thanks, Coach."

"All right, guys, let's practice our passing drills: bounce, chest, high, and low passes. Let's go over the three-man weave and practice our pick-and-roll drills. When the point guard and power forward are running the pick-and-roll, I want the small forward and shooting guard to be on the wings. For those of you who may not know what the wing is, it is the top right and left corners of the half circle surrounding the rim. Follow the ball. So, guys, move into the corner if Shay goes near the rim. Shay, if you pass the ball to the rolling power forward, you cut toward the basket or the open spot to allow for a third pass option."

"All right, Coach, we got it," the players yelled out in unison.

"Well, then show me," Coach Scott said that as he chuckled.

"All right, guys, I'm at the top of the key," Shay said.

Coach Scott placed the other players.

"Are you going to guard me again?"

"Yeah, Shay, you…"

"Big. Big mistake," Shay said jokingly as he tried to invoke a better mood for himself.

Shay dribbled the ball in his right hand. Coach Scott yelled out to the power forward, "Move up three feet above the foul line."

"Okay, Coach," the power forward yelled.

"Shay, go now. Take your defender right into the body of the power forward."

"Okay, Coach," Shay said as he lowered his left shoulder and moved quickly toward the power forward's body.

"All right, wing men, follow the ball."

"Okay, Coach," they yelled.

Thud! The bodies banged together as Shay guided Chris into the power forward.

"Okay, roll now," Coach Scott yelled.

The defense played the passing lane well. Shay passed the ball anyway. The ball was stolen by the defense.

Shay held his head in frustration.

"It's okay, Shay. What could you have done differently? Sometimes, the most important thing is how you respond when things do not go according to planned."

"I could have passed the ball to the shooting guard or small forward that were in the corners."

"Okay, good. What else could you have done?"

"I guess I could have shot the ball," Shay said.

The Crossover that Won the Game

"Shay, you had the open shot because Chris did not get around the pick fast enough. You have to learn how to take what the defense gives you and maximize on the opportunities. As a point guard, I need you to take smart shots and make good passes."

They ran the pick-and-roll drill several more times. Shay failed many times, but he finally figured how to read the defense and make decisions based on their reactions to the offense. Shay went on to make many shots and attain several assists during practice.

"Okay, guys, that's a wrap. Good job in practice. We leave for Win, Lose, No Draw Middle School in a little more than one hour. Relax a little bit and then we will be on our way."

Game Time:
Win, Lose, No Draw Middle School
versus
New Perspectives Junior High School

"All right, guys, wake up! Enough sleeping! It is time to go in here and do the best that we can. We are in their gym, but we still have to play our game."

"Hey, Coach, who will be starting tonight?" Shay asked.

"At point guard, we will start you, Shay."

Shay smiled. "I like the sound of that, Coach."

"At shooting guard, Chris will start. At small forward, Liam will start. At power forward, Michael will start, and at center, William, you will start."

"All right, guys, we can do this," Liam said in his heavy Asian accent.

"Shay, we are going to school them with our pick-and-roll play."

"It will definitely take a team effort, guys. Win, Lose, No Draw is a tough team."

"We will do our best, bros," Chris said in his Latin accent.

The team walked down the long hallway, through the gymnasium, and then into the locker room. Before exiting the gym and going into the locker room, Shay paused and thought to himself, *I really hope Daddy is in the stands watching me play tonight.*

Chris put his arm around Shay's neck. "Come on, buddy. Let's go. Everything will be all right."

Shay walked into the locker room and prepared to listen to Coach Scott's pregame speech.

◆ ◆ ◆

"All right, team, first of all, thank you for being here. I want you to know that how you play tonight's game is dependent on you. Whether you win or lose, you decide the amount of effort you put into your performance. Do I have faith in you? Yes, I do have faith in you…in all of you! But! Yes there is usually a 'but' whether we like it or not. So I will ask again…do I have faith in you? You already know that the answer is yes. But what good is it if I have faith in you, if you do not have faith in yourself?"

"It is no good, Coach Scott," Shay yelled out.

"Correct, Shay! The most important thing is that you have faith in yourself. Faith fuels fire. The fire necessary to burn through any circumstance, challenge, and conflict, and anything that tries to stop you from reaching your end goals in life. The end goal is not always winning. Any positive outcome is a winning result. Never give up. If you give up, you will never know what the result would have been. If you continue to pursue your goals, no matter how many times you lose, eventually, you win. I've heard that it's not about whether you win or lose, but how you play the game. Just as you are going to play a basketball game, life is akin to a game. In neither is there ever a draw. You will either win or lose. Enjoy small victories and know that you may lose some battles, but the war is usually far from over. You are under my supervision to learn new perspectives that carries you not only through basketball games but through all of life's greatest and toughest moments. With that being said, leave your all on the floor out there tonight, guys. Bring your hands in here, guys. Faith, Confidence, Determination on 3."

"One…two…three, Faith! Confidence! Determination!" the team and Coach Scott yelled out.

The team began walking back toward the gymnasium when Coach Shay put his hand on Shay's shoulder.

"Shay," Coach Scott called.

"Yes, Mr. Scott?"

"Your success is dependent upon you. The people you want to share in your success and sometimes your failures will be nowhere around at the times you need and desire them most. But do not change who you are or how you behave because they choose not to appreciate that jewel God has made you to be."

"Thanks, Mr. Scott," Shay said as he smiled slightly. The two of them walked into the gymnasium and began pregame drills, shoot around, and the layup line.

"Great job on the pick-and-roll play, guys," Coach Scott said to the starting five. "Michael, just roll a little faster to make the defense have to either follow you or give Shay an open shot."

"Okay, Coach," Michael responded.

"To my center, William. I need you to be on the opposite side of Michael and Shay in order to give an additional pass option," Coach Scott said.

"All right, Coach," William replied.

"Chris and Liam, if you run this pick-and-roll drill correctly, you may get a lot of open shots in tonight's game," Coach Scott said.

"All right, let's try that once more."

The starting five players ran the pick-and-roll once more. "Great job, guys. Let's not overrun it so the other team do not figure out one of our key weapons."

"Okay, Coach," the players replied almost in unison.

"Form a layup line, guys, and be sure to shoot some jump shots. Chris and William, shoot especially from the corners and wings. Shay, shoot some three-pointers from the top of the key and the foul line."

The team continued to practice while Shay took long in-depth stares into the bleachers. Oh, how he hoped his dad would show up.

"Come on, Shay. Shoot that three-pointer you've been working on," Chris said with a hint of sarcasm.

"I'm sorry, man. Pass me the ball and I'll show you what I've got," Shay replied.

"Okay, here goes!"

Chris passed Shay the ball. Shay missed the shot. This became a pattern during pregame drills.

"Hey, Shay, focus. Keep your eyes on the court and rim after the ball is passed to you. Nothing or no one in the stands will help you make the shot," Coach Scott said to Shay.

Little did Coach Scott know, if my dad was here it would make a big difference. It may very well help me play better, Shay thought.

Shay made a few shots but remained inconsistent during warm-ups.

"Shay, you can do it. We believe in you," the starting five players surrounded Shay and attempted to raise his belief in himself.

"All right, guys, bring it in. You've prepared well! You've heard the pregame speech. So let's give it our all. Remember, faith fuels fire and never give up. Please consider small victories. Faith! Confidence! Determination! On 3."

"One...two...three! Faith! Confidence! Determination!" the players and Coach yelled out in unison.

Starting 5 for New Perspectives Junior High School:

>Point guard: Shay
>Shooting guard: Chris

Small forward: Liam
Power forward: Michael
Center: William

Starting 5 for Win, Lose, No Draw Middle School:

Point guard: Ricky
Shooting guard: Keith
Small forward: Sam
Power forward: Jackson
Center: Jovan

Quarter 1

The referee threw the ball high in the air at the start of the game. With eyes fixed on the ball, Shay watched with more anticipation and anxiety than ever before. *Smack*! William hit the ball to Shay.

With eyes scanning the bleachers, Shay asked himself, "Where is Daddy?"

"Over here!" Chris yelled from the right wing of the court. Shay's defender put his forearm on Shay's left side. Shay ran two steps to the right and spun quickly to the left. The defender hopped right back in front of Shay.

"You're not going anywhere, kid," Shay's defender taunted.

Shay did an in-and-out dribble, then crossed the ball quickly to the right, then passed the ball to Chris. Chris's defender hopped in front of Chris, stealing the ball with his left hand. As Chris started to get in front of his defender, the defender put the ball quickly behind his back and ran the length of the floor, making a layup, setting the momentum of the game in Win, Lose, No Draw's direction.

The Crossover that Won the Game

"Shay, when the defender is guarding you closely, consider ball faking high and then bounce passing to create distance between the ball and the defender," Coach Scott yelled from New Perspectives' bench.

"It's not going to matter, I know how to shut him down," Ricky, Shay's defender, yelled.

Shay wasn't intimidated, but he struggled to play effectively because he continued to think about his dad not being at the game. Shay had a look of defeat that those who knew him hadn't seen in a really long time.

Pat! Pat! Chris tapped Shay on the back.

"Hey, buddy, you can handle this and you can handle him. Make sure he knows that he cannot handle you," Chris told Shay. Chris and Shay slapped hands and pounded fists.

Shay brought the ball toward the half-court line as he randomly stared into the bleachers looking for his dad. Tears began to well in Shay's eyes.

"I must go on," Shay told himself. Shay put the ball in his left hand, then put his right hand in the air. Sticking up one finger, he motioned Michael to run the pick-and-roll play. Shay crossed the ball quickly to his right hand and lowered his shoulder.

"I'm about to shut you down," Ricky said as he taunted Shay.

Shay smirked as Michael moved forward and Shay guided Ricky into his body. Shay burst right as Ricky tried to fight to get around Michael's body.

"Nice roll, Michael," Coach Scott yelled from the bench. Just was Shay was about to pass the ball, he saw Michael's defender put his hands up.

73

Here comes Ricky! Shay thought to himself. Ricky was too little too late as Shay sunk the mid-range jump shot.

"You got that one, bum, but not next time!" With his face six inches from Shay's and his arm pressed against Shay's arm, Ricky taunted Shay.

"I don't fear you!" Shay defended his honor.

"You better!" Ricky began to speak as Shay hurried down the court to get to his defensive position. Ricky was inbounded the ball.

"You better fear me!" Ricky continued to taunt Shay.

"I was taught not to succumb to fear, so bring it on!" Shay responded.

"You ready!" Shay reached his right hand in and stripped the ball out of Ricky's left hand as he was about to attempt his move.

"See, you talk too much!" Shay said as he was trying to create distance between him and Ricky and make the layup. Everyone's eyes stared in awe as Shay began maneuvering through the air and doing his creative layup. The thing he did not expect is what happened next. The ball goes higher and higher when…

Bang! The ball bounces hard off of the backboard. Shay could not believe it. Ricky had blocked his shot and the crowd went wild with oohs and aahs. Shay stared into the stands.

"At least Daddy didn't watch me get embarrassed," Shay said as he shook his head in disbelief. "Time to hustle. Have to play defense," Shay told himself as he tried to get back in front of Ricky. Ricky put the ball behind his back, faked left, and then quickly went right. Just as Shay was moving back in front of him, he pulled up for a three-pointer. *Swish*! The crowd continued to cheer.

The Crossover that Won the Game

Shay heard a loud whistle blowing. Coach Scott called timeout. "Guys, we have to play defense. Shay, do you need a break?"

"No, Coach, I do not."

"All right because not only do you seem a bit exhausted, you seem distracted as well. I am going to give you another chance, Shay, because I believe in you."

"Thanks, Coach," Shay replied.

"All right, Shay, get the ball up the floor," Coach Scott yelled from the bench.

Banging bodies against Ricky, Shay used his forearm as a guard against Ricky's defense. "Back up, Ricky!"

"Or else what?" Ricky asked.

"This is what," Shay said as he put the ball behind his back using his right hand and then did an in-and-out dribble.

"That's not going to do anything," Ricky responded.

Shay quickly crossed the ball back to his right hand as Ricky broke his fall using his hands against the hardwood floor.

"You can't stop me. The only person that can stop me is me," Shay told Ricky. Shay stepped gracefully past Ricky and sunk the three-pointer. Shay stared Ricky square in the eyes as he backpedaled down the court. Shay glanced into the bleachers as he could not shake the pain of not seeing his dad present at the game.

"Good shot, Shay. That's just what we need," Liam said.

"Yeah, Shay, Ricky cannot guard you. Take him to school all game."

"Thanks, Chris," Shay replied.

"All right, back on defense!" Coach Scott yelled while clapping his hands.

"I wish my dad could have seen that shot. It was epic," Shay said to himself. "Well, maybe next game he will be here." Shay tried teaching himself how not to miss or need his father, but the undeniable truth was that children need their fathers.

Shay got back in his defensive position as he prepared to guard Ricky.

"You got me that time, Shay. I'll pay you back though," Ricky taunted Shay.

Ricky began doing a behind-the-back crossover. Shay was determined not to let Ricky score. Shay slid his feet well and watched Ricky's waist closely. As Ricky tried crossing the ball back into his right hand following the behind-the-back crossover, Shay stayed right in front of him.

"Hey, man, you better back off of me," Ricky told Shay.

Shay didn't say a word but continued playing defense close to Ricky. Ricky became frustrated, lowered his shoulder, and knocked Shay down. With Shay on the floor and an open look at the basket, Ricky swished the mid-range jump shot. Shay hopped up quickly and got in Ricky's face.

"What was that, man?" Shay yelled.

Ricky put his hand in Shay's face. "Just play ball, son."

"I'm not your son." Shay pushed Ricky. Shay and Ricky stood face-to-face, and the referee blew his whistle.

The Crossover that Won the Game

"Shay, this technical foul is on you! One more and you are out of here! Yes, ejected from the game."

I can't believe this. He ran me over and then teased me, Shay thought.

Shay watched as Ricky made the foul shot. Shay felt like his heart was in his stomach. He just shook his head. As he's trying to recover, he hears another whistle.

"Time out," Coach Scott yelled. "Shay, you're out of the game. I am not sure what happened to you out there, but I think you need to take some time to cool off."

"All right, Coach," Shay said.

The second quarter seemed to last forever. "Coach, can I go back in the game?"

"No, Shay, you must learn that there is a consequence for losing control," Coach Scott told Shay.

Shay sat and watched as New Perspectives Junior High School fell deeper and deeper behind to Win, Lose, No Draw Middle School. The score at halftime was 40–22.

"Okay, guys, it's not over yet. We are going to keep playing hard. We can get back in this game. Defend your opponents. Execute the plays we have worked on during practice. Shay, you're going back into the game. And I need you to remember that you should not let someone's actions cause you to behave uncharacteristically. All right…Defend! Execute! Defense on 3! 1…2…3."

"Defense!" the team yelled almost in unison.

"Hey, Shay, we need you, bro," Chris said.

"Yeah, buddy, I'm back in this," Shay said as he and Chris pounded fists.

Third Quarter

Ricky brought the ball up the court. Shay met him at the half-court line. Ricky crossed the ball from his left to right hand in front of his body.

"You haven't learned yet, have you?" Ricky said.

"No! And I won't," Shay said as he stripped the ball with his left hand. Shay grabbed the ball with his right hand. Shay sprinted down the court and did a reverse layup to avoid Ricky blocking his shot. Score: 40–24.

Shay stole the ball as it was inbounded by Win, Lose, No Draw. Shay leaped and banged bodies with Ricky shooting a left hand layup. Lying there on the ground, Shay watched as the ball went through the net.

"Yes!" Shay yelled as Michael grabbed his hand and helped him to his feet. Shay smiled as heard the referee blow his whistle. Shay sunk the foul shot, completing the three-point play. This brought the score to 40–25.

"All right, guys, good job, but get back on defense," Coach Scott said.

Shay played tight on Ricky. As he got surprised by a screen, Liam stepped over to help Shay, but Ricky quickly passed it to his teammate that Liam was responsible for defending. Louis swished the three-pointer. Score now 43–25.

"That's all right, guys, keep playing hard out there," Coach Scott told the team.

Shay brought the ball up the court. He crossed the ball quickly between his legs and twice in front of Ricky. Shay ran Ricky right into the screen

The Crossover that Won the Game

that Michael set. With Chris and Liam spreading the floor, Shay faked a pass to Chris, then shot an alley-oop to Michael after he rolled to the basket. Score: 43–27.

The crowd cheered loudly disrupting the concentration of the inbound player for Win, Lose, No Draw. Coach Scott called for a 1-2-2 full court press. The ball flew through the air toward the half-court line. Shay watched and Ricky watched as he ran toward the ball. Just as he was about to grab the ball, Shay jumped and intercepted the pass. Ricky quickly got in front of Shay. Shay ran toward the basket. With Ricky body to body, Shay quickly stepped back. Timing Ricky's jump, Shay leaped with enough time to release a shot before Ricky could block it. *Swish!* Score: 43–30.

Ricky caught the inbound pass. He put his hand up, motioning for the team to slow the pace of the game down. The team made several passes before finding their center, Jovan, open underneath the basket. Layup successful! Score: 45–30.

At the half-court line, Shay began calling a motion 1 play. Chris ran around a screen set by William. Michael stepped up to set a screen for Shay. He then rolled off and set a screen for Liam who ran near the basket and faked like he was receiving a pass. Chris ran all the way over to the other side of the court. Approaching the left corner, Shay passed the passed the ball to Chris who pulled up for the three-pointer. The ball hit off of the right side of the rim and Jovan grabbed the ball and passed it to Ricky. New Perspectives Junior High School did not see shooting guard, Keith, and power forward, Jackson from Win, Lose, No Draw Middle School sprinting toward the opposite basket. Ricky launched the ball to Jackson who quickly passed the ball to Keith in order to confuse New Perspective defenders. Keith made the uncontested layup. Score: 47–30.

"Time is ticking away, guys. I want pick and rolls off the ball and isolation for Shay, if no pass option opens up," Coach Scott said during a timeout.

"Here we go, guys. We got this," Shay said as they walked back onto the floor. Shay brought the ball up the court.

Shay quickly crossed the ball from his right to left hand in front of Ricky. "You believe you can stop me?" Shay asked Ricky.

"I always believe in myself," Ricky replied.

10..."All right, well, I have ten seconds to show you that your belief will not help you stop me."

9...Shay put the ball in between his legs.

8...ball now in his right hand.

7..."You're not going to do anything with that ball," Ricky told Shay.

6...Shay called for the off-the-ball pick-and-roll play.

5...Shay dribbled the ball behind his back as he watched the plays happen to no avail.

4...Shay waved the play.

3...Shay hopped right, put the ball behind his back into his left hand. Ricky hopped with Shay. With Ricky erratically waving his hands in Shay's face and the clock reading 2, Shay faked left, then quickly crossed right. Creating just enough space, Shay jumped and quickly released his shot, and the snap of the wrist was heard like the snap of the net as the clock buzzed. Score: 47–33.

The players from New Perspectives Junior High School slapped hands as they went back to the bench. Shay heard several compliments but stared into the bleachers, wondering why his dad failed him once again.

The Crossover that Won the Game

Fourth Quarter

"Okay, just one more quarter...one more quarter!" Shay told himself. "I know we can win this game, but I just want it to be over. I do not want to play another moment while wishing Dad to be here and he's not. Why can't I just fall asleep and—"

Coach Scott interrupted Shay's daydream, "Shay, snap out of it. This is not the time for daydreams. We need you. One more quarter...one more quarter, then you can sleep, dream, daydream, do whatever makes you happy, but for now, I need you to go out there and give your best effort."

"Okay, Coach," Shay replied.

"It's New Perspectives' ball," the referee yelled.

"Michael, you're inbounding the ball," Coach Scott yelled.

With hands waving in his face, Michael ran along the baseline, trying to make a good pass to Shay. As Michael released the ball, Ricky stole it. He quickly passed it to Keith who made the three-pointer. Score: 50–33.

Hands once again waving in Michael's face, Shay motioned for Michael to throw the ball up high. Shay grabbed the pass and began sprinting down the floor. Ricky grabbed Shay's jersey. Shay crossed the ball in between Ricky's legs, then behind his own back. Shay hopped left, squared his feet, jumped, and sunk the three-pointer. "It's not over yet, Ricky," Shay said. Score: 50–36.

"Okay 2-1-2 press, guys. 2-1-2 press," Coach Scott yelled from the sideline. Shay and Chris set up near the foul line of their own basket. Michael set up at the half-court line, and William and Liam set up near the opposite foul line. As the ball was inbounded by Keith, Michael leaped in front of Jackson and stole the pass. After making one dribble, he passed the ball to Shay. Smiling in Ricky's face, Shay touch-passed the ball to Chris.

"Come on, Chris, we need this," Shay encouraged Chris. Chris jumped and released the ball. All eyes intently watching the ball for what felt like forever. The ball hit the rim and bounced high, barely missing the top of the backboard, the ball hit the rim and eventually fell through the net. Score: 50–39.

"Yes!" Shay yelled as he and Chris slapped hands.

"We got this!" Chris reassured Shay.

"Come on, man. It's not over yet," Shay reminded Chris.

"Oh yeah, I know it's not over. No one on your team can stop me so count your blessings now," said Ricky as he attempts to frustrate some of New Perspectives players.

"You may as well give up now, Shay. The game is in my hands now. The real star!" Ricky continued taunting.

Shay just stared Ricky square in the eye. He glanced occasionally at Ricky's waist to watch which direction he was intending to go. Not a word spoken, Shay just thought about the absence of his father. With a tear beginning to well in Shay's left eye, Ricky began his move. Ricky faked left…

"Where you going, bro?" Ricky asked. "I'm over here!"

Shay stood still. Ricky crossed the ball back into his right hand. With the shot clock winding down, Ricky crossed the ball quickly into his left hand. He hopped left. As Shay stepped left, Ricky quickly put the ball behind his back, leaving Shay behind.

"Ooooh! Ahhh!" the crowd began to cheer.

The Crossover that Won the Game

"Gone," Ricky said.

"Never give up," Shay remembered. "The only person that can beat me is me!" Shay meditated briefly on these words as he reached quickly around Ricky's back, tapping the ball into Liam's hands.

"Over here! Over here, Liam!" Shay yelled and clapped as he ran toward New Perspectives' side of the court.

"I got him!" Sam yelled as he hustled to get in front of Shay.

"Not really!" Shay responded as he did an in-and-out dribble and put the ball around Sam's body, catching the ball with his left hand. He quickly crossed the ball into his right hand. "Count those two points," Shay said as he got in Sam's face. Score 50–41.

"Shay, stop that!" Coach Scott yelled.

"Jovan, take the ball out," Coach Gene from Win, Lose, No Draw yelled from the bench.

"Over here!" Keith yelled.

Liam watched Jovan closely, and just as the ball was released, he made his move toward Keith from across the court. Liam stole the ball and touch-passed it to Shay who touch-passed it to Chris. Chris's three-point shot swished the net and further hushed the crowd. Score 50–44.

"Okay, guys, get back on defense. Great job! Keep up your level of intensity," Coach Scott told his team.

With hands waving, bleachers pounding, and yelling heard from every area of the gymnasium, Jackson managed to inbound the ball to Keith.

"Over here," Ricky yelled from the three-point line opposite their basket. Shay stayed body to body with Ricky and then...*thud*! Shay fell to the ground when suddenly running into a pick set by Sam.

"Liam, come on, man, you got to call out those picks," Shay yelled as he slowly got up from the floor. "I'll guard your man. You stay on Ricky!"

Sam hit Shay with an elbow to his right side.

"You better watch it, man!" Shay said.

Sam wrapped Shay's right arm with his left arm and shoved Shay. Shay hurried over to Sam and gave him a quick elbow to his left side as he was catching the ball.

The whistle blew rather loudly. "Foul! No elbows, Shay!" the referee said.

"Ref, did you see all that he did to me?"

"This is not a discussion!" the referee replied.

"He hooked my arm, he pushed me. Geez, he even hit me in the side with his elbow," Shay said in a stark tone of voice.

"One more comment, Shay, and you will be ejected!" Shay watched as Sam sunk both free throws. Score 52–44.

"Shay, run the P and R between you and William," Coach Crossover yelled after the second free throw went in.

The Crossover that Won the Game

Shay brought the ball up the floor. "All right, William, P and R at 3." Shay called a pick and roll play to start at the three-point line. Shay ran Ricky off of William's body.

"Over here, Shay!" William yelled as he rolled toward the basket with a smaller Ricky defending him. Shay ran quickly toward the foul line, then quickly stepped back behind the three-point line with Jovan guarding him.

Shay laughed as he squared his shoulders, jumped, and quickly released the ball over the hands of the much taller Jovan, center for Win, Lose, No Draw Middle School. Score 52–47.

With forty-five seconds left in the game, it was now or not at all for New Perspectives. Ricky brought the ball up the floor. Shay squared his feet and spread his hands wide.

"Defense! Defense!" the crowd roared. Boy, was Shay glad to hear the fans supporting them. As determined as Shay was to stop Ricky from scoring, he had no idea what awaited him. Surprised by a pick from Jovan, a basket for Win, Lose, No Draw seemed promising.

"Michael, you have to help!" Shay yelled as he struggled to get up from the hardwood floor.

"I'm on it, buddy!" Michael responded as he sprinted from the left side of the floor. Ricky leaped, lifted his right arm high for a beautiful finger roll. Michael leaped with hopes of stopping Ricky in his tracks. Everyone watched as the ball went higher and higher and higher, and Michael rose higher and higher and then…*smack*!

"Rejected!" Michael yelled, and William caught the ball and quickly passed it to Shay.

"Chris, you go right there." Shay pointed Chris to the three-point line. "Liam, I need you on my right!" Michael set a pick for Shay as Chris and Liam crossed behind William's back. Shay hopped out toward the left side of the court. Shay quickly crossed right. Watching Ricky's waist, Shay quickly crossed back right. With Ricky behind him, Shay made his start toward the basket. Keith stepped over to help cover Shay, and Jackson waited for Shay to attempt his layup. With hands in his face and bodies skewing his view of the basket, he remembered where his teammates were placed. Shay leaped, banged bodies with Jackson, and passed the ball behind his back and Keith's back to Chris. *Swish*! The crowd went wild as Chris made the three-point field goal from the left corner. Score 52–50.

"Great shot, Chris. Good way to be in position!" Shay said as he gave Chris a high five.

Ricky stands four feet beyond the three-point line, trying to allow more time to come off of the game clock.

"Don't guard him that close, Shay," Liam yelled out.

"Fifteen seconds remaining on the clock. Don't give up, guys," Coach Scott screamed to his guys as he paced quickly up the sideline.

14…13…12…11…10. Ricky just continued bouncing the ball.

9…8. Ricky passed the ball to Keith.

7…Shay watched Keith and Ricky simultaneously. Ricky ran toward Keith for the pass.

6…"Shay, look up! Chris yelled at the top of his lungs.

Shay barely got his fingertips on the ball.

The Crossover that Won the Game

"Shay, pick and roll with William and run the motion 1. Overtime!" Coach Scott yelled.

Shay took one last glance into the bleachers. Shay just shook his head in disbelief. *Dad really didn't show up!* Shay thought to himself. *I will make him proud anyway.* Shay finished his internal dialogue.

4..."Over here," Chris yelled to begin the motion 1. Shay simply didn't feel like running an off that play. He lost confidence in Coach Scott's ability to make the final decision.

3...Shay crossed between his legs from his left to his right hand. He quickly put the ball behind his back into to his left hand.

2...Shay faked the drive and stepped back.

"That move won't work this time!" Ricky said.

1...Shay leaped, and just as the clock was approaching 0, he released the ball. The players, coaches, and crowd watched with anticipation and varying hopes. Heads turned, eyes widened, jaws dropped, and so did Shay in great dismay as his shot hit the front of the rim. Game over and now disappointment, regret, and fear of failing will haunt him!

Postgame Speech

"Hey, guys! Do not hold your heads down. You played a great game, and when it was over, an amazing team happened to have two more points than another amazing team. I am so proud of how hard you guys played. You did exactly what any coach would ask of you...that you leave it out on the floor and that you give your all! Shay, you chose to do something different than what I asked of you. Can I promise that we would have gone into overtime if you had executed the play I designed? No, I cannot! But what I can tell you is that sometimes you have to listen to and trust other people even if you think your method or strategy is superior. However, my friend, you played with confidence, and no one should be upset at you for that. If the shot had gone in and we won the game, I would have had the same conversation with you, Shay," Coach Scott told the team.

Shay sat quietly, staring at the floor. Distraught Shay did not want to make eye contact with anyone in the room.

"Shay, look at me!" Coach Scott said with enthusiasm.

"Yeah, Coach?"

"I noticed that you were frustrated, and for some reason, you continued looking into the bleachers. But you know what?"

"What, Coach?"

"You never gave up. I remember how hard Coach Crossover worked to build your self-esteem. I also remember how hard you worked to become a better player."

"You are right, Coach Scott!" Shay said as he smiled just a little.

"Now those are the moments that define people," Coach Scott said.

"Thanks, Coach!"

"You're welcome, Shay! Never give up. Remain confident and know that failure simply makes you stronger and teaches you what to do and what not to do in order to succeed. Shay, you have the ingredients of a champion and I need you to know and believe that."

"Okay, Coach!"

The Crossover that Won the Game

"No matter how many times you lose, guys. You always win from within. Winning begins in here," Coach Scott said as he tapped his heart.

"Yeah, that's right!" the team roared. "We are winners!"

"All right, go home, and get a good night's sleep to be ready to do well in class tomorrow. No practice. Take a day off and think about all of things I said. I want tomorrow to be something like a mental practice. It is time to transform our minds and defeat our mental enemies. Love all of you, guys. I will see you soon!" Coach Scott concluded his postgame speech.

All of the other players hurried out of the locker room while Shay walked slowly toward the exit. Shay sat down on the bench and waited for his mom to arrive.

The Morning After

"Good morning, son!"

"Good morning, Mom!"

"How are you today?"

"I'm all right, Mom!" Shay replied.

"You're only all right? Wait…before you answer! Tell me what is bothering you."

"I just do not understand why Daddy didn't show up to the game last night. You didn't show up either, Mom, but I feel like I really need Dad's support!"

"Shay, I apologize, but you know I have to take care of your little sister, and sometimes, I have to babysit some of the grandchildren also. You want to eat when you get home, don't you?"

"I understand that you are busy, Mom, but I need support," Shay said as he choked on his words.

"I know you do, son," Mom said as she patted Shay on the back. "I will try to be at the next game. I will have to bring your little sister though."

"I would be so happy if you came to the last game of the season. If you have to bring Angel, then I understand," Shay said in a tone showing his disappointment.

"Can we call Daddy?" Shay asked.

"Sure we can!" Mom replied.

"Mom, I don't think he is going to…"

"Hello," Daddy said as he finished clearing his throat.

"What's up, Dad?"

"Not much, son! How are you?"

"I am not doing well."

"Why is that, son?" Daddy said in a concerned tone of voice.

"You weren't there!"

"Wasn't where, son?"

"At my game last night!"

"I am sorry, son. I was so busy and I didn't get your message in enough time to reschedule other engagements."

The Crossover that Won the Game

"Well, Dad, I have another game in a couple of days!"

"Well, son, I will be there! I have to change a few things around in my schedule, but I will be there to support you."

"Thanks, Dad! That would mean a lot to me," Shay said as he smiled.

"You're welcome, son. I have to run now, but have a great day, and I will see you in a couple of days. Okay, son! Oh, before I forget, what time is the game?"

"The game is at 5:00 p.m."

"All right, I will see you there!"

"Bye, Dad!"

"Bye, and have a great day!"

"Thanks, you have a great day also."

Their good-byes rang out simultaneously as the phones hung up.

"Hey, Mom, guess what?" Shay said, leaving his mother in anticipation.

"What?"

Shay just smiled. "Are you ready for this, Mom?" Shay asked.

"Come on, Shay! What is it?"

"Okay, I guess I will tell you." Shay laughed. "Daddy will be there!" Shay said enthusiastically.

"Be where, son?"

"At my game in two days!" Shay smiled.

"Well, son, that is great. You will play great. I just know it."

"Thanks, Mom."

"You're welcome, son. Get out there to catch your bus, all right!"

"Okay, bye, Mom. I will see you later," Shay said as he hurried out the door.

The school day went by rather quickly. Shay was very excited that Daddy would be at his final game of the eighth grade season. Shay was fired up and ready for practice.

"Hey, Chris, what's up?" Shay asked.

"Not much, bro! What's up with you?"

"I'm just excited, man."

"About what, bro? I want to know what's making you so excited!"

"My dad will be at the game tomorrow!" Shay said with a lot of expression in his voice.

"Whoa, that is awesome. I haven't seen him at any of the games. I can tell how excited you are though!"

"Yeah, man, I am very excited!"

The two friends slapped hands.

"Well, congrats, bro!" Chris said.

The Crossover that Won the Game

"All right, man, enough about that. It's time to go in this gym and run these plays!" The boys laughed.

"Hey, guys!" Coach Scott lightly tapped the boys on the arm.

"Yeah, Coach?" the boys asked in unison.

"Time for some awesome practice, not talking!" Coach Scott said as he laughed along with the Shay and Chris.

"All right, well, we do have a big game ahead of us tomorrow night!" Shay said.

"Yeah, you're right, Shay! Let's get in there for practice," Chris responded.

"Good idea!" Coach Scott interjected.

The three of them walked into the gym and began preparing for their big game.

"All right, guys, we are going to continue with the plays that we used last game," Coach Scott told the team. "I will also introduce a couple of new plays. We played a great game in our last game, but Win, Lose, No Draw defended pretty well overall. We have to be quicker when setting the pick, and whichever guard has the ball must run his defender as close to the player setting the pick as possible. To my players setting the pick, roll immediately."

"Coach, are the wing players switching sides or just spacing the floor?" Shay asked.

"Great question, Shay! I want my wing players to simply space the floor. On P&R2, the wing players, shooting guard and small forward. The power forward will always play the low box area to give the option of an additional outlet pass. If the power forward notices a shot will be taken, he must get in front of his man, protect the basket, and secure the rebound," Coach Scott replied.

"Coach, who will be starting at our next game?" Liam asked with his broken English.

"The same players from our last game will start. I hope to utilize our sixth man a bit more though," Coach Scott said.

Ace smiled. "I hope so, Coach! I have been practicing."

"I know, Ace, and your hard work will be rewarded. Just know that I will always make the decisions that are best for the team!" Coach Scott replied. "All right, guys, let's start running these plays. We have once again made it to the championship. You should be proud of yourselves!"

"Yeah! That's right because we are awesome," several players yelled out.

"All right! All right! We have a big game tomorrow night. I have faith in you, guys, but my gut feeling is the time that works the hardest will win this championship game. Are you guys ready to work hard?"

"Yes!" the players responded.

♦ ♦ ♦

"Great practice, guys! The pick and roll was done very efficiently. All of our motion plays have a very high chance of being successful. Execution is important. How hard you play is up to you. I can tell you this though: if you give your all out there tomorrow, I am pretty confident that you will win. At the least, they will have to play really hard to beat you guys. I want

The Crossover that Won the Game

you guys to study the play books tonight. Get a good night's sleep and make sure you eat a hearty breakfast."

"Okay, Coach, thank you for the kind words and good practice. I will see you tomorrow," Shay said.

"Shay, the good practice was a result of all of you guys' hard work," Coach Scott said with a smile.

The players began to exit the gym as Shay punched Chris in the shoulder. "Hey, man, we are going to do good tomorrow!"

"Yeah, bro, I think we can even beat Win, Lose, No Draw tomorrow!" Chris said with excitement in his voice.

"It would be awesome if we could win the championship!" Shay replied.

"Definitely!"

"Oh and…"

"Oh, and what?" Chris asked.

"I am going to make Ricky pay for all the crap he was talking last game!"

"Oh, you must," Chris said as he and Shay pounded fists.

"And my dad will be there so I definitely have to show him that I can play!"

"Shay, you will take him to school. You are an awesome player!"

"Thanks, Chris! I always appreciate words of encouragement. They fuel my fire, bro!" Shay said with enthusiasm.

"You're welcome! Well, I will see you tomorrow."

"All right, Chris, see you tomorrow!" Shay replied.

♦ ♦ ♦

"Hey, Mom," Shay said as he hopped in the car.

"Hey, son, how was practice?"

"It was really good. I think that we will play really well tomorrow."

"I hope that your team does very well, son."

"There is another reason that I am excited!" Shay said with hope that Mom would ask what he was excited.

"And why are you excited?

"Because Daddy will be at the game," Shay said with a huge smile on his face.

"Well, son, I surely hope he comes. I can tell how excited you are," Mom replied.

"Will you be there, Mom?"

"I will do my best," Mom said in a soft voice.

"Well, I hope so, Mom! Hey, Mom, can I ask you a question?"

"Sure, Shay."

The Crossover that Won the Game

"Can I use your phone to call Dad?"

"Sure you can, son. Here is my phone!"

◆ ◆ ◆

"Hello!" Dad answered in a deep voice.

"Hey, Dad, it's Shay!"

"Hey, son, how are you?"

"I am doing pretty good, Dad! How are you?"

"Son, I am doing well. I've just been working hard!"

"You're always working hard, Daddy," Shay replied.

"So, Shay, what did you want to talk about?"

"Well, Dad, do you remember what is happening tomorrow night?"

"Hmmm, let me think…"

"Come on, Dad! You really don't know what's going on tomorrow night?"

"Ha! Ha! Ha! I'm just joking, son. Your basketball game is tomorrow!"

"Will you be there, Dad?"

"You better believe it, son. I will be right there supporting my boy!"

"Thank you so much, Dad. You have no idea how much that means to me!" Shay replied with joy.

"Are you going to play hard and make some shots for me, son?"

"Oh, you better believe it, Dad," Shay said as he and Daddy laughed.

"Well, son, thanks for calling!"

"You're welcome, Dad."

"Son, I will see you tomorrow!"

"Bye, Dad, see you tomorrow!"

"Bye, son!"

♦ ♦ ♦

Mom pulled into the driveway and requested Shay's help with the groceries.

"Boy, do not run into that house and leave me to carry all of these groceries by myself. Learn the value of serving and being a gentleman. Be sure to always treat others the way you would like to be treated. That is called the Golden Rule. You understand, son?"

"Yes, I do, Mom. I'm sorry!"

"It's okay, son. I do not expect you to know everything, but myself and everyone else expects you to be a person who is teachable and capable of changing behaviors when necessary."

"Thanks, Mom!"

The Crossover that Won the Game

"You're welcome!"

"You know what, Mom?"

"What's that, son?"

"I wonder if Coach Crossover will be at the game!"

"Well, why don't you give him a call, Shay? I am sure that if he knew you had an important game and his schedule allowed him to be there, he would be right there in the bleachers supporting you!"

"You're right, Mom! I am going to give him a call once we finish taking the groceries into the house!"

"All right, Mom, all done! Can I use the phone again?"

"Sure, but call him from the house phone because my battery is a little low."

"Okay, Mom, thanks!"

♦ ♦ ♦

"Come on, Coach Crossover, answer the phone. It rang like six times already…"

"Hey! My buddy Shay! How are ya?" Coach Crossover said jokingly.

"I am doing well. What have you been up to?"

"I have just been volunteering at Confidence Elementary!"

"I thought you worked there, Coach!"

"Oh! Well no, I do not work there. I just love to help others and hopefully be a positive impact in their lives."

"Wow, I did not know that. That is really amazing!"

"Thanks, Shay!"

"Coach, are you busy tomorrow night at 7:00?"

"Well, Shay, I believe I am free!"

"That is great, Coach. Would you like to come to my championship game versus Win, Lose, No Draw?"

"Oh! Of course! I would love to watch you play."

"That would be very nice, Coach Crossover. I can't wait for you to see how much I have improved."

"Shay, I can't wait! I will be there, buddy!"

"Thanks, Coach Crossover. I can't wait to see you!" Shay said with a huge smile.

"Okay, I can't wait to see you either. I will talk to you later, Shay. Bye for now!"

"Bye, Coach, see you tomorrow!"

♦ ♦ ♦

"Is he coming, Shay?" Mom yelled from the kitchen where she was preparing dinner for her and the kids.

The Crossover that Won the Game

"Yeah, Mom, that means you, Dad, and Coach Crossover will be there," Shay said with a smile.

"I can't wait to see you play, son. You bounce the ball enough in the house." Mom laughed.

"Uh, I'm sorry, Mom!"

"Well, son, now it is time to see some of those crossovers on the court."

"I am going to show you guys a few, Mom!" Shay said with confidence.

"I am looking forward to watching you play, son!"

"Thanks, Mom!"

"You're welcome, son! All right, guys, time to eat dinner."

♦ ♦ ♦

"Thanks for dinner, Mom. It was very tasty. Chicken wings are my favorite!" Shay said with a smile.

"You're welcome, son!"

"All right, well, I am going to take a shower, call some of my friends, then go to bed so I can be rested for the game tomorrow!"

"Good night, son!"

"Good night, Mom!"

"Oh, Shay, make sure you brush your teeth also!"

"Okay will do! Night," Shay said as he made his way toward the staircase.

"Night, son," Mom said as Shay hurried up the stairs.

◆ ◆ ◆

Shay finished all of his nighttime routines. He had a few conversations with friends. Shay and Chris talked the longest of all. They talked about their excitement and hopes for the championship game tomorrow night. Shay had an overwhelming sense of excitement because the most important people in his life would be at the game to support him. Shay slept peacefully that night. He arose bright and early and ready for his day! Even more so, he was ready for his big game. The school day was over in a flash, but it seemed to take forever because of how excited Shay was to play the championship game in front of his fans and some of his most important supporters.

From the night before, to the school day that felt like an eternity, to the commute by bus to the game, the most frequent topic of conversation for Shay was playing in the championship game and his excitement about Coach Crossover, his mom, and most importantly, his dad being present at the game.

Shay listened intently to Coach Scott's pregame speech as he always had, but he was anxious to get out there and wave to Mom, Dad, and Coach Crossover. What he remembered most about Coach Scott's speech was this: "Your victory depends on you. Results are the black and white of effort, but success is always dependent on you and perspective! Play hard, give your all, and success will be the inevitable result!"

Shay smiled as he scanned the bleachers and saw the hands of Mom, Dad, and Coach Crossover waving at him. It was his time! Shay waved back, and smiled, then thought to himself, *This is my time, and the only person who can stop me is me!*

The Crossover that Won the Game

The starting five for both teams took the floor, and it was time to play ball!

Championship Game
New Perspectives Junior High School
versus
Win, Lose, No Draw Middle School

Starting 5 for New Perspectives Junior High School:

> Point guard: Shay
> Shooting guard: Chris
> Small forward: Liam
> Power forward: Michael
> Center: William

Starting 5 for Win, Lose, No Draw Middle School:

> Point guard: Ricky
> Shooting guard: Keith
> Small forward: Sam
> Power forward: Jackson
> Center: Jovan

First Quarter

Win, Lose, No Draw won the jump ball. Sam caught the tip and quickly passed the ball to the teams point guard, Ricky.

"Shay, it's about to be—" Ricky was stripped by Shay in the middle of his sentence.

Shay sprinted up the floor and made the contested layup.

"I guess it's going to be a long game for you, Ricky!" Shay said with an air of confidence.

"All right, guys, we are playing intense defense like that all game long!" Shay told New Perspectives' players.

"Good job, guys. Keep up the intensity. We have a long game ahead of us!" Coach Scott yelled from the bench.

"Space the floor, boys!" Ricky yelled to his teammates. Keith positioned himself on the right wing. Sam ran from the left wing to the left corner while Jackson made his movement forward to set a pick for Ricky. Jovan remained near the basket.

"Pick coming on your right side!" Michael yelled.

Ricky quickly moved right and then crossed the ball between his legs into his left hand. He banged bodies with Shay.

"You will never be able to guard me!" Ricky said as he quickly passed the ball to Sam who sunk the three-pointer. Score: WLND 3–NP 2.

"Come on, Liam, you got to stay with your man!" Shay said out of frustration.

"Thanks, Shay. I will pick it up!"

Liam inbounded the ball to Shay. The two of them walked up the court together.

"Hey, Liam, when I get to the three-point line, I am to run the IF3 play. I will hold up my right middle, ring, and pinky fingers."

"All right, team, let's go!" Shay yelled as he held up the middle, ring, and pinky fingers on his right hand.

New Perspectives' players spaced the floor as Shay began to take Ricky off the dribble. On the left side of the floor, Liam ran toward Shay and Ricky to set a pick. He then curled back and ran off of a back pick set by Michael. Shay quickly burst past Ricky going left, then bounce-passed the ball in between the defense giving Liam the open layup. Score WLND 3–NP 5.

"Keep executing like that, guys!" Coach Scott told his team.

"Guys, it is okay! Make sure you talk to each other when picks are coming!" Win, Lose, No Draw's coach said.

"Okay, guys, let's run them off the court. We beat them once and we can beat them again!" Ricky said.

"Are you sure, Mr. Big Mouth?" Shay asked.

"You will see, man!" Ricky responded. Ricky hopped right and then quickly put the ball behind his back. Shay stuck his right hand in to tap the ball away from Ricky. Shay ran quickly toward the basket.

"Get your hands off me!" Shay said as Ricky grabbed his jersey.

"It won't be that easy, Shay!" Ricky responded.

Shay slapped Ricky's hand away and continued toward the basket giving New Perspectives a 7 to 3 lead over Win, Lose, No Draw.

"It doesn't have to be easy. It just has to be worth it!" Shay told Ricky as he ran back down the court, overhearing yelling as he transitioned back into a defensive set.

"Yeah, you better go, boy. You are awesome, Shay!" Mom yelled from the bleachers. Dad sat next to Mom, watching intently. Coach Crossover sat nearby, wondering who was yelling for his buddy, Shay.

"I am going to ask them at halftime!" Coach Crossover told himself.

"Three-pointer!" the referee said while holding both arms in the air. Score: WLND 6–NP 7.

Coach Scott remained quiet but knew his team needed to defend the perimeter better. "I believe that they will figure it out on their own!" Coach Scott said to himself.

"Okay, William, P&R!"

"All right, man!" William replied.

"Get to your positions!" Coach Scott yelled.

"Now, William, now!" Shay called for the pick. William ran quickly and placed his frame to the left side of Ricky. Shay ran quickly toward the basket.

"Roll, William!" Shay yelled.

"He's never going to get around Jovan!" Shay said.

Ricky hustled around William and made his way back in front of Shay. Shay faked left, then continued right, creating space between him and Ricky. Shay smiled!

I got this! Shay thought to himself. Jovan stepped closer toward the basket. Shay leaped and let the ball go. The ball floated higher and higher! Jovan floated higher and higher. Jovan's hands were high in the air as Shay landed while watching with expectation of success.

"Get that garbage out of here!" Jovan said as he blocked Shay's shot.

Jackson grabbed the ball and passed it to Ricky. Ricky ran quickly along the right side of court.

The Crossover that Won the Game

"Get back on defense!" Coach Scott yelled.

Ricky passed the ball to Sam who quickly passed the ball to Keith. Keith put the ball behind his back immediately. Stopped short of driving to the basket and swished the mid-range jump shot. Score WLND 8–NP 7.

"Okay, guys, there are only six seconds left in the quarter. Shay, the offense is running through you on this play!" Coach Scott said.

Shay bounced the ball at the three-point line, waiting for Ricky to flinch.

"Are you just going to stand there?" Shay asked Ricky.

"You're not even doing anything, man!" Ricky responded.

With the clock reading 3, Shay bounced the ball between his legs. Clock reading 2, Shay faked hard right. With Ricky now right in his face, Shay crossed the ball quickly into his left hand. One second left in the quarter, Shay jumped and released the ball with a perfect snap of the wrist. *Swish!* Shay smiled as he stared Ricky in the eyes.

"It's going to be a different game! I hope you're ready!" Shay said as he walked off of the court.

"Great shot, Shay!" Coach Crossover yelled.

There were several cheers for the heroics Shay had shown so far.

"He sure is a good player, Ruby!" John, Shay's dad, said to his wife.

"Yes, he sure is!" Mom responded.

"Who is that guy over there that keeps cheering for Shay?" Dad asked.

"I believe that is Shay's sixth grade coach, Coach Crossover!"

"Oh, okay. I'd like to meet him!" Dad said.

"We can go sit with him at halftime!"

"Okay!" Dad responded.

In the huddle prior to starting the second quarter, Coach Scott was giving New Perspectives a brief pep talk.

"Okay, you guys are playing really well. Keep up the same intensity. Shay, I like your confidence and wise play. Team, you are moving the ball really well. Continue to play hard and move without the ball. Let's go out here and give our all and our best in this second quarter. Okay, fight on 3."

"1...2...3...fight!" New Perspectives team resounded throughout the gymnasium.

Second Quarter

When New Perspectives Junior High School yelled "Fight," that is exactly what they meant. The two teams traded baskets for much of the second quarter, but Shay and the team refused to give up.

"Okay, listen, we are down by 7, but this quarter is not over yet!" Shay told the team.

"Over here, William! Pass the ball high!" Shay said as he attempted to catch the inbound pass over Ricky.

"This quarter belongs to me, Shay!" Ricky said.

"Hmmm, we'll see about that!" Shay replied.

The Crossover that Won the Game

Shay jumped and caught the ball. He faked right and then went left.

"You will not be scoring anymore this quarter! That's a promise!" Ricky told Shay.

Shay motioned for Liam and Chris to cross to opposite sides of the court. Liam and Chris ran as William and Michael set picks for them. Shay crossed to the right and then spent left. He noticed Chris out of the corner of his eye. Shay made the quick bounce pass.

"I got this, Shay!" Chris said as he motioned for the ball. *Swish!* Chris sunk the three-pointer! Score WLND 27–NP 23.

"I guess you forgot that there is no 'I' in team, Ricky!" Shay said as he backpedaled down the court.

"Stay aggressive on defense!" the coach from Win, Lose, No Draw yelled from the bench.

Shay stopped backpedaling and got as close to Ricky as he could without fouling him. "Determination," Shay told himself.

Ricky crossed the ball quickly in front of Shay's face, then from left to right.

"I'm right here, Ricky!" Shay said.

Ricky faked right, then continued bouncing the ball in his right hand. Shay squared his feet and spread his hands wide. Ricky crossed the ball quickly to his right hand, then bounce-passed the ball quickly to Jackson who cut to the basket after faking as if he was going to set a pick on Shay.

Score WLND 29–NP 23.

Persistence, Shay thought to himself. "Hey, guys let's keep playing hard. Persistence is what we need right now!" Shay told his teammates.

Shay brought the ball down the court. At the half-court line, Shay began calling a motion 2 play. Liam ran around a screen set by Michael. William stepped up to set a screen for Shay. He then rolled off and set a screen for Chris who ran near the basket and faked like he was receiving a pass. Liam ran all the way over to the other side of the court. Approaching the left corner, Shay passed the ball to Liam and quickly cut to the basket.

"Over here!" Shay called out.

Liam faked the shot, then passed the ball to Shay.

"I got this!" Shay said as he jumped and scooped the ball under Jackson's arms, making the fancy finger roll layup. Score WLND 29–NP 25.

"That was luck!" Jackson said.

"No, that was in your face!" Shay said as he smirked.

"Great execution and patience, guys," Coach Scott yelled from the bench.

"Guys, defense wins games!" the coach from Win, Lose, No Draw yelled from the opposite bench.

Ricky brought the ball up the court and motioned for Keith to come around the back of him to grab the ball. Shay saw Keith coming and lay in wait like a lion for his prey. Shay lunged around Keith's back as he grabbed the ball from Ricky. Shay tapped the ball out of Keith's hand and sprinted the opposite direction.

"Over here, Chris!" Shay yelled as he ran down the court.

The Crossover that Won the Game

Chris passed the ball to Shay and hustled down the court beside him, approximately seven feet to the left. "I'm here to help if you need it, bro!" Chris yelled.

Shay noticed Chris running beside him. Shay crossed the ball to his left hand very quickly in front of Keith. Shay leaped, and it looked as if he was about to deliver the finishing blow of the first half. Then suddenly, while in midair, Shay passed the ball to Chris. Chris leaped and released the ball...

Bang! Ricky smashed into Chris's body as he tried to block his shot. Chris lay on the floor, breathing and watching the ball fly through the air with great expectation.

The referees' whistle blew loudly. "Foul on the play!" the referee yelled.

Swish! The ball went through the net. By this time, Shay had ran over to give Chris a hand up. They slapped hands and embraced. "Great shot, Chris! Now make this foul shot and we go into halftime with a tie score. You can do it, man. Just relax and focus!"

The sweat dropped from Chris's forehead as he informed the referee that he would not be able to shoot the foul shot as he was shaken up from being knocked to the ground. Coach Scott informed Shay that he would be shooting the foul shot.

"Ace, you will be starting the third quarter!" Coach Scott said.

The sweat rolled down Shay's cheeks, dripped to the floor, and clouded his vision. Shay bounced the ball three times. Now holding the ball in both hands, Shay told himself, "My moment is now. Our moment is now! This is for me, for the team, for those who believe in me and those who do not and perhaps never will believe!"

Shay sunk the foul shot. Score WLND 29–NP 29.

Halftime

"Okay, guys, I am going to keep this short and sweet: keep fighting! Keeping playing as hard as you're playing! If you do that, we will win this game. Go out there and have a productive halftime shoot around. Execute and fight, fight...fight!"

The team worked on layups and reviewed their plays and second-half strategies.

"Hey, Ace, are you ready?" Shay asked.

"Man, I don't know. I am pretty nervous!" Ace responded.

"You may be nervous, but we are a team. You can do it! We will get this victory together. Guess what?"

"What?" Ace answered.

"The greatest basketball player to ever live was nervous before every game! He has six championship rings. Won several scoring titles and he is currently the third all-time leading scorer in NBA history. You want to talk about nervousness? No, let's talk about turning anxiety into adrenaline and performing!"

"Wow, thanks, Shay! Which player are you talking about?"

"Ha! Ha! I am disappointed, my friend...none other than the great MJ!"

"Oh my goodness, I should have known that!" Ace said as he shook his head.

"Put your game face on because it's game time!" Shay said in closing.

On the other side of the court, another conversation was developing.

The Crossover that Won the Game

"Hey, Coach Crossover, how are you?" Mrs. Ponder, Shay's mom, startled Coach Crossover.

"Hello there, Mrs. Ponder. How are you?"

"I am doing well Mr. Crossover. How are you?"

"I am doing well. I am really admiring how hard Shay is playing!"

"Hey, meet my husband!" Mrs. Ponder said.

"I'm John!"

"Nice to meet you, I am Mr. Charlie Crossover!"

"It's nice to meet you as well!" John responded.

"He is playing really hard!" all parties said in unison.

"He is playing really well also!" Coach Crossover said.

"Well, you taught him a lot, sir!" Mrs. Ponder said.

"Thank you, ma'am, he's a great kid and it will always be my absolute pleasure to be involved in his life and help in any way that I can!"

"We really appreciate you!" Mr. and Mrs. Ponder replied.

"Hey, let's sit together!" Coach Crossover said.

"We don't want to impose!" Mrs. Ponder replied.

"Oh, don't be silly. I came alone and it would be great to cheer for Shay together."

"Yes, that would be nice!" Mr. Ponder responded.

"Yes, I concur!" Mrs. Ponder said as she chuckled.

The three of them decided to sit together for the remainder of the game to cheer for someone they knew and loved.

Third Quarter

"All right, Ace, let's do this!" Shay said after Ace inbounded the ball to him.

"I don't know if I am ready, man!" Ace replied.

"Hey, you have to be confident, man. I can tell you stories of how confidence changes both perspective and performance. I have faith in you, my friend," Shay said as he hurried the ball beyond the half-court line.

"Over here, Shay!" William yelled from the low post.

Ricky waved his hands relentlessly in front of Shay's face. Shay ball faked high and then bounced the ball low to William. William and Jovan banged bodies. William spun left and then slapped the backboard, giving New Perspectives a 31–29 lead over Win, Lose, No Draw.

"All right, guys, we are going with a P&R on the weak side. Strong side, space the floor!" Ricky told his teammates.

Jackson set a hard pick on Shay. Shay fought to get around the pick but fell to the floor. Michael stepped up to guard Ricky. Ricky crossed the ball quickly to his left. He then hopped left and swiftly crossed the ball between his legs.

"I'm cutting!" Jackson yelled. Ricky chest-passed the ball to Jackson who touch-passed it to Sam in the corner. Sam sunk the three-pointer from the corner. Score WLND 32–NP 31.

The Crossover that Won the Game

"Great execution, guys," the coach yelled.

"Hey, guys, just keep playing hard," Coach Scott yelled. "Michael, you inbound the ball. Ace, you get down the left side of the floor. Liam, you go to the right corner, and, William, you go to the low post on the left."

Ricky met Shay at the half-court line. Shay saw Ace out of the corner of his eye. Shay burst left and went to pass the ball to Ace when suddenly, Ricky stuck his hand out and stripped the ball. Ricky sped down the court and Shay chased after him. The two ran neck and neck and Ricky leaped. Shay leaped shortly after. The rose higher and higher as Shay swung to block the shot immediately after Ricky released the ball off of the backboard giving Win, Lose, No Draw a 34–31 lead over New Perspectives. Ricky stared Shay up and down and then up and down again.

"You thought you were going to block my shot? Ha! Ha! Why would you even waste your time on a thought like that?" Ricky taunted Shay.

Shay hung his head low in frustration for how poorly New Perspectives Junior High School had begun the second half of the championship game. Shay also hung his head in desperation for his team to do better.

"Pick your head up, Shay!" Mom yelled.

"Yeah, it's not over yet!" Coach Crossover yelled.

Dad just sat quiet as he usually did. Shay looked up into the bleachers and smiled.

"All right, guys, same idea but just look for different options," Coach Scott told New Perspective players.

The players took their positions. Ricky ran a man to man full court press against Shay.

"I'm not worried about your defense!" Shay said.

"I am going to strip that…"

Shay crossed quickly to his left. Just as Ricky recovered, Shay spun quickly to his right.

"You are not going any…" Ricky began saying as Shay took off to his right, then crossed the ball in between his legs into his left hand. With Ricky slightly to the right, Shay had just enough space to take the three-pointer! Shay squared his feet beneath his shoulders, leaped, and released. Ricky stood watching as the ball snapped the net. Score: WLND 34–NP 34.

"Maybe you should do more playing than talking, Ricky!" Shay said as he backpedaled down the court.

Shay watched as the ball was being inbounded to Ricky. Shay quickly jumped in front of Ricky and stole the ball. With Ricky trailing and Sam closing in, Shay stepped right then to the left and passed the ball behind his back to Ace who had spotted up in the right corner. Ace released the ball and sunk the shot and gave New Perspectives a 36–34 lead over Win, Lose, No Draw.

"Yes!" Ace shouted.

"Great shot, Ace! Keep moving and getting open. I will get you some good shots, man!" Shay assured Ace.

Ricky brought the ball up the court. "Crisscross, guys!" Ricky yelled to Keith and Sam.

Just as they crisscrossed, Ricky burst toward the basket, leaving Shay to trail behind.

The Crossover that Won the Game

"Never ever give up!" Shay told himself.

Shay allowed adrenaline to supersede exhaustion, persistence to supersede pity. Ricky jumped and so did Shay. As the ball rose, so did Shay and…

Bang! Shay blocked the shot off of the backboard. William grabbed the rebound and quickly passed the ball to Shay. Shay dribbled through two defenders, but the ball was knocked out of his hands from behind. Sam grabbed the ball and quickly passed it to Keith who made the three-pointer.

Score: WLND 37–NP 36.

Shay sat on the floor. When he heard "Timeout!"

The New Perspective players solemnly walked toward the bench.

"Guys, pick your heads up and get some pep in your step! We are playing well. I only have three words for you: patience, persistence and passion! How bad do you want to win? How badly do you want to be champions? You have a little over one quarter left to play. We all know you are champions, it's time to show all who are not yet aware. Guys, it happens right here and it happens right now!"

"All right, Ace, space the floor," Shay said.

Ace ran along the right side of the floor. William set the pick and Ace curled around his body. Setting up on the right wing, Ace made the three-pointer. Score WLND 37–NP 39.

New Perspectives players did not get back on defense fast enough. Ricky brought the ball up the court and passed the ball to Keith who was wide open. Ace ran toward him. Keith ball faked and went around Ace as he jumped. Keith's three-point field goal gave Win, Lose, No Draw a 40–39 lead over New Perspectives.

Shay brought the ball up the floor. "Michael, run the post play!"

Michael got in position. He motioned for the ball up high, but Ricky obscured his vision and ability to make a good pass. "Down-low," Michael yelled.

Michael reached for the ball, but Jackson was too quick. Jackson stuck his hands in the path of the ball. After stealing, he quickly passed the ball to Keith who passed the ball to Ricky. Ricky crossed the ball quickly to his right and lobbed the ball to Sam who made the uncontested layup.

Score WLND 42–NP 39.

There are ten seconds left in the quarter! Shay thought to himself. Shay pointed to the floor, motioning William to set the pick.

"Right there, Will!" Shay ran quickly around William's body and then lobbed the ball over Jovan.

"Good pass, Shay!" William said as he attempted the finger-roll layup. The ball rolled off the other side of the rim. Four seconds now remain. Sam grabbed the rebound and quickly passed the ball to Jackson. The players watched the ball flying through the air from half court. New Perspective players hearts sunk as Jackson made an unbelievable shot. Score WLND 45–NP 39.

Fourth Quarter

"Okay, guys, this is your moment. We have one more quarter. Just ten more minutes to give everything we've got and see if it pays off!" Coach Scott said to the team.

"Coach, can I say something?" Chris asked.

The Crossover that Won the Game

"Of course, you can!" Coach Scott replied.

"My fellow teammates, you mean so much to me. I have 100 percent faith and belief in you. We have all worked so hard. I really wish I could be out there with you, but I will be cheering you on and I will be with you in spirit. Go out there and win a championship for us."

"Thank you, Chris!" Coach Scott said.

"Oh and, Shay, no one can stop you but you!"

"Thanks, buddy," Shay said while smiling.

Jovan inbounded the ball to Ricky.

"Man to man press!" Coach Scott yelled.

Shay guarded Ricky body to body. "Go for the steal, Shay!" Chris yelled.

Shay reached his left hand in and tapped the ball away from Ricky. Ricky hopped over to get in front of Shay when suddenly, Shay put the ball in between Ricky's legs, then made a layup at the front of the basket. Ricky just looked at the ball drop through the net.

"Do it again, guys!" Coach Scott yelled.

Again, Shay defended Ricky body to body.

"Get off me, Shay!" Ricky demanded.

"You're going to have to make me!" Shay replied.

"Okay, I will!" Ricky said as he knocked Shay down after hitting him in the chest with his left elbow.

Shay got up slowly as he watched Ricky run the length of the court and make several passes that lead to a layup for himself.

"Come on, ref," Shay raised his voice. "He hit me right in the chest with an elbow!"

"Shay, technical foul," the ref replied.

Shay stared at the floor as Ricky made the foul shot. Score: WLND 48–NP 41.

Shay brought the ball up the floor. Shay looked around briefly. "I am going to make Ricky pay for that!" Shay returned the elbow to Ricky.

"Foul," the referee said as he blew his whistle.

"Substitution," Coach Scott called out. "Shay, you need a little break!"

"Coach, I need to be in there right now. It's the fourth quarter and we are losing by 8!"

"Shay, I understand this, but if you are frustrated and making poor decisions, as a result, you will not help yourself or the team. I'll get you back in there, but you have to calm down a bit!"

"Okay, Coach!"

Shay watched as his team continued to struggle. "The score is 55 to 41, Coach Scott! Can I go back in?" Shay asked.

"In a moment, Shay," Coach Scott replied.

"Hey, Coach, can I have a moment with him?"

"Hey, my friend, sure you can," Coach Scott replied.

Shay looked up and smiled. Much to his surprise, Coach Crossover had come to the bench to talk to him.

"Hey, Coach Crossover," Shay said.

"Hey, Shay, so I will be brief because I know how much you want to go out there and support your team."

"Thanks, Coach Crossover!"

"Do you remember how hard you worked to learn how to do a crossover efficiently?"

"Yes, Coach Crossover, I do!" Shay replied.

"It will always be your hard work that brings you success. Complaining will not bring you success! Getting upset at others without finding a solution to the problem will not bring you success. Always look within self. It is there that you will find your strength. It is there that you will know what you have to do to achieve the best possible results. And if you ever need advice talk to your parents, Coach Scott, or me. You know that I will always only be a phone call away. And God is always ready to hear from you also, Shay. I, Coach Scott, your fans, your team need you to show your frustration and anger through some butt-kicking basketball playing," Coach Scott said as he chuckled.

"Thank you very much, Coach Crossover!" Shay replied.

"Shay, people will criticize and you know what?"

"What?" Shay answered.

"Life will not always be fair! But you have to make the best out of every situation or circumstance. Now you have five minutes left in your final game for New Perspectives Junior High School. You are the only one who can choose how to spend those five minutes. Simply give your best and as always you have my support. If you need any support, I will be right over there," Coach Crossover pointed over to where he had been sitting with Shay's parents.

Shay stared in the direction Coach Crossover was pointing. Shay smiled and waved to his parents. "Thanks, Coach Crossover. I am more than ready now," Shay said while smiling.

"All right, Shay, I see that you are ready and well equipped to perform! Get ready, Shay!" Coach Scott said. "And thanks a lot, Coach Crossover!"

"You're welcome! Anything for my best buddy, Shay," Coach Crossover said.

"All right, Shay, you're going back in!"

"Thanks, Coach!"

"Hey, Shay," Chris called out.

"What's up?"

"You can do it, bro!" Chris said as him and Shay pounded fists.

"You're right, man, I can!"

Shay subbed into the game with extreme confidence.

"All right, guys, we can do this!" Shay told his teammates.

The Crossover that Won the Game

Shay brought the ball up the floor and motioned for Michael to set the pick.

"Right there on his body, Mike!" Shay said.

Michael set a solid pick and Shay began his movement. Michael rolled quickly to the left and raised his left hand for the ball.

"Look up, Michael!" Shay said as he lobbed the ball.

Michael jumped, caught, and released the ball before gravity brought him back to the floor. Score: WLND 55–NP 43.

"Okay, team that is what I like to see! I am totally excited about your high level of play," Coach Scott told New Perspectives players.

"Space the floor and make good movements!" Ricky yelled to his team.

Win, Lose, No Draw players began running their play. Ricky began bounce-passing the ball to Keith when Ace stepped in and stole the pass. Ace moved left around Keith's body, then passed the ball over Ricky's head to Shay. Ace continued to run the floor. Shay put the ball behind his back, hopped right, then quickly went left.

"Get ready, Ace!" Shay yelled as he swiftly passed the ball.

"I'm ready!" Ace replied as he raised his hands to catch the pass. Ace caught the pass and laid the ball softly off of the backboard. Score: WLND 55–NP 45.

Ricky brought the ball up the court. "Run the motion 1, guys!" Ricky told the team.

Sam crossed to the other side of the court and used a pick set by Jackson. Jovan moved to the high post as Keith faked as if he was going to set a pick for Ricky, then went back door and ran toward the basket. Ricky shot a quick pass to Keith. Keith leaped while looking at William. William jumped with hands high, attempting to block Keith's shot. Keith scooped the ball under William's arms and converted on the beautiful finger roll layup. Score: WLND 57–NP 45.

"Stay in the game, guys! It's not over yet," Coach Scott told the team.

"Space the floor, guys!" Shay yelled out as he bounced the ball at the half-court line. Shay dropped his hand and made his move toward the basket.

"You're not going anywhere, man!" Ricky said.

"Oh, you want to bet?" Shay asked. Shay stared at Ricky's waste. He ran right and then quickly switched directions. Ricky stuck his foot in Shay's path. As Shay fell to the ground, Ricky picked up the ball, ran the length of the court, and made an uncontested layup. Score WLND 59–NP 45.

Shay smiled as he watched Ricky make the layup. "He will pay for that!" Shay told himself.

"Okay P&R! P&R!" Shay yelled out. Shay ran Ricky off of Michael's body and faced Jovan at the basket.

"You cannot stop me!" Shay said as he reversed the ball from the right to the left side of the rim.

"Two points!" the ref yelled! Score: WLND 59–NP 47.

New Perspectives set up the full court press. Jackson passed the ball into Ricky who tried to pass the ball over Shay's head. Shay leaped and knocked the ball into Ace's hands.

The Crossover that Won the Game

"Look up, Shay!" Ace yelled as he passed the ball back to Shay. Shay touch passed the ball to Liam as Ricky ran to defend the drive. *Swish!* Liam drained the three-pointer. Score: WLND 59–NP 49.

Ricky managed to catch the inbound pass despite the efficient defense of New Perspectives Junior High School.

"Pick off the ball, Sam!" Ricky motioned for Jovan and Jackson to play the high post as Keith ran off of Sam's pick. Keith broke free from Ace. Keith released the jump shot.

"Box him out!" Shay yelled as he watched the ball bounce off the rim. William grabbed the rebound and passed the ball to Shay.

"Fast break, guys," Shay called out. Shay ran with determination. Ricky guarded him closely. Shay seen Michael on his right side and slightly in front of Jackson. Shay shot the alley-oop and watched as Michael slapped the glass as Jackson barely missed the block. Score: WLND 59–NP 51.

"2-1-2 Press!" Coach Scott yelled out.

New Perspectives players set up the 2-1-2 press. Shay tapped the ball out of Sam's hand. Sam stepped so close to Shay that they were body to body.

"You guys never learn your lessons, do you?" Shay asked.

Sam stared at Shay and shook his head.

Shay hopped right. "You will today!" Shay said.

"I doubt it!" Sam replied.

Shay faked a crossover to the left, then quickly to the right.

"I'm right here!" Sam said.

Shay pump faked and made his move as Sam landed and struggled to get back on defense. Shay headed right and went directly at William and floated the ball over his hand. Score: WLND 59–NP 53.

Ricky brought the ball up the floor.

"Get back on defense, guys!' Shay yelled.

Shay ran body to body with Ricky. Ricky felt Shay close to him and leaped to draw the foul. Shay jumped along with Ricky. The shot missed and Shay kept his hands straight in the air. Ricky landed and fell to the ground!

"Foul!" the ref yelled.

"I didn't touch him, ref!" Shay pleaded.

"Young man, don't contest my call! I will eject you from the game and it's almost over."

Shay shook his head and watched as Ricky made the first foul shot. Ricky missed the second shot and Michael grabbed the rebound. Score: WLND 60–NP 53.

"Motion 1!" Shay yelled from the half-court line. Shay watched as the play unfolded. Shay made his move toward the middle of the foul line and noticed Ace in the right corner. Shay passed the ball across the court and watched as Ace released the open three-pointer. Score: WLND 60–NP 56.

The Crossover that Won the Game

"Okay, guys, we are right where we need to be at this point! Keep fighting!" Coach Scott yelled as he ran up the sideline.

New Perspectives set up their half-court press to preserve energy for the last minute of the game. Ricky passed the ball to Keith.

"Post play, Jackson!" Keith yelled out.

Keith passed the ball to Ricky and ran to around Jackson's body to the other side of the court. Ricky ran toward the basket and passed the ball to Jackson. Jackson banged bodies with Michael.

"Game over, buddy!" Jackson said as he spun and floated the ball toward the basket. New Perspectives watched as their dreams began to slip further and further away. The rolled and rolled and rolled some more before it fell out of the basket. Michael grabbed the rebound and passed the ball to Liam. Liam ran up the court and passed the ball to Shay who passed the ball back to Liam.

"There's only twenty seconds left, Liam. You got to nail this, man!" Shay told Liam.

Liam made the mid-range jump shot. Score: WLND 60–NP 58.

Ricky brought the ball up the court and Win, Lose, No Draw began running the clock down. 15…14…13…12…11…10…9. Ricky took his eyes off of the ball and Shay tapped the ball away. Shay and Ricky both dove on the floor for the ball. Shay gained possession and called timeout with seven seconds remaining.

"Okay, guys, we have one shot here! Shay, I am putting this one on you. You have worked so hard. Run the isolation play. Guys, space the floor. If

Shay cannot get a good shot, run the off the ball pick and roll on Shay's cue. We have faith in you."

Shay nodded his head as he breathed heavily.

Shay held up his left hand. He dropped it, then bounced the ball from left to right. With four seconds left, Shay burst quickly to his left and began driving in for the layup. Ricky held his hands up and stayed body to body with Shay. Two seconds remain and Shay suddenly hopped back behind the three-point line, leaving Ricky feet away. One second remain Ricky leaped and so did Shay. Tenths of a second remained as Shay let the ball roll softly off his fingertips. The clock dropped to zero and Shay watched his dream fly through air. Shay couldn't think, couldn't speak, he just knew what he had so sincerely hoped for...

The ball continued to fly through air and the players continued to watch with varying hopes, dreams, and expectation. Wait no more! The dream came true. Ricky and his fellow teammates buried their heads in disbelief and Shay leaped for joy shortly before being tackled by his fellow teammates. He went down a hero.

"Hey, guys, your son really played a great game. He has learned to trust in his abilities and to not allow fear to inhibit him!" Coach Crossover told Mr. and Mrs. Ponder.

"We personally thank you for investing into his life. We know that it will have a long-lasting effect on him," Mr. Ponder said.

"It has always been my pleasure!" Coach Crossover responded.

"You're going to be around to continue helping him, right?" Mrs. Ponder asked.

"I plan to always be in his life. I will be pretty busy this next school year though, but I will try to make time for him whenever possible!"

"He would really like that!" Mr. Ponder said.

"You know, Mr. Ponder, Shay really wants to spend more time with you!"

"You are right, Coach Crossover. I plan to rearrange my work schedule to be available more often to spend more time with him!'

"That's great, sir. Well, guys, I am going to go talk to Coach Scott and say a few words to Shay before you take him home."

Coach Scott and Coach Crossover discussed the strategies used for the game and various future plans.

♦ ♦ ♦

"Hey, buddy, where are you going?" Coach Crossover said as Shay bolted passed him.

"Oh, hey, Coach Crossover!"

"I just wanted to talk to you before you left!"

"Sure!" Shay replied.

"First, I wanted to say that you played a great game. I admire your newfound confidence. You were fearless out there, kiddo!"

"Thanks, Coach Crossover. I've held dear to the lessons you have taught me!"

"Shay, you should be really proud of yourself. You have matured so much, and with a positive attitude, you will eventually be a winner regardless of what happens in your life. I will be working on something exciting during next school year so I will not have as much free time but we will still hang out sometime."

"Thanks! Coach, what will you be working on?"

"It is a surprise, but it will be a once in a lifetime experience for you! I promise!" Coach Crossover told Shay.

"I am very excited!"

"So have you decided on a school for next year?"

"No, I haven't done that yet. I will be choosing a school this summer along with family vacations and a lot of sleep!" Shay said and they laughed.

"Well, Shay, congratulations on your big victory tonight."

"Thanks, Coach Crossover!" Shay said as he took off toward his parents and embraced the both of them.

"Great game, son! Let's go to a nice restaurant and talk about your victory, summer plans, and where you will go to school next year…"

Book 5
Ninth Grade

Prologue

Shay and his parents sat down at the restaurant and ordered their meals. Shay was excited to be having dinner with both of his parents. He was very happy that Dad invited him and Mom out to eat.

"Guys, did you see that last shot?"

"Son, that shot was awesome. You know what I admired?"

"What's that, Dad?"

"I admired how hard you played! Hard work usually pays off and yours did. Good job!"

"Thanks, Dad!" Shay said with a smile.

"You guys know what Coach Scott told me and the team?"

"What did he say?" the parents said in unison.

"He said in his deep voice, 'Okay, guys, this is your moment!' I think that life is about capitalizing on moments, seizing the day, carpe diem!" Shay said with a chuckle.

Shay's parents laughed. "Quite the philosopher!" Dad said jokingly. "Son, keep making the best out of life and you will find the success you are looking for!"

Shay's mother told him how proud she was of him. The family talked and planned a summer full of fun, which was what Shay had desired. Shay was promised a trip to Disney. He had been wanting to go to Disney ever since he was a young boy learning the ABCs in his kindergarten class.

Their food finally arrived. The family shared a meal. Jeremiah couldn't be there because as he put it, "I have to go see my friends because we have so, so much more fun when our parents are not around!"

"So, son, where will you go to school next year?" Mom asked.

"I am not sure yet, but I am thinking about going to Lion's Heart High School!"

"Why is that?" Dad asked.

"Because my friend Chris may be going there!"

"Are there any other reasons?" Mom asked.

"Nah!" Shay laughed. The laughed together, ate together, and simply enjoyed each other's company.

Shay continued to practice hard. He was nervous about the new challenges of going to a new school, making new friends, and trying out for the basketball team, not to mention playing at a higher grade level if he made the team. One thing Shay knew is that belief in himself was the necessary option.

Section 1

Frowning, Shay stared upward at his opponent in disbelief. It was like David against Goliath! Never had he played against such huge players. *Wow*, he thought to himself. *What is the solution to this equation?*

The Crossover that Won the Game

"Now anytime you come through the lane against me, I assure you that the results will not change! You will always find yourself on your back looking up at me," George laughed, causing the other players laughing as well.

Embarrassed, puzzled, he laid on the hardwood floor for what seemed like an eternity. "It's comfortable down here," he reasoned.

"A winner never quits and a quitter never wins," a voice said as the friendly hand of Coach Denise reached down and helped him off the floor.

◆ ◆ ◆

The rest of the tryouts went by in a blur. Shay had so much on his mind. He loved basketball with passion, yet his mother had already threatened him that he would not continue to play unless he raised that C average to a B. To him, that seemed next to impossible because he hated math with a passion, and to just receive a C was a pain.

5:00 the Next Morning

The loud ringing startled Shay out of his sleep. He reached over and grabbed the alarm clock, but to his surprise, it wasn't the one that was ringing. Confused, he looked over to see his new cell phone ringing loudly.

"Hello?" he said sleepily as he grabbed his phone and placed it on speaker phone.

"It's Dad, son. How are you doing this beautiful, early morning?"

Now the handsome smile appeared on his face, even though he was still sleepy. He sat up straight and said, "I'm fine, Dad, how are you?"

"I'm fine, son. I know it's very early, but I wanted to call you before I went to work. There's something your mom and I spoke about…"

"I know, Dad, I'll get my grades up. At least I'll do my best, I promise!"

"Well," his dad started, "if you don't improve in math, you will not play basketball."

"What?" Shay questioned.

"Do not yell at your dad."

"Oh, now you're my dad? You don't live with us, you hardly ever come to my games and events for students and parents. Now you try and come into my life and dictate whether or not I play basketball?"

Through the other end of the phone, the father listened with a contrite heart. Who was he to tell the child he could not play basketball? Well, he is Shay's father, whether he's present or absent, and he will be treated as such.

"Listen, son," he said and paused. "I know you're upset and hurt by my absence. I make no excuse for my previous conduct, or lack thereof,"

Like an angry person trying to calm down, Shay counted down from 10 slowly. His little chest was heaving up and down. He realized that he had just spoken years of pent-up anger. The words his dad just spoke were true, he was his father and respect would always be due to him. Running his right hand through his hair, something he always does when he is frustrated and trying to calm down, he started his apology.

"Sorry, Dad! So much is bothering me. I never knew I had so much anger built up inside of me due to your absence. You could never imagine what it's like to hear the other children say, 'Hey, my parents and I are going to Disney this summer' or 'My dad is teaching me to drive, and he even said he'd buy me a car when I turn sixteen.' It's painful to see both parents

The Crossover that Won the Game

yelling in the stands, showing how proud they are for the basket their son just made. And…and…and…"

The tears that were built up in his brown eyes now fell, but he would never know the tears that were building up in his dad's eyes.

"Son, I have a surpr—"

"Shay, Shay, it is 5:00 a.m. Get up and get ready for school!" his mother yelled.

"Okay, Mom. Dad, what's the surpr—"

The three rapid knocks at the door interrupted the conversation. "Hang up that phone right this minute and get ready for school. In fact…" she said kindly, "I'll do it for you."

"Good-bye," she said, "my son has to get ready for school. You don't call people this early in the morning." She politely hung up the phone.

Shay sat there, baffled. "Ma…"

"Up and out! You can pick up your phone on the kitchen table on your way to school." With that, mother and phone were gone like magic.

"Maaaaa…" he called again, but his word was lost with the closing of the door. Lost in his mind like Alice in Wonderland, he shook his head in shock. "Man, what was the surprise that Dad had for me?" he asked himself.

The Ride to School

Shay stared out of the passenger side window, stewing about the events of the morning. As the car pulled up to the school, Shay reached for the door handle.

"Hey," his mom said as she gently grabbed his shoulder, "please let this be the last time I catch you on the phone that early. You understand me?"

"Yes, Ma. I have a question for you, though."

"Sure, son."

"If I was living with Dad and you called me at 5:00 a.m., would that be acceptable?"

"Of course," his mom said and giggled.

"Great," he giggled, "what's good for the goose is good for the gander. That was Dad." He smiled and winked, kissed his mom on the cheek, and headed for his first class, math, leaving her with her mouth agape.

♦ ♦ ♦

"A goose is flying 60 mph on a cool winter night. If he is going 60 miles away and leaves at 6:00 a.m., what time would it be when he arrived if he landed for 5 seconds?"

Shay took his #2 pencil and tapped on the side of his desk. "I hate math," he said under his breath.

Second Practice

"Okay, remember what I told you: Have confidence and faith in yourself," the coach told Shay.

"Sure, Coach," Shay said. He wasn't as confident as he was when he played for Confidence Elementary. "These guys are just too big," he reasoned with himself.

The Crossover that Won the Game

"Rick, you inbound. Shay, you play point guard," the coach said.

Apprehensive, Shay caught the ball. With one tall opponent in front of him, he crossed the ball between his legs and took off down the court. With a huge smile on his face, he went for the layup. Then, with what seemed to be a magic trick, a tall player on the opposing team leaped and knocked the ball in the opposite direction, sending Shay cascading to the shiny wooden floor.

"Well, do you believe me now?" George said.

"You're too little to come through this lane!" He laughed once again, this time harder than before.

Maybe he's right, Shay thought.

"Get back up, Shay!" He heard a voice yell from the sideline. Shay looked at Coach Denise and began feeling comforted by her encouragement.

"I really hope she believes in me like Coach Cross…"

"Shay, I believe in you, but that means nothing if you do not believe in yourself!" Coach Denise ironically interrupted Shay's comment.

Shay hopped back to his feet to face this giant hovering over him.

"It's about time you got up, coward!" George said.

Face-to-face, Shay stared down at the floor. "A winner never quits!" Shay remembered some of the words of Coach Denise.

"I'm no coward," Shay said as he intentionally bumped into George.

"All right, back on defense, Shay!" Coach Denise yelled.

Shay stripped the ball from another player trying out and took the ball up the court.

A quitter never wins! Shay thought as he looked at George waiting as a predator did for his prey.

"Don't come in here, little boy!" George taunted Shay.

"Nothing makes a failure but a try!" Shay said as he jumped simultaneously with George.

With hands positioned high to block the shot, Shay faked the ball high, then scooped the ball under George's left arm. Shay smiled as he watched the ball drop through the net. Shay smiled at George as he backpedaled down the court.

"I may get knocked down, but I will get back up every single time!"

"I like this kid," Coach Denise said to herself. "I admire his heart!"

"Shay, come here!" Coach Denise called out.

"Yes, Coach Williams?"

"Please call me Coach Denise!"

"Okay!" Shay replied.

"I admire your heart. Know that people will taunt and try to tear you down, but you have to simply do your best. Are you ready to work with me?

"Oh yes, I am, Coach!"

"Then I am ready to work with you! I cannot say that you have certainly made the team, but make sure you check the roster!" Coach Denise said as she and Shay shook hands.

"All right, guys, wrap it up," Coach Denise said before Shay had a chance to respond.

Shay began running toward the door to tell his mom about the final day of tryouts when a familiar person stepped in front of him.

"Move, man! I have to go!" Shay said.

"Hold up, I just want to tell you something!"

"Okay!" Shay replied.

"Good shot!" George winked, smiled, and walked away.

"Th-than-thanks!" Shay stuttered a little as he backed up, shocked that George said something kind to him. He turned and ran out of the door.

◆ ◆ ◆

"Hey, Mom!"

"Hey, son! How was practice?"

"It was good!"

"That's all you have to say? Tell me more about it, son!" Mom said as she chuckled.

"Well, this gigantic guy named George continued to knock me down and saying hurtful things when I was on the floor looking up. Coach Denise said that a quitter never wins and a winner never quits. She was right. I jumped right into George's body and scooped the ball underneath his left arm. Then he knew I was no longer afraid of him," Shay said with self-assuredness.

"That is very good, son!"

"Oh, and guess what?"

"What's that, son?"

"I am not totally sure, but I think I made the team!" Shay said excitedly.

"I know that you love basketball, son, but if you do not raise your math grade to an A, you will not be allowed to play!"

"Ugh! Dad said the same thing!" Shay said angrily.

"Respect your mother, son! I understand how you feel, but education must come before basketball!"

"But, Mom, what if I go to the NBA?"

"Son, I would never tell you that you cannot do something, but without good grades, you will not get accepted to a college where a lot of scouts will even spend time looking at the players!"

Shay did not respond. He did not want to admit it, but he knew his mother was right. He knew he had to focus on education, especially ninth grade math. Shay subconsciously wished Daddy would call so they could finish their conversation that took place earlier in the day. Just as Shay opened

The Crossover that Won the Game

the door and began walking in after his mother, he heard a sound that made him smile.

♦ ♦ ♦

Ring! Ring! Ring! Shay ran toward the phone, almost falling as he went to answer.

Practically out of breath, Shay answered, "He...hel...hello!"

"Hey, son, how are ya?"

"Hey, Dad, I am doing pretty good!"

"I am glad to hear that! So how were tryouts?"

"Dad, I want to apologize for how I acted earlier!"

"Son, I forgave you the moment you spoke those words to me. I understand that I have not been there, but I really hope that you will give me a chance to be a better father to you. I love you, son!"

"Thanks, Dad, but I'm not ready to include you in all of my life. You may disappoint and hurt me again!"

"Son, give me a chance, I'm begging!"

"I'll let you know if I make the team. Come to my games and maybe I will give you a chance!"

"Son, I still have..."

"No more broken promises, Dad! I have to go! I have homework to do!"

"I hope its ma—!" Daddy's statement was interrupted by the sound of the dial tone after Shay hung up the phone without further warning.

"Shay!" his mother called.

"Yes, Mom?" Shay answered, startled.

"I overheard some of your conversation with your father!"

"Okay..."

"Your father may not have always been there for you, but you still have to respect him. I do not want you to hang up on your father again. That's very disrespectful. Do not talk to him as if he is one of your peers. He is your father and he is an adult. Respect him!"

"But, Mom!"

"No but! Respect is nonnegotiable!" his mom replied.

◆ ◆ ◆

There were students yelling and screaming. They dropped pens, pencils, backpacks, and laughed just as loud as they yelled. Friends playing cards and telling stories about the night before. Energy level ran high on this bright and beautiful morning! The bus driver whistled loudly as he transported the students to Lion's Heart High School. He chewed on his toothpick as if it was his morning breakfast. Shay did his best to quiet the noise around him.

I really wish all of these passengers would quiet down and simply enjoy the ride, Shay thought to himself.

Shay was unable to quiet the noise within himself.

"Math is going to be difficult today, but I know I can succeed if I work hard enough. That's what Coach Crossover says. I am starting to think that my dad believes in me also. He doesn't seem to be giving up!" Shay smiled as he was having this thought.

Erttttt! The bus came to a screeching stop. All of the students hopped off of the bus and ran toward the door.

"Time to face my giant!" Shay mumbled.

"Still having nightmares about me, Shay?" Shay felt a hand on his left shoulder.

Shay looked to his right. *Familiar voice!* Shay thought to himself. "Ha! Ha! No, George! You are quite gigantic, but I will continue to face you when necessary!" The boys laughed and slapped hands. "I have another giant to face!"

"Who? I am the tallest player on the team!"

"It's not a who, it's a what!" Shay replied.

"Well then, what is it?"

"Math!"

"Oh, I totally relate!" George replied. "I know a great tutor though. I will have her give you a call!"

"Thanks, man! I will see you after school to check the list to see who made the team!" Shay said as he lowered his eyes.

"Hey, man, stay positive. Keep your head up!" George replied.

The boys said their good-byes.

Math Class

Ms. Reynolds started class the same as she did every other day.

"Welcome to another fun day of algebra. I hope you have been counting down the minutes to our time together. I hope you are well-rested and well-prepared. Remember today is your day, you choose how it will go! Now turn your eyes toward the blackboard!"

The math problem of the day is: Use the quadratic formula to find all roots of the equation $2x^2-3x-2=0$

Ms. Reynolds spoke and Shay listened. Most of what she said sounded similar to a foreign language to Shay. Shay put his pencil down, leaned back in his chair and folded his arms. Shay began to slouch when he heard Ms. Reynolds's voice.

"Hey, Mr. Ponder! Are you giving up?"

"Somewhat! I just don't understand this material!"

"Have you asked for help?"

"No, I have not!" Shay said in a frustrated tone of voice.

"Okay, well, I will be calling your house later to speak to you and your parents!" Ms. Reynolds said.

Though Shay was physically present, his mind was somewhere else.

The News

Shay walked the long and seemingly lonely hallway. He watched as many players rejoiced at the news they were on the team. Shay's moment of truth came as he scanned the list. Shay hung his head and began walking past all of the people in the hallway though he only visualized his destination—the door that lead to the front of the school.

"Hey, man!" Shay was stopped by two hands on his shoulders.

"Sorry, George, I wasn't even paying attention!"

"Oh, I see, you're trying to get your chance to knock me down now, huh?" George replied.

Shay didn't laugh much. He just looked at George with a smirk and said, "All right, man, have fun at practice! I have to go now!"

"Hey, what are you talking about? Aren't you coming?"

"I didn't make the team!" Shay replied.

"Why don't we go and check the list together? Maybe you overlooked it!"

Shay and George, the new comrades, walked together down the not-so-lonely hallway.

"I really do not want to be disappointed again, man!"

"I am going to check for you and me, my friend!"

George scanned the list up and down several times until finally he saw Shay's name in the middle of the list.

"Hey, man, there it is! Look right here!" George said as he pointed at Shay's name.

Shay's face glistened, and after eradicating disbelief, he jumped for joy. "Thanks, George!" Shay ran off to call his mom, dad, and Coach Crossover.

Standing outside of the school, Shay listened to the phone ringing in his ear as he waited for his mother to answer the phone.

"Hello!"

"Hey, Mom! Guess what?"

"You sound so excited, I can't wait to hear your news!"

"Get ready, Mom," Shay warned.

"I'm rea—"

"I made the team!" Shay yelled, interrupting his mother.

"I am so happy for you, son. I know how much you wanted to participate on the team. All right, son, I will see you after practice."

"All right, Mom, thanks! Got to go!"

"Bye!" Shay listened to the dial tone and prepared to call Dad.

"Hello!" Shay's dad answered.

"I have news for you!"

"Anything, son!"

"I made the team," Shay said in a tone lacking enthusiasm.

"Well, son, that's great!" Dad said excitedly.

"Will you come to some of the games?"

"Son, I certainly will!"

"Okay, Daddy, I will find out and let you know!"

"You know I am rooting for you, son!"

"Well, here's your chance to prove it!" Shay said in a matter-of-fact tone.

"I will, son!"

"Talk to you later, Dad!"

"Bye, son!"

Remembering what his mother told him about respect, he replied, "Bye, Dad!"

One more conversation, Shay thought. Shay pressed one key on his phone. *Glad to have Coach Crossover on speed dial*! he thought. The phone rang and rang and rang, but Coach Crossover did not answer.

Beep! "Hey, Coach Crossover, it's your best buddy Shay! I wanted to give you my good news. Let's talk when you get a chance. Could really use some guidance as I take on this new challenge! Hope to ta—"

Beep! "You have reached your time limit for recording!" Shay's message was interrupted. He hung up, hoping for a return phone call from Coach Crossover.

Practice
"All right, Shay, it's time for practice!" Coach Denise told Shay as she rounded up all of the players on her team.

"Okay, Coach D, here I come!"

The team ran several drills and were introduced to a variety of plays. Coach D kept an eye on Shay while simultaneously observing all players to pick the starting five.

"All right, guys, work on foul shots and jump shots for the remainder of practice!" Coach D told the team.

Conversation with Teacher
"Hello!"

"Good evening! This is Ms. Reynolds, Shay's math teacher! How are you?"

"I am doing well. Thanks for asking! How is my son doing in your class?"

"He is doing all right, but he's struggling somewhat! Is he home?"

"No, I was just about to head out the door to pick him up from basketball practice!"

"I will be brief, Mrs. Ponder! Though I am Shay's teacher, I am also a tutor. I would like to work privately with Shay to help him better understand concepts and the practical application of algebra."

"That sounds like a great idea, Ms. Reynolds. I would like to personally thank you for your willingness to tutor Shay. Please let me know if there is anything I can do to help!"

"You're welcome! I've heard that it takes a village to raise a child. With us working as a team, he is highly capable of getting an A in my class. I look forward to scheduling an appointment!"

"We will be in touch soon, Ms. Reynolds. Thanks for calling. I have to go pick Shay up now, and I will make sure he gives you a call!"

"Good-bye, Mrs. Ponder!"

"Bye, Ms. Reynolds!"

Conversation between Mom and Shay
Mom had a peaceful drive on the way to pick Shay up from practice. She wanted what was best Shay and knew that she had to make sure he was aware.

"Hey, Mom! Practice was so hard today. Coach D made us run and learn three new plays. I do not know if I will be able to learn them fast enough. I want to play a lot, but this will be a long, very long season!"

"Just do your best! If you give your all, then you will be victorious regardless of the outcome!"

"But they're so big, tall, and strong!"

"Well, you have to find a way to stand a little taller, be a little stronger, and be enough of who you are to face whatever comes your way, no matter how big you think it is!"

"Thanks, Mom! I will try to keep that in mind when I am staring at guys twice my size!" Shay said sarcastically.

"One day, you will grasp the analogy, my child! Oh, before I forget, you have to call Ms. Reynolds. She has offered to tutor you in math!"

"Oh, that is awesome!"

The rest of the car ride was serene. Shay and his mother enjoyed the tranquil nature of day. The wind was gently blowing, the leaves rustled, and the sun welcomed the two of them home. In just several hours, it would be time to navigate yet another day.

Mom and Shay ate dinner and reviewed plans for tomorrow.

"How is your food?" Mom asked.

"It is good. Thank you!"

"I want you to call Ms. Reynolds after dinner! Okay?"

"Okay, Mom, I will!" The two of them finished eating and Shay completed his nighttime routine: wash dishes, shower, brush teeth, and read. "All done! Time to call Ms. Reynolds!" Shay said to himself.

Ring! Ring!

"Hello!"

"Hi, Ms. Reynolds! How are you?"

"I am doing very well! Is this Shay?"

"Yes, it is! Mom said that I had to call you in order to schedule an appointment!"

"Well, it is nice to hear from you. Great way to take initiative, Shay! Did you make the team?"

"Yes, ma'am, I did!" Shay said with enthusiasm.

"What are the best days and times for you?"

"Well, we practice late on Tuesdays and Thursdays! Can we meet then?"

"Young man, this is your plan. Your mom and I talked about the importance of you learning responsibility. Tell me when you would like to meet and I will accommodate your schedule!"

"Well," Shay lowered his voice. "I am having a lot of trouble understanding algebra so I guess we should meet three days a week. Tuesday and Thursday before practice and Fridays during study hall!"

"All right, Tuesday, Thursday, and Friday it is! We will monitor progress right after your first game in two weeks!"

"Okay, Ms. Reynolds, see you tomorrow!"

"Bye for now, Shay!"

"Bye, Ms. Reynolds!"

The Next Two Weeks
Shay met faithfully with Ms. Reynolds. Shay continued to struggle to understand algebra, but as reported by Ms. Reynolds, he had made some progress.

"Shay, you are beginning to really understand algebra. Keep working hard and you will get that grade up to an A in no time."

Shay knew he needed at least a B to play in the first game. Shay worked diligently with Miss Reynolds over the next two weeks.

Shay's dad still attempted to bond with him. Shay remained resistant and kept their conversations short and sometimes sweet. Deep inside, he wanted a better relationship with his dad, but he couldn't stand being hurt again. Shay joyfully told Daddy and Mom about his progress in math. He would be playing in the first game.

First Game of Season
"All right, team, you have worked very hard. It's time to make sure our hard work pays off. Based on what I have seen in practice, these five players will start the game: Aaron, point guard; Deron, shooting guard; Oliver, small forward; Michael, power forward; and George, center. All right, guys, hands in here! Hard work on 3."

"Hard work!" the team yelled and began to file into the gymnasium.

"Hey, Coach D!"

"Yes, Michael?"

"I know you haven't had a lot of time to watch Shay play, but he is a really good player. I was on his team last season and…" Michael began telling of Shay's heroics and phenomenal game time moments.

The Crossover that Won the Game

"Michael, I appreciate your input, but I have to make my decisions based on what is presently happening."

"I mean no disrespect, but you're making a mistake! That kid has heart, Coach D."

"And as everyone has to do, I will learn from my mistake if you are right! Now let's play hard and I will keep an eye on Shay!"

Shay sat and watched as his team, Lion's Heart High School, sunk deeper and deeper. At the end of the first quarter Lion's Heart was losing 8 to 20.

"Coach D, I believe I can make a positive impact on our team's performance if you sub me into the game!"

"Be patient, Shay. I will get you in the game when it is appropriate!"

Why doesn't Coach D give me a chance to show her she can put faith in me? Shay thought.

Shay continued to watch the team struggle to perform. Coach D yelled out a plethora of plays, and Shay visualized every step in his head. He was anxious to ask Coach D to put him in the game but decided against it. Shay watched with wide and nearly teary eyes as he realized neither Coach D nor his team believed in him. All he wanted was a chance. The score at halftime was 31–16. Shay had yet to play in the game.

Halfway through the third quarter, Coach D would give Shay the chance he had been waiting for.

"Shay, you're in. You're playing shooting guard!"

"But, Coach, this is not the position I typically play!"

"Do you want to play or not?" Coach D replied. Shay walked timidly along the sideline.

Shay watched as Aaron brought the ball up the court. "Over there, Shay!" Aaron yelled.

Shay began running across the baseline when the center stuck out his hip and knocked him down. Shay slowly got up when he heard...

"Get up, you miniscule coward!" the gigantic player said. Shay wanted to slap him but knew that would be inappropriate. Shay continued to run to the opposite corner.

"Over here!" Shay yelled. Aaron ignored him and shot the ball.

"Have some faith, man!" Shay said as he and Aaron was running down the court after the missed shot.

"I'm the point guard! Not you!"

Shay ignored Aaron and continued running up the court.

"Look up, buddy!" Michael yelled!

Shay turned around and nearly fell as he tapped the ball away from his opponent. Shay put the ball behind his back, then crossed quickly in front of him.

"You're not going anywhere!" his opponent taunted.

Shay ran quickly down the court. Leaving his player behind, Shay leaped. Out of his peripheral, Shay saw a familiar frame coming toward him. "I can do this!" he told himself.

The Crossover that Won the Game

Bang! Bodies collided. *Smack!* Shay's body hit the floor. Shay's opponent passed the ball and began running down the court. Shay saw Deron approach the table to sub back in the game.

I have to do something! he thought.

With the opposite team pressuring the ball, Aaron was unable to get the ball and Shay became the second option. Shay caught the ball. He knew he could withstand the pressure, but he really wanted to score to prove himself to all those around him. Shay did several crossovers just to get the ball beyond half court. Standing at the top of the three-point line and watching as the players moved according to the play that Coach D called, Aaron came to relieve Shay of his point guard duties. Shay waved him off. He continued seeking approval. The clock was winding down. *This is my moment!* Shay thought.

"You're not going anywhere!" Shay's opponent told him.

Shay crossed the ball in between his legs and looked at the clock. Five seconds remained.

"Over here, Shay!" Aaron yelled from the left corner. Shay ignored Aaron and faked left. His opponent hopped. Three seconds remained, and Shay was quickly crossing right as the clock was ticking. Shay ran toward the basket and met body to body once again with the opponent that knocked him to the floor. Shay, while staring at his opponent's hands, reversed the ball and made the layup. The clock read 0 and the third quarter concluded.

"0! I will always face my giants and conquer every fear!" Shay spoke, staring up at his opponent.

Back at the bench, Shay heard the words he rarely desired to hear.

"You're sitting! Deron, you're back in!" Coach D said.

Why won't she give me a chance? Shay thought to himself.

"You played all right, Shay, but there is no 'I' in team!"

Shay watched unenthusiastically as Lion's Heart High School was crushed by their opponent. Shay did not play any of the fourth quarter.

"I can't believe this!" Shay said as he walked directly out of the gym once the buzzer sounded!

"Hey, Shay! Shay, wait up!" Michael said as he ran behind Shay.

Conversations about Game
"Hey, Michael," Shay said in a low tone of voice. "What's up?"

"I just want you to stay encouraged, friend. I know Coach D didn't let you play much, but there is always next game!"

"Thanks, Michael, I appreciate that. I am having trouble learning and executing those plays. It's even harder because Coach D only plays me for a few minutes at a time!"

Michael could hear the frustration in Shay's voice. He put his hand on Shay's shoulder. "You're a great player, man, and one day, Coach D will be thoroughly convinced!"

"Thanks, man! Hey, you are a good player also. It's not just about me!" The two laughed and said their good-byes as Shay hopped into the backseat of his mother's car.

"Hey, guys! Dad, I didn't know you were at the game!"

"Son, I told you that I was going to try to a better father!"

"Well, this is a good start. Thank you for coming even though Coach D didn't let me play much."

"It was still great seeing you out there! Never stop working hard and your moment will come!"

"Thanks, Dad! Thanks, Mom, for coming to the game. Hopefully, I will play more next time!"

"Just like your dad said, never stop working hard and your moment will come! One day, that coach will regret not giving you more playing time a lot sooner!"

"We will see about that!"

"Stay positive, Shay! Are you hungry?"

"Yes, I am!"

"Wait a minute!" Dad interjected. "Can I join you guys?"

"I really don't want..." Shay began to speak.

"Son, it is all right if your dad joins us for dinner?"

The three of them ate dinner and did their best to have normal table-time conversation. Shay displayed a façade of anger toward his Dad. Shay was indeed angry at his dad for not being a better father at other times in his life. However, deep inside, Shay had more feelings of joy than anger. Shay was happy that for the first time in a long time, he and his parents was eating dinner as a family. Jeremiah walked in from his friend's house and changed the dynamic for a moment.

"Hey, Mom and Dad! So I heard you kept the bench warm?" Jeremiah said, staring at Shay.

"You know, why don't you ever say anything nice, positive, or encouraging?"

Jeremiah was lost for words. Initially, Dad sat quietly and watched this interaction.

"I can say what I wa—" Jeremiah finally began responding.

"No, son! No, you really can't say what you want," Daddy said. Shay smiled but tried to hide it by negating the smile with a frown. "People have feelings! Shay is your little brother and—"

Jeremiah interrupted his father, "Now you want to tell me how to treat Shay! How about you be the father we need you to be?"

Shay shoved his plate and saucer toward the middle of the dining room table and headed upstairs. "Ironically, I've suddenly lost my appetite!" Mom and Dad's calling out to him was lost in the wind as Shay ran up the stairs to escape the anguish that encompassed him.

"I am going to go talk to Shay!"

"No, Ruby! Let's give him a moment to himself!" her husband said.

Dad was extremely frustrated, but he knew that Jeremiah was right. "Okay, you are entitled to your feelings and opinions and I would never try stripping you of them, but I will make you a proposition."

"Okay, I am literally all ears, Dad!" Jeremiah said sarcastically.

"For every day that I come around, that equals one day you have to be nice to Shay. That means only positive and encouraging words! That

The Crossover that Won the Game

means helping him with his homework and treating him like a little brother who is loved dearly!"

"Fine!" Jeremiah said as he and Dad shook hands.

Through the music, Shay faintly heard footsteps coming up the stairs. *Bang! Bang!* Shay heard the knock on the bedroom door. "Come in!"

"Son, I know I haven't been a strong presence in your life these last few years, but I am here now! I want to rebuild our relationship. I remember reading to you and strumming the guitar and telling stories at bedtime to help you fall asleep!"

Tears began to well in Shay's eyes. That anger shield was slowly dissipating. "I do not want to be let down again!"

"I understand, son, but—"

"No, Dad! There is always a 'but' with you and I'm sick of it!" Shay interrupted.

"Son!"

"Son? Call me that when you are ready to be a real father!" Shay said angrily as he put his headphones back in.

Dad really wanted to reach Shay, but he knew he had to let Shay go through the healing process on his own time. He wanted to make sure he addressed Shay's leaving the dinner table during a conversation. Dad wrote a note:

"Anger is normal, but facing your problems is nonnegotiable!"

Dad left the note on Shay's dresser and kissed Shay's forehead. He went downstairs to speak briefly with his wife from he had been separated from for a few years.

"Maybe not tonight, but we really have to talk."

"I agree, John!" Ruby, Shay's mom, responded.

The two embraced and said good-bye. Shay heard the door slam, jumped up, and stared out of the window as he watched his dad drive away.

"It's like he's walking away all over again!" Shay said and then closed his eyes for bed.

Shay slept only a few hours that night. He tossed and turned with several thoughts about his family. He wanted his dad close, but similar to someone struggling with borderline personality disorder, he continued to push him away. He sincerely wished Jeremiah wasn't so harsh. He finally fell asleep.

Shay woke up bright and early to sun beaming into his bedroom window. Endorphins released naturally, it was time to get ready for school. Hygiene intact, feet now moving quickly toward the bus stop, Shay just wanted this day to be over.

Tutoring
"How has your day been?" Ms. Reynolds asked.

"It has been long and kind of boring!" Shay replied.

"How are you feeling about math?"

"I am feeling somewhat more confident!"

"Shay, you seem a little down!"

"It was a long night and I didn't sleep very well. I just had a lot on my mind!"

The Crossover that Won the Game

"Would you like to talk about it?"

"No, but thank you! I will probably call my dad when we are finished."

"Just so you know I am not only your teacher and tutor, I am a part of your life to make a positive difference. If you ever need to talk, let me know."

"Thank you!" Shay smiled. "I will!"

Ms. Reynolds and Shay worked diligently to help him understand algebra, specifically using the appropriate formula to solve quadratic equations.

The Next Month
During the next thirty days, Shay continued to go to tutoring. His math grade soared and he now had an A. Shay and Ms. Reynolds continued to develop a bond, and Shay felt comfortable talking to her about personal matters. Ms. Reynolds encouraged Shay build a relationship with his father. Shay told her that he wasn't sure he was ready. Ms. Reynolds told Shay that he would know when the time was right. Shay was conflicted about when the ideal time would be. Ms. Reynolds would frequently tell Shay that he doesn't have to wait for the ideal time, he just has to have two hearts that are prepared.

Daddy continued trying to reach out, but resistance seemed favorable to Shay. Despite Shay's detachment, Dad was a man of his word. He came by the house almost every day. Shay couldn't understand why Jeremiah had been so nice to him lately, but he certainly preferred this version of his brother.

Shay was still frustrated about not playing much in the games thus far, but his primary focus was primarily on the team's final game tomorrow. Coach Crossover and Shay had a couple of meaningful conversations, but overall, he had been pretty busy with some project he kept quiet about.

Shay felt ready for tomorrow's game, but admittedly, he was equally as ambivalent. Shay knew he had to give his all.

"Win or lose, facing problems is nonnegotiable, overcoming fears is probable, and slaying the giants that lay in wait is all dependent on me."

Shay was appreciative of all he had learned from other people, but he knew it was up to him to use the things he'd been taught.

Final Game
Swish! Shay watched as their opponent, Malcolm X High School, took the lead.

"I know I'll be out there on the floor, but I do not have to go alone. I can take everything I've learned, both physical and mental!" Shay remembered words spoken by Coach Crossover.

"Shay, you're in!" Coach Denise yelled down the bench as Shay was in the last seat, in deep thought.

It's still the first quarter! Shay smiled as he thought.

"You're playing point guard!" Coach Denise and Shay smiled as he approached the scorer table. Shay kneeled, with hand on table, as he waited to go into the game. Shay and Aaron slapped hands as they traded places.

"Right there, George!" Shay stood at the top of the key as he pointed to the right low post. Shay ran to the left, then crossed right when his opponent elbowed him to the ground. Shay lay there on the ground as he watched the ball go through the rim.

"A real fighter gets knocked down seven times and gets up eight!" Shay heard a voice yelling from the bleachers. Shay turned and looked, it was his dad. Shay smiled and knew he had to get back up.

The Crossover that Won the Game

Shay watched his opponent closely as he brought the ball up the floor. He remembered what his dad said, "Anger is normal, but facing problems is nonnegotiable!"

Shay was angry and his opponent's behavior certainly was a problem. Shay crossed the ball and ran left. With his opponent lunging in, Shay put the ball behind his back and into his right hand.

"Take what the defense gives you and maximize on opportunities!" Shay remembered what Coach Scott said to him last season. Shay noticed that none of Ricky's (his archnemesis) teammates came to help so he did as Coach Crossover and Coach Scott taught him. He squared his feet under his shoulders, leaped, and released the ball with the snapping of his wrist. *Swish*!

"Three-pointer good!" the referee yelled. Score LHHS 10–MXHS 15.

The crowd yelled, but Shay was most concerned with impressing his father. Amid his daydreaming, Shay found himself staring up at gym lights once again.

"Get up, Shay!" Shay noticed the hand that reached down to help MXHS increased their lead to 17–10.

"Thanks, Michael!"

"Let's go get these guys!" Michael said.

Shay jumped up. He was no quitter. He brought the ball down the court.

"Now, Michael!" Shay said as he put the ball between Ricky's legs and leaped, releasing the lob pass to Michael. Michael dunked the ball through the hoop concluding the first quarter with finesse. Score: LHHS 12–MXHS 17.

"Aaron, you're back in the game! Shay, stay close to me, pal. I am enjoying the improvements you have made. So confident, fearless, and proficient!"

Second Quarter

Shay observed the game closely. One thing he learned from past experiences is that he had to be a student first and foremost. *Every expert was a novice prior to being someone's student*! he thought.

Shay wondered when he would get back in the game, but decided that learning was just as valuable. Lion's Heart High School making the playoffs did not seem promising. The score at halftime was 22–34 in favor of Malcolm X High School.

Halftime

"Guys, the game is not over yet. We can still win this. We need this win to make the playoffs (sectionals). Most importantly, team, have fun and enjoy playing. If we lose, at least, leave it all on the floor. Sometimes, life offers second chances, but there will be times when you face situation in which all you have is that moment to achieve a desired goal. These next two quarters is your moment. I love all of you guys and it has been so much fun getting to know you, let's never forget those moments. But in this moment, all we have is now. One Chance on 3."

"1…2…3, One Chance!" the team yelled.

Third Quarter

Half of the third quarter passed and Shay was still sitting on the bench. He had learned enough for one game he thought. He was ready to help his team. Lion's Heart High School was playing well but simply couldn't defend Malcolm X High School very well. Ricky was still as amazing as Shay recalled from Junior High School, but Shay had finally learned to fear no one. Every giant has a weakness…

"Shay, you're in!"

The Crossover that Won the Game

Al, the small forward, passed Shay the ball from out of bounds.

"You're finished, Shay!" Ricky yelled out.

"Haven't you learned from last year's showdowns that you can't stop me?"

"Watch me!"

"You perpetuate the myth that there is an 'I' in team!" Shay said as he quickly passed the ball to George who made the mid-range jump shot. Score: LHHS 30–MXHS 38.

Ricky brought the ball up the court. Shay had watched Ricky get past Aaron with the same move several times. He would cross left, back right, fake right, then spin left. Aaron would be lost and Ricky would either score or make an efficient pass.

"Corner!" Ricky yelled to his teammate.

Shay kept his eyes on Ricky's waist. Like record on repeat, Ricky crossed left and quickly crossed right. Shay stumbled slightly but recovered as Ricky started to go right. As Ricky spun, Shay tapped the ball loose with his left hand and took the ball up the court. Shay jumped and slapped the glass, watching the ball fall through the net, bringing the score to 32–38.

"Good job, Shay! Keep doing what you're doing!" Coach Denise yelled from the sideline.

Ricky brought the ball up the floor. Pretty frustrated about being stripped by Shay, he was determined to get revenge. Ricky crossed left, then faked left, quickly crossed right, then leaped, and shot the three-point shot. Ricky watched as the ball flew through the air. Shay's heart leaped for joy as he saw the ball bounce off of the rim.

"Over here, Michael!" Shay yelled.

MXHS got back on defense. Shay dribbled the ball in his left hand. He could not get Ricky off of his body. Shay went to put the ball behind his back when Ricky's teammate came from Shay's blind side and stole the ball. After three quick passes, MXHS scored again, bringing the score to 40–32.

"Don't even think about coming near the basket!" Shay's opponent said.

Shay looked up at this figure symbolic of the Giants of Jotunheim staring down at him as he gave this directive. He stood in opposition to Shay, but just as Thor did in Norse mythology, Shay intended to slay this giant.

Shay had a fearless look in his eyes. "Spread the floor!" he told his team.

Shay crossed right and then faked left. With enough space between him and Ricky, Shay ran straight toward the giant that attempted to emasculate him just a short time prior. Shay jumped. Knee cocked, no fear, bodies clashing like opposing universes, Shay looked down at his opponent as the ball fell through the rim.

"Remember me! I guess you're now the 'not-so Jolly Green Giant!'" Shay said as he walked away. Score LHHS 34–MXHS 40.

"George, look up!" Shay yelled. George stole the ball, touch-passed the ball to Shay who touch-passed the ball to Deron who sunk the three-pointer. Score LHHS 37–MXHS 40.

The buzzer sounded and Shay was back where he started, on the bench!

"Coach, I can bring this victory home for us!"

The Crossover that Won the Game

"Shay, you played very well and I admire your fearlessness, but it's your time to sit down."

This was hard for Shay, but he had no choice except to watch the game from the bench. The team played well, but the score remained close. With less than one minute left in the game, Lion's Heart trailed by 1. Al inbounded the ball to Aaron who brought the ball up the court. Aaron passed the ball to Michael who ran the ball toward the basket. With the defense collapsing, he passed the ball back out to Aaron. Aaron leaped and released the ball, intending to deliver a dagger into the heart of Malcolm X High School. The ball snapped the net, bringing the score to 53 (LHHS)–51 (MXHS).

"Back on defense, guys! It's not over yet!"

"Defense! Defense!" the crowd yelled.

I am usually the one that plays in the crucial moments! Shay thought as he frowned and folded his arms.

"Set the pick right there!" Ricky yelled.

Ricky ran around the pick and passed the ball to his teammate. Ricky ran along the baseline and circled back to the top of the key. Ricky grabbed the ball back from his teammate.

"Spread the floor!" Ricky told his team.

Ricky began running toward the basket. "Pick right here!" he yelled. "You cut to the basket!"

Ricky ran around the pick. Aaron fought hard to recover and contest Ricky's shot. As Ricky went right, Aaron slowly but surely got back in front of him. With three seconds remaining, Ricky quickly stepped back. Two seconds remaining, Ricky jumped as Aaron gave the last of what he had to get back in front of him. One second now remaining, Ricky released the ball. The clock now reads 0 and Lion's Heart High School watches as their season hangs in the ballads, dependent on one moment, one shot, one last hope.

Heads hanging low.

"Shay, do not get up and leave like you did before! We win as a team, lose as a team and walk out of this gymnasium…as…a…team!"

Shay sat there, unable to conquer the thought that he could have defended Ricky better. Somehow, he knew that he had to learn to trust other people in moments that mattered.

"Hey, Aaron, you did the best that you could, man. That was a hard pick they hit you with. I'm not sure who else would have been able to recover as fast as you did!" Shay said with advertent humility.

Aaron lifted his head. "Thanks, man that means a lot to me!" He smiled. "But you know what?"

"What?"

"We all know that you can defend Ricky better than me!"

Shay wished Coach Denise would have heard that, but she was busy talking to parents and other faculty members.

"We win as a team, and we lose as a team. We played hard, and we left our all on the floor like Coach Denise said. And a wise coach once told me that sometimes it's not whether you win or lose, but rather how you play the game!"

The Crossover that Won the Game

"Hey! Hey now! I think I know who said that!" Shay heard a familiar voice and laugh as his feet suddenly changed directions.

Shay ran and hugged his beloved friend and coach. "Hey, Coach Crossover! Aaron, I will talk to you later, man!"

"Hey, Shay! Are your parents here?"

"Yes, they are. Mom! Dad! Over here!"

Coach Crossover and Shay's parents talked for a few minutes about Shay's growth, both athletically and academically. They gushed about how proud they were of Shay.

"Hey guys, can Coach Crossover bring me home?"

"Oh sure!" Mom replied...

"Sure son!" Daddy responded with a seemingly upset voice. "I will be at the house when you get there buddy!"

"Okay." Shay said stoically as he turned quickly back to Coach Crossover.

Shay and Coach Crossover talked about the school year and Shay's feelings about the game. Shay's parents headed to the cars. They drove home where they would finish their conversation and wait for Shay to return. Shay and Coach Crossover walked to the restaurant across the street from the school.

"I've tried everything humanly possible to connect with Shay, he's just so distant," John shared with his wife.

"That's really something. I remember when you used to have the answers to everything. When you used to have empathy for others. Try to understand how the child feels. You've been gone out of his life before he was walking, but you know what? I've forgiven you. However, it's not my forgiveness that matters, it is Shay's," she said.

She knew he was hurt by the reality of her words, and for the first time ever, she saw water build up in his eyes. *Wait!* she thought. *This man never cries. I guess the saying is true, "Change is the only thing in this world that is constant."*

Not wanting him to be embarrassed that she saw him teary eyed, she walked away and said, "I'll put on a pot of coffee. I think I know who may be able to help you."

⋅ ♦ ⋅

"Shay, listen to me," Coach Crossover said as Shay sat at the table across from him venting. He smiled, he was so knowledgeable in the area of helping father and son reunite. These are the times he felt he was in the wrong profession. Perhaps he should have been a therapist, but his love for basketball and children led him to believe he was right where he was destined to be.

"What's so funny, Coach?" Shay questioned.

"You know how when you do something wrong and your mother scolds you?"

"Yeah," Shay answered, unsure where his coach was going with this conversation.

"And then she forgives you. A lot of the time she does this because she understands that you're a child and you don't know any better."

"Okay, Coach," Shay smiled, "get to the point."

"See, that is one of the problems a child has. They don't listen, they're impatient and unforgiving."

"I'm sorry, but how do you feel I'm unforgiving? It's like you're taking my dad's side...He left me!" he explained, raising his voice an octave.

"Please, I told you about those anger issues. I know you're hurt, and that's understandable. Let me explain something to you, though. Your dad made a mistake. The things we do in life are learned behaviors. How do you know his dad didn't do the same thing to his wife and kids?" Coach Crossover paused, letting Shay mull over what he had said.

"When you do wrong, you want others to forgive you, right?"

"Sure," he said, falling right into the coach's trap.

Coach smiled, and Shay shook his head as he realized that he'd just been cornered.

The ringing of the cell phone startled Coach Crossover. He grabbed the phone, puzzled at who could possibly be calling. His eyes widened, and he was at a loss for words as he looked at the screen.

"What's wrong, Coach?" Shay asked, his voice concerned.

"Shay..."

"What is it, Coach?"

Running his fingers through his gray hair, he said, "It's your dad..."

Book 6

Tenth Grade and Camp

"You're a deadbeat dad!" Shay screamed through the cell phone as a spray of saliva inundated the air.

"Don't ever ca—"

The phone was abruptly snatched away from his hand, "Don't you ever speak to your dad like that again. Whether he is good, bad, or indifferent, he's still your biological father and you will respect him as—"

"He is not my dad!" Shay spat, "he is just the one who donated—"

"Enough!" Coach Crossover said before speaking into the phone. "Sir, please give us thirty minutes and your son will call you back with a different attitude."

John, Shay's father, did not know what to say or think. Here was a coach, a white coach at that, having the type of relationship with his son that he wished the two of them could have.

"Wow!" he said audibly. "If I could turn back the hands of time, yet time awaits no man. That time is gone forever. Like vapor, it's gone."

"Listen," as though he heard neither of their statements. "Yesterday is the past, and today is the present, and that's why they call it a gift. Let us work on this gift. You and Shay have to work on the present and let the past remain the past. I will not always be around, my days are numbered," Coach Crossover said, revealing no emotions whatsoever.

"What?" John said through the phone.

"What?" Shay echoed.

Coach acted as though he didn't hear them. "Give me some time to speak with Shay and he will call you later with a different attitude," he said before hanging up the phone, leaving John feeling as guilty as a child who had just gotten caught with his hand in the cookie jar.

"Coach, I—"

"No, you have already spoken earlier. I think it's fair that you allow me to speak now. If you remember nothing else I've shared with you, please remember this old adage: be quick to listen and slow to speak."

"What's an adage?" he questioned.

"It's just an old saying that society uses, Shay."

"Yes, Coach."

"Although your dad has not been there and assumed the role as Dad, he's still your father. Each day, he is a day older. One day, he will fail to exist. The last thing you want is for your dad to pass away and you guys never had the chance to make amends. Or you never had the chance to tell him, 'Dad, I forgive you for your absence and I love you.'"

"But, Coach, how could I love him when I do not even know him? I don't love him."

"Hahaha." Coach Crossover laughed.

"What's so funny?"

The Crossover that Won the Game

"You're just fifteen years old, and you know nothing about love. Get to know the man, and I promise you, one day you will thank me for the advice I have given you today."

"How do you know so much about father-son relationships? Have you ever walked out of a child's life? Did your dad ever walk out on you? Oh, you probably do not even have children, and you and probably grew up in a nice two-parent home with the lovely white picket fence," Shay spat. "Answer me that, Coach, the cat has your tongue?"

The coach turned his head as a way of not allowing Shay to see the pain that he felt was now visible. *If the kid only knew he...* he thought. He began to reminisce on some years that he that he dare not share with Shay. In fact, he would not share this with anyone. He had to quickly take the sudden focus off of himself and put it back to where it belonged: on Shay. He smiled and ran his hand through his aging grey hair.

"In life, son," he said and began to smile. "Try and never answer a question with a question. Now," he said and paused, "If I remember correctly, the focus was you, not me. Now if you would please do me a favor?"

"Sure, Coach."

"Please call your dad and listen to him. Approach this thing with an open mind. Remember, even adults make mistakes. Oftentimes, we mature and earnestly endeavor to rectify our errors. If I am reading this correctly, your dad has matured and now realizes his errors in abandoning you. It appears as though he is truly trying to make up for his mistakes. Does this make any sense?"

"Kinda sorta," Shay said with a smirk. "You know, Coach," he said and paused. "You've been in my life, not John. When I am having female problems, it is you I turn to, not John. Coach Crossover, when I seek advice, it is you who is there for me, not some man who just decided he would dona—"

"I've heard enough," Coach Crossover said, raising his voice up an octave. He may be John to others, but to you he is Dad. And do not ever let me here you call him a man who donated. Do I make myself clear, young man?"

Shay was taken aback that the man who was dearest to him would yell at him. Well, not yell, but raise his voice up an octave. This man was his father figure, his true role model, surely his best friend and confidant. His tiny chest heaved in and out, tucked his bottom lip, and clenched his sweaty fist. Coach smiled at Shay. "Count from ten to one backwards and take deep breaths. Now close your eyes and think of pleasant moments."

Against his own will, he complied.

"Now imagine your dad on the basketball court with you, going over drills with you and not me. Think of him throwing you a football and baseball and saying, 'I am proud of you, son. I am so sorry that I was not there for you in the past. I made a mistake as people always do. Please forgive me and know that I love you and will always be there for you. Yes, son, I am here for the duration…'"

The water began to build up behind Shay's eyelids.

Coach continued on. "Now imagine him telling you, 'I will always love you and you will always be a special part of my life. I will give you the world. If you need a liver, I will gladly give it to you. If you need my heart in order to live, and that meant I had to die, I will give my life for you and not even give it a second thought. I love you just that much.'"

The Crossover that Won the Game

Now the water began to pour out of Shay's eyes. Clear blue tears were streaming down his cheeks. "Out of all things I could give you in life, the one thing I cannot give you is that father-and-son connection. That is a connection parents have, and no stranger can make that connection. If I could, I would not even try because that would be stealing an opportunity that your dad rightfully deserves."

With that said, he removed his hand off of Shay's shoulder as an indication that he had imparted on him all of the knowledge he could. He had given him the formula to the problem, but only they could use it to find the solution.

Shay opened his eyes as the clear blue water began to cascade down both of his brown cheeks. "Thank you so much for being so tolerant and loving to me. I am not a bad kid, sometimes I am just in that gray area of life. My dad's absence really hurt me."

Coach swallowed hard. This was truly an emotional moment, he had never heard Shay speak from the heart the way he did tonight.

"If you do not mind, I would like to walk home so I can call my dad and speak with him. You are right, I will only have one dad. You could never take his place, nor can he take yours," he said as he turned to leave. "Oh, and, Coach?" he said and paused as the tears continued to cascade down his face freely.

"Yes, Shay?" Coach answered, unsure of his own voice.

"Never ever forget to remember that you are the best coach in the whole wide world," he said through a choked voice and began to trot away.

Coach Crossover blinked and stared as his own tears now fell. *Oh, how I love him and wish I were his dad*, he thought.

Shay was truly touched by Coach Crossover's love for him. He was shocked by how stern he was with him, but deep inside, Shay knew that Coach Crossover was right. "I have been somewhat rude to my dad and I do not want to miss an opportunity to love him. If I do not find the strength to forgive my dad, I will never truly know the love he has for me. I'll give this relationship another…"

Ring, ring, ring! Shay's thought was interrupted by the ringtone on his cell phone. Much to Shay's surprise, it was his dad.

"Hello!" Shay said.

"Hi, son! I want you to listen for a moment, okay?"

"Okay!" Shay said, puzzled.

"I know that I haven't been there for you and for that I am very sorry. I cannot do much about the past, but today, I want to do all that I can to be the dad you want and need. I want to comfort you when you're sad. I want to te—"

"Dad, I am fifteen!" They both laughed.

"Okay, Shay, I want us to create our own stories!"

Shay began to cry gently. God heard his prayer that his dad would hear and understand the cry of his heart. He loved Coach Crossover, but he readily agreed that he could never replace his dad.

"I feel things for my dad that I could never feel for Coach Crossover. The love I have for my dad is very different. I would give my li—"

"Shay! Hello, Shay, are you there?"

"Oh yeah, I'm sorry, Dad, I was just thinking!"

"What's on your mind, son?" Dad said in a deep voice. Shay remained silent.

Shay slowly and inconspicuously opened the door. Now standing behind his dad in the living room, Shay began to speak.

"I love you and I need a..."

Shay's dad quickly turned around. Startled and excited, he grabbed Shay and pulled him close.

"Hug!" Shay barely got the word out of his mouth as he finished his sentence.

The two of them embraced one another and shared tears. Through the sobs, they continued their conversation.

"You surprised me, son!"

"I know, Dad. Ha! Ha! I am very glad that you are here right now!"

"There's no place I'd rather be!"

Shay's dad proved that during the summer of Shay's sophomore year in high school. He made sure to spend time with Shay every day during the summer. Ruby and John had several in-depth conversations about the future of their family. They both agreed that, at least for Shay's sake, there would have to be some changes. Shay's dad agreed that he would no longer be in and out of Shay's life.

Dad practiced basketball with Shay.

"Son, you really are good!" he would frequently say.

"I guess you won't be missing anymore games!" Shay laughed as he teased his dad.

"Not if I can help it!"

Shay couldn't believe it. His dad showed up without warning and began giving demands.

"Get dressed now! No questions, there are no time for answers."

Shay never liked demands without reason, but he knew his dad must have had an acceptable reason. Before Shay knew it, his dad had made one of his dreams come true.

The plane ride was new for Shay. *I'm kind of excited but also nervous*, he thought. *Are we moving to another state? What does Dad have up his sleeve?* Shay put his chin in his right palm and continued to mull over this adventure. The plane finally stopped.

"Orlando, Florida! No way! Could it be?" They, as a family, had just walked through the gates of Disney World! The grass was greener than Shay had ever seen, the water was so clear Shay thought he just might have a sip to cool off in the 95-degree weather. Magic Kingdom was memorable. Shay stood awestruck at the gigantic rides. Shay loved animals, but the zoos in Rochester, New York, paled in comparison to Animal Kingdom, a section within Magic Kingdom. "So this is Disney World?" Shay screamed as he splashed in the clear blue water of Typhoon Lagoon. "It must take magic to create something this awesome!" Shay said, speaking of all the wonders found in Magic Kingdom. Shay smiled one of the biggest smiles that day of summer before his sophomore year. Shay felt as if he was 15 going on 5, but this was a once in a lifetime experience.

The memory created was truly one that Shay would always remember. Dad had more surprises for Shay, but he kept the suspense high and the information top secret.

Shay didn't talk to Coach Crossover much over the summer, but when they did speak, Coach would always say the same thing.

"Oh, my buddy, just you wait! I am working on something big!" Then he would laugh a familiar laugh.

It was bright and early on this Saturday morning. The school year was approaching and Shay wanted all of the rest he could get. Much to his dismay and surprise, he would be arising earlier than desired. *What is that big truck doing in the driveway?* he thought.

Staring up at the face staring down at him.

"I'm home, Shay!" His dad was officially moving back in.

Shay had learned a few things about treating others the way he wanted to be treated. Dad, Jeremiah, Shay, and a few movers put their arms to work and made sure he was all moved in.

First Day of School

Today marked the first time that Shay's dad would watch him get on the bus.

"Dad, I am fifteen years old. I do not need you to drive me to the bus stop!"

"We have some lost time to make up for!"

"I am happy that you want to make up for lost time, but uh…this is embarrassing!" Shay laughed.

Dad laughed simultaneously. "I understand, son! I will see you when you get home. Have a good day at school!"

"Thanks!" Shay said as he slammed the car door and walked toward the bus stop.

Dad didn't move.

"Dad...go!" Shay motioned with his hand.

"Not today, son. I will not embarrass you tomorrow, but this one time, I am watching my main man board the bus on his first day of school."

Shay smiled. "Okay, thanks! Bye, Dad!"

Shay looked at the familiar and not-so-familiar faces. The bus ride was pretty rambunctious as the students reacquainted themselves with old friends and took liberty to meet new ones, all while talking about their summer. This time, Shay was left with no feelings of envy. Shay hopped off the bus and walked toward the glass doors of Lion's Heart High School.

Bang! Shay turned to look as someone bumped into him. "Hey, watch where you're..." Shay began to speak.

"You know who I am, bro!" a voice spoke from behind him.

Shay could recognize that voice from a mile away. "Chris?"

"What's up, bro?" Chris replied.

The two friends chatted over breakfast and were happy to discover that they had several classes together. The first day of school was very busy. Learning the names of the new teachers and a few students and learning the locations of his classes made for a busy day. Shay was very excited to have his buddy Chris there with him, though. From his conversation with George that day, it seemed like their bond from last school year was still intact. All players agreed that they would be trying out for the Junior Varsity team. Walking out to the school buses, Shay and Chris had their last conversation of the day.

"How was your season last year, Chris?"

"It was rough, Shay!"

"I think we may share a similar story, bro!"

"We rarely played, and when we did, we paid!" the two said in unison and shared a laugh at the memory.

"We should work out together this year though! It will be just old times!" Chris said.

"Yeah, let's do that. Hey, man, I will see you tomorrow!"

The two friends said their good-byes and boarded the buses. Their friendship flowed as if they hadn't missed an entire school year and several months apart.

Shay's dad helped him with his homework. Dad still worked many hours to support the family, but something was different this time, he made sure he was home in time to have dinner with his family. The family gradually grew closer.

"John, it has been nice to have you around more often!" Shay's mom said.

"It's been a great feeling to be with my family."

There was now a strong male presence to direct Jeremiah and Shay's arguments.

"You're brothers! You should love each other and treat each other with respect! Jeremiah, Shay is your younger brother and whether you believe it or not, he needs your positive words and support. The words you say to him will undoubtedly have a long-term impact on his life."

Often, Jeremiah would be without a response to dad's beckoning. Shay was glad that Daddy was standing up for him. Shay was getting bigger and arguments had a greater propensity for getting physical if Jeremiah continued to tease him. Every so often, Dad would have to diffuse situations.

"Stop it now! If the two of you cannot deal with disagreements in a civil manner, then find me or your mom!"

"Dad, I am sick of him teasing me!"

"Shay, I know, but there are healthy ways to handle it!"

Dad had a long heartfelt conversation with Jeremiah. Jeremiah remembered his promise that he made to dad during last school year. "You will treat your brother with respect and kindness or your mother and I are taking your car away!" That was a big deal to a twenty-year-old!

"Shay, if I see you get in your brother's face again, I am taking your basketball!" Certainly taking Shay's basketball was akin to momentarily removing a best friend and Shay would not let that happen.

The three of them connected over shoot-around at the basketball court near their house. The walks home were much more pleasant than before. It was refreshing to have his dad practicing basketball with him and telling him how proud he was of him. Shay had imagined it and it was finally

The Crossover that Won the Game

happening. He could never forget that night in Coach Crossover's car. The father-son connection is one that no stranger could give. Shay was just as happy that Jeremiah speaking much needed positive words of affirmation. It didn't bother Shay that James was too busy working to come around much.

The school year was progressing smoothly for Shay. Dad and Mom helped with homework and Shay took advantage of additional help from school faculty when necessary. Shay and Chris's relationship continued to grow. Their big day had finally come...tryouts!

Tryouts

Shay was happy to have his best friend there with him. *What a source of moral support*, Shay thought. But he knew that Chris's support would have nothing to do with whether or not made the team. Shay brought his very best to tryouts. No one believed in him besides his buddy Chris. The bigger players knocked him down and guards defended him better than he cared to admit. Shay loved all of the family activities that he did this past summer, but he knew he needed to practice more than he did. Shay showed that he was decent shooter, but the coach didn't seem impressed. Shay did, what he thought to be, amazing crossovers. No one really noticed. It was like his presence was ghostly at best. Shay made passes to the best of his ability, even a full court pass that landed the team a point.

What more can I do? Shay thought to himself. "One thing I know is that I am going to give my all, do my best...and let the chips fall where they may!" Shay told Chris during a water break.

"You're playing very well, bro. If you do not make the team, I will be very surprised!"

"Well, I will say a prayer for you too, my friend. Well, let's get back in there so we can finish tryouts and get home for R and R."

Decision

Shay and Chris completed their school day and began their unforgettable walk. The two of them shared so many emotions: anxiety, excitement, fear, premature joy accompanied by premature sadness. *Clunk! Clunk! Clunk!* Their feet finally came to a stop and their eyes finally met the truth...

"I don't even want to look, bro!" Chris said.

"I don't want to either, but it's our only option!"

Chris scanned the list several times and, much to his dismay, did not see his name.

"Your turn!" Chris said sadly.

"Hey, bro, I'm sorry that you didn't make the team!"

"It's okay! There's always next year!"

"My turn, huh?" Shay asked rhetorically. "No way!" Shay stomped his foot and crossed his arms. "I can't believe I didn't make the team!"

Chris put his hand on Shay's shoulder.

"It's okay, bro! We will get through it the same way we got through difficult moments during eighth grade. Remember, when you were frustrated about whether or not your dad would be at the game, and I put my arm around your neck and told you that everything would be all right?"

"Yeah!"

"Well, here it goes again! Everything will be all right!" Chris said as he put his arm around his best friend's neck.

"You're right, buddy, everything will be all right!" Shay said as he and Chris walked toward the buses.

Shay was quiet during the ride home. He was still in disbelief that he would not be playing basketball for Lion's Heart this year. He knew that he had to triumph beyond this moment. From the role models and experiences he'd had, he knew he could not let failure stop him. He didn't have a complete recipe for success, but he was sure that effort was one of the ingredients. He wasn't quite sure what to do next.

Ring! Ring! Shay's cell phone began sounding off as Shay opened the door. *Could not be better timing!* Shay thought to himself as he plopped onto the couch.

"Hello!"

"Hey, Shay, how are you?"

"I am doing…uh…well…not so great! How are you?

"The concern is not me right now! What's wrong?"

"Well…I didn't make the team!" Shay responded while holding back tears.

"Shay, I am so sorry!" Coach Crossover responded.

"I need some advice, Coach!"

"I will give you advice. You know that I always want what's best for you. I do have a project beginning in a couple of weeks that may be of great benefit to you!"

"What is it?"

"Have your dad call me. I want him to deliver the news to you. I am also going to try something different!"

"What? I'm confused!"

"Have you called your dad yet?"

"No! You and I always talk about things when I am frustrated," Shay responded.

"And I will still be someone that you can talk to, but I want your dad to be the first to give you advice. Give him a call, then call me back!"

Shay was astonished!

Coach Crossover called John before Shay could. He did not tell John what Shay would be calling about, but only that he needed to talk. Coach Crossover talked to John briefly about the basketball camp that he would be running for fourteen- to eighteen-year-olds that would debut in one month.

Shay began calling his dad while Dad was talking to Coach Crossover.

"Hello, son!"

"Hi, Dad, I just need to talk about today!"

"What's wrong, son?

"I didn't make…the…" Shay began to cry.

"Son, would you prefer to have this conversation face-to-face?"

"That would be great!"

"Okay, son, I'll see you soon!"

Had John just made an empty promise? He was aware that he had three hours left on his shift, but he was equally aware that it was his duty to be there for his son. *Knock! Knock! Knock!*

"Yes, John, what is it?" the supervisor asked as he opened the door.

"Sir, I know I have three hours remaining on my shift, but my son is distraught about something and, Mr. Jackson, he needs me!"

"I really do not have anyone to cover the rest of your shift, but I am not going to stand in between a man and his family!" Mr. Jackson said as he lifted his brown-skinned hand. "You can make the time up, John!"

"Thanks a lot! I will see you tomorrow!"

John closed the office door, gathered his belongings, and headed toward his car.

"Hey! I'm home!" Dad yelled as he walked in the house.

Shay was still sitting in the same place as when he called his dad. "Hey, Dad! I'm in here!"

Dad looked and began walking toward the living room.

"You talk, I listen?" Dad said as he sat beside Shay.

"Yeah, that would be nice!" Shay responded.

"I'm all ears, son!"

"Well, I didn't make the team. I know that tryouts were challenging, but I believed I played well enough to make the team, at least."

"Why do you think you were cut from the team?"

"I don't know! Maybe I am too weak, too slow and...or too small!"

"What if you were not meant to play for the school this year?"

"Why wouldn't I be?"

"First of all, son, you're not too weak, slow, or small. In fact, you are a phenomenal player, but what if you are able to learn more by not playing than if you would have played this year?"

"How so, Dad? That doesn't make any sense!"

"I talked to Coach Crossover and he has a basketball camp beginning in two weeks! Are you interested?"

"Of course, I am!" Shay's eyes lit up and his frown was now a smile!

"He will be happy to hear that, Shay! I will let him tell you all about it."

"Thank you, Dad. I really appreciate you taking the time to talk to me!"

"Hey, what are dads for?"

"Well, I can think of many..."

"Oh, stop it..." The two of them laughed and embraced.

"Hey, I am going to call Coach Crossover back so I can hear all about this camp!"

Phone Conversation with Coach Crossover

"Hello!"

"Hey, Shay! How are you feeling?"

"A lot better now. Thank you so much for persuading me to call my dad!"

"You're welcome! Like I said before, you and him share something very special and both of you should enjoy it while you can!"

"Okay, Coach…what's this I hear about a basketball camp?"

"Well, I've been waiting for you to ask!' The two of them laughed. "The camp will begin in one month. The age range will be fourteen to eighteen. Are you ready for the challenge?"

"Ehhh, I don't kn—"

"The answer is yes, Shay. God will never put any task before us that we cannot handle," Crossover said in a deep and animated voice. "Sometimes, bad things happen for good reason. You will be exposed to potential future competition. You will have to play against students that are bigger, stronger, and perhaps…"

"I experienced that last season! They were bigger, stronger, and yes… sometimes quicker!"

"This camp will be a safe place for you to be challenged. You will lift weights and run drills, learn more efficient ways to dribble the ball, and I can guarantee you an improved jump shot. You will feel prepared for any challenge that may come your way. Now I ask again, Shay...are you ready?"

"Yes, I am!"

"Well then, I look forward to seeing you in a couple of weeks."

"Okay, see you soon, Coach!"

The two said good-bye and briefly listened to the silence before setting their phones down. Shay was excited about the camp and really hoped it could prepare him for varsity next year. The next two weeks were hard for Shay. He would hear his fellow schoolmates talking about how much they were looking forward to watching the basketball team play. Every once in a while, Shay would hear the basketball team discussing plays and strategies for high performance. The sound of the basketball hitting the hardwood floor created a sort of hypervigilance inside of Shay. He knew he would defeat the demons that haunted him daily.

Shay focused on school and developed a closer relationship with Chris. Shay was overjoyed when he found out that Chris would be able to attend the camp with him.

"We're going to rule the court during varsity season!" Chris said!

Shay just smiled and stuck out his fist for Chris to pound it. Shay admired Chris's positive attitude. It was certainly the kind of attitude Shay needed. For now, the façade of belief would have to suffice.

Shay's relationship with his dad continued to improve. He helped Shay with his homework, and if he didn't know the answer, well, he would call his brother, Shay's uncle who was an eleventh grade math and English teacher. Shay and his family were really proud of his grades. Math was his only B, but it wasn't due to a lack of effort.

The Crossover that Won the Game

Dad wasn't much of a basketball player, but he still indulged Shay over games of horse, 21, and shoot-around. "All right, son, I am whooped, so we must resume another day, but hey, your first day of camp is tomorrow."

Camp

"All right, for all of you who don't know me, my name is Coach Crossover and this is Coach Denise!"

"I thought she was coaching basketball at Lion's Heart?" Shay questioned internally.

"My day job was coaching ninth grade boys at Lion's Heart High School. I think I see a couple of familiar faces!" Coach Denise said while scanning the crowd and fixing on Shay.

"All right, let's learn and laugh. Let's play hard, but let's play fair! Oh, and negativity is not allowed. What you believe about yourself is essential to who you become, and before anyone asks, Crossover is really my last name!" He laughed while looking at Shay. "As epic as it would be, I...did... not...give myself...that name!" Coach said, remembering Shay's twenty-one questions from their first meeting.

The coaches divided the teams and started with passing drills. They taught the boys how to truly make the best pass in the moment.

"It's much like life, having a variety of skills and a broad knowledge base will enable you to make the best decision in life's most crucial moments," Coach Denise said.

"Embrace simple because there are times when fancy will land you a first-class ticket on the bench!" Coach Crossover spoke covertly to the boys that thought a nice crossover was more important than being able to do a bounce pass correctly.

Coach Crossover was not feeling well but gave his all to impart what he could to these groups of boys that were counting on him. "Okay, one game of one-on-one!" Coach Crossover scanned to make sure the teams were evenly matched.

Shay brought the ball down the court and, much to his surprise, was quickly stripped. *Here we go again, déjà vu! Oh my gosh, he is so fast!* Shay thought he saw his future flash before his eyes. Indeed, some of the fellow campers were the boys he would eventually play against.

"Shay, there is no giving up here!" Coach Crossover said.

Shay brought the ball down the court again. He crossed the ball from left to right, then moved swiftly past his opponent.

Bang! Shay first banged bodies, then banged against the floor. Shay lay there for what felt like forever.

"I hope this hand is familiar to you! Get up, kid! I told you last year that you have a lot of heart. Never forget who you are!" Coach Denise helped Shay up.

"Funny how we seem to keep meeting…this way!" Shay laughed as he brushed his shorts off.

"All right, tiger, go get 'em!"

The rest of the day was pretty much the same. Shay continued to get knocked down. He never stayed there though. He knew he had to get stronger. In the coming weeks, Shay began lifting weights with the help of fitness instructors that volunteered.

"I'm feeling stronger, Coach!"

"By the time camp concludes, you will be knocking those big guys on their behinds!" Coach Crossover patted Shay on the back.

Shay walked slowly to the car.

"What's wrong, son?"

"Aside from being knocked down, scraped up, and straining to lift weights, well…nothing!"

"Every time you get knocked down, son, the stronger you will become… if you truly want that! Give it your best tomorrow!"

Shay remembered his dad's words when he was face-to-face with his least favorite player. The two banged bodies. Shay did two crossovers between his legs while stepping back. "Time to make him fear me!" Shay pump-faked!

"I don't fall for those!"

Shay put the ball behind his back, faked right, and then quickly crossed the ball in front of him to his left hand. His least favorite player was now lying on his back, shocked and staring at Shay. Shay dropped the ball into his chest and walked away. Little did Shay know he had gotten a little stronger!

The players put on ankle weights and worked on agility and speed. Shay lifted weights and his confidence began to increase. Shay and Chris were growing closer and closer, and both were improving a great deal in the sport they loved. Walking down the hallway and out of the door, Shay shared a piece of his heart with his best friend.

"As much as I am enjoying this camp, you're my best friend and your company is priceless. Bro, your friendship has become invaluable to me. Thank you for being a friend!"

Chris returned the accolades. "Thank you for being a friend! I think I've heard that somewhere before!" Chris laughed.

The two shook hands. "Well...now it's our signature phrase." In unison, they spoke, concluding in laughter.

As the two separated and cars drove away, Shay was happy about the progress he had made and how much closer he was growing to Chris. Certainly, Shay wished he was playing basketball for the junior varsity team, but he had begun to believe that there was a greater purpose behind being cut from the team. Personal growth had always been important to Shay, and friendships just the same. The camp offered both. There was clear connectedness and Shay's growth was visible to all whom he interacted with. During sports or matters unrelated, Shay's maturation was revealed.

"You think you're all that, huh?" Jeremiah asked as the family was finishing their dinnertime conversations.

"That's enough, son!" Dad interjected.

"It's okay. Let him speak!" Shay responded.

"You heard what I said before!"

"Well, brother, I've actually learned humility these last couple of weeks."

"Blah, blah, blah!"

"I'm not going to entertain your immaturity!"

Dad was interested in seeing which direction this conversation would take. Anxious to chime in, but also very aware of the educational benefit to simply listening, he did just that, simply listened.

The Crossover that Won the Game

"Go to all of the camps you can find and you still won't be better than me!"

Shay was tired of listening to his brother rant. He sincerely wanted to walk away from the dinner table, but he would no longer back down from any challenge.

"There's a court right in the backyard. We can play right now if you're really ready." Shay had fury in his eyes like never before. Today was his day and this was a moment he had to make count.

The two brothers along with their father took a walk that neither of them would ever forget. Destination: the backyard; it was time to solve this dilemma and put years of anger to rest.

Jeremiah moved the ball very quickly in front of Shay's eyes. Shay tried to time the bounces to move in for the steal, but to no avail. Jeremiah put the ball between Shay's legs and completed a finger roll layup. "You're just a little bum. You think believing in yourself makes a difference!"

"Never stop believing in yourself." Shay remembered the words of his friend and confidant, Coach Crossover. Shay secured his defensive stance in front of Jeremiah.

"You're no good. It's all right though, I have enough game for both of us!" Jeremiah ran past Shay, and just as Shay regained composure, Jeremiah released the ball and sunk the long-range jump shot.

"You're a really good player, son. Never let anyone tell you otherwise." Shay remembered the words of his dad.

Now standing face-to-face with Shay, Jeremiah used his height advantage to add to his demeaning behavior. "I thought I told you before just to give up."

Shay turned and walked away. "You're finally learning your true colors I see!" Shay didn't say a word. He bent down, picked up the ball slowly, and with a walk similar to the grim reaper made his way closer to Jeremiah.

"I'll never give up!" Shay handed Jeremiah the ball. Dad admired Shay's heart.

Jeremiah dribbled the ball in his left hand. He was astonished at his younger brother's newfound confidence. He quickly crossed the ball to his right hand. As he went to run right, Shay tapped the ball out of Jeremiah's hand. Shocked, he lunged in to take the ball back from Shay. Just as he lunged in, Shay spun to the left, leaving Jeremiah behind as he made the layup. "The score is 2–1," Shay said. "Play to 7?"

"That's fine with me!" Jeremiah responded sarcastically.

Shay dribbled the ball slowly and intently in front of Jeremiah's face.

"You're not ready for me yet!" Jeremiah used discouraging tactics. Just as Shay began his movement around Jeremiah's body, he sidestepped, greeting Shay with his elbow. Shay lay on the ground, breathing heavily, and grimacing from the effect of foul play, he remembered the outstretched hand and words of Coach Denise: "A winner never quits, and a quitter never wins!"

"That's 3–1!" Jeremiah said as he shot a jump shot while Shay lay there on the ground.

Shay got back up. He was determined to stand strong. Jeremiah missed his next jump shot and Shay grabbed the rebound. He crossed the ball quickly between his legs, faked the drive, and stepped back for the mid-range jumper.

"Still don't have a jumper I see!"

The Crossover that Won the Game

Jeremiah's ranting seemed to last forever. As Shay stepped in front of Jeremiah, his brother used his strength to run him over. The score is now 4-1, and actually, we are only playing to 5.

"Does it really make you feel better about yourself to bully me?" Shay asked.

Dad had seen enough, so he walked over and patted both boys on the back. "You guys have to work through this one on your own. I have to go see your mother!"

Shay and Jeremiah were baffled. Dad walked into the house, the boys didn't know it, but he would be watching the game from the window inside, looking over the backyard.

There was a sort of awkward silence. "Cat has your tongue? I've never done anything to you, but you continue to treat me like the little brother that you never wanted!" Shay said with both tears in his eyes and fury in his heart. For him, this would be the moment the new day began.

Jeremiah stared at his baby brother. For the first time, he saw something in his little brother that he'd never seen before...himself! He saw himself when he used to be the one getting bullied. *Wow!* he thought to himself, as he remembered how much that hurt.

"You always have so much negative to say to me, speak now. Have I struck a nerve somewhere?"

Jeremiah turned his head and blinked his eyes to fight back his own tears. What the heck was wrong with him? Bullying a little kid, his own flesh and blood nonetheless! He felt like such a coward. Then, as a man who had just received a second wind, he gathered his composure and turned. He was the strong one, and Shay was the weak one. Tears falling faster, Jeremiah put the ball behind his back and pulled up for the jump shot. Shay stripped the ball with his left hand.

Dribbled the ball behind his back once, then drained the jump shot. Wiping his many tears, Shay stared Jeremiah square in the eyes.

"I'm waiting…you seem to enjoy tearing me down, so let me hear it!"

"I'll tell you what, little bro," with his hand on Shay's shoulder he spoke in a more kind tone.

"Get your hand off of me! What?" Shay questioned as his tears continued to fall.

"The score is 4–3. If you make this last basket, I'll take you to the mall and buy you the newest Jumpmans, take you out to lunch, and…"

"What else?" Shay asked in a choked voice.

"I'll apologize and never bully you again," Jeremiah said.

"You're on!"

Jeremiah smiled, but he was stuck between a rock and a hard place. Shay was much too little for him. He could overpower him any time and any way he'd like, but it was his baby brother.

"Your ball," Jeremiah said.

Shay put the ball on the ground. Jeremiah backed up. *I'll be nice and be the good big brother and allow him to win*, he thought.

"No, the bullies I dealt with did not give me a break," he reasoned.

He ran toward Shay as he bounced the ball twice. Jeremiah reached as Shay crossed the ball over. Then he took the ball between his legs and

The Crossover that Won the Game

behind his back. Once again, he did a crossover and leaped for the jumper. Jeremiah crashed bodies with Shay, but it was too late. They both fell to the ground, and the ball soared through the air as Jeremiah stared in disbelief.

"Miss!" he yelled.

Shay's smile widened as he jumped off the ground, hoping this would be the first time he beat his big brother in something.

"Really, look at how the ball soars," Shay said, turned with his fists in the air, and walked away.

Book 7

The ball hit the rim while Jeremiah was still yelling the word, "Miss!" Then, bringing his worst nightmare to life, the ball fell through the net. Shay never turned around because he just knew. "Sometimes you just know," Shay said to himself. He knew the ball would go in, just like Jeremiah knew that his demise was approaching, so to speak.

John released his wife's hand and hugged her. "I knew Shay would one day defeat Jeremiah," he laughed.

In the Victorian-style living room, Mom and Dad stood at the window, staring and smiling. John turned and held his wife's hand. Eyes fixed on the ball, John smiled and said, "That's my boy…"

"I think this will be a humbling experience for Jeremiah," his wife said with a grin as John ran out the door.

Shay held his head high. He did not have to turn around to see the results of his final shot. If Coach Crossover taught him anything, it was to believe in himself. In his heart and mind, he knew that the shot he made was truly a result of the crossover that won the game.

The trotting of footsteps did not even faze him because he knew it was Jeremiah. *Oh well. He got what was coming to him*, he thought.

The strong hand placed on his right shoulder caused him to stop. Actually, he couldn't move even if he wanted to; the hand was too strong. He tried to move forward, but to no avail.

♦ ♦ ♦

Jeremiah was now sitting up with his head between his hands. "Unbelievable!" he said in awe.

• • •

"Never look down on a man when he's dejected unless you're going to help him up. Go help your brother please," his dad pleaded. "Look at him, he's pitiful."

"But, Dad!"

"Please, son, I promise you he will never forget this moment. Trust me."

Reluctant, Shay agreed. "Okay, Dad. We are trying to build trust in each other, right?"

"Right, son."

• • •

Shay stood in front of Jeremiah with an outstretched hand. "C'mon, big brother," he said as he helped his brother up.

"Thanks," Jeremiah said.

"Sure."

"Hey, Shay?"

"Yeah?"

Jeremiah looked into the heavens, then right at Shay, and smiled. "I thought Michael Jordan retired?"

"He did," Shay said.

"No, you're next in line," he said as he placed his arm around his baby brother. "Let's shower, go to the mall, and pick out your Jumpmans, and grab some lunch."

"Sure, but...but...but..." he stammered.

"I'm sorry for bullying you," he said as they continued to walk with his shoulder around Shay.

"Thanks."

"For what?" Jeremiah asked.

"For being a man of your word. Will you really stop bullying me?"

"Yes, and you know what?"

"What?" Shay asked.

"A bully is really a coward."

Shay laughed. "I know."

Shay and Jeremiah went inside to get cleaned up. "Hey, I have to make a call before we go!" Shay said.

The ringing of the alarm clock did not startle Coach Crossover. Why should it? He had not been able to get a good night's sleep the last few weeks. His mother told him this would likely happen. Coach Crossover became sad as he thought about his deceased mother. *God rest her lovely soul!* he thought. *She was correct.* He felt his right kidney trying to relieve the pain. He could not even make it out of bed to see Shay in summer camp. What he was faced with was his problem. He had told no one but his diary. He tried to smile, but the pain was overwhelming. *Well, I am getting up in age. Truth be told, although time awaits no man, no one really wants to...* Coach Crossover's thought was interrupted.

Ring! Ring! Ring!

"Who is it?" he asked himself. He could no longer let the phone ring. The caller was persistent so it had to be important. He answered on the eighth ring. "Hello..."

"Well!" Shay said, "Are you getting old or something? You used to answer by the third or fourth ring."

"Hello, Shay, how are you?" Coach Crossover said, trying to disguise his pain.

"I'm...I'm fine. I won't be long. I just hadn't seen you in at least a couple of weeks and I wanted to see how you were doing!"

"That's nice of you, Shay. I am doing—"

"Oh, sorry, Coach, I have to go. I am at the mall with my brother, Jeremiah..."

"What?" Coach asked, arching an eyebrow.

"Yes, he bet me that if I beat him in a game of basketball, he would take me to the mall to buy me the latest Jumpman sneakers, take me to lunch, and not only that, he promised to apologize and never bully me again!"

"That's great, Shay, I'm happy for you!"

"Okay, Coach! It was nice to talk to you. I'll talk to you later and hope to see you at camp!"

"Shay!"

It was too late, Shay had already hung up the phone.

I really hope Jeremiah keeps his word! Shay certainly deserves happiness and to be treated with respect! Coach Crossover thought.

While Shay was at the mall and Coach Crossover was managing his pain and trying muster up the strength to go to summer camp, Coach Denise was preparing for next season.

Coach Denise sat in front of her television reviewing tapes from the previous season. She noticed something for the first time, Shay's ability and skills. She recalled the words of Michael, "Why don't you let Shay play more? He really is a great player." Although she knew this, she was really, somewhat biased toward short players. But today, that would change. Shay would be starting next season. As she watched Shay's last couple plays of the game, she had to admit that Shay was a pretty good player and smart too. Drove the ball fearlessly toward the big man, then made a great touch pass the very next time down the court. She picked up the phone and dialed her brother.

"Hello!" he answered on the third ring.

"Hey, big brother! How are ya?"

"Good! Will you be at camp later?"

"Yes, I will. Hey, remember that player you coached at New Perspectives Junior High School?"

"Shay?"

"Yes!"

"Yeah, I remember!"

"Well, I underestimated Shay's ability and intelligence. I am going to start him next season."

"If you give that kid a chance and be a source of positivity for him, he will shine like your brightest star! Well, little sis, I have to go now. Sorry that I have been so busy lately, but I will see you at camp later," Coach Scott said as he hung up the phone.

Summer Camp
Final Day

The purplish sun shone above the mountaintop as Shay rode his bike to camp. Mom was very preoccupied with some other really important matter, and Dad was at work. Jeremiah had already made plans with some of his friends. "Exercise is good anyhow!" Shay reasoned. He smiled; he had a feeling that he would have a great day at camp. It pleased Shay that Jeremiah was transforming into a better big brother. He had spent several hours working with Shay to improve his skills. He even promised to visit the camp today. Shay looked forward to seeing Coach Crossover.

Shay hopped off of his bike, wrapped his chain around the bike and light pole, snapped his lock shut, and began running toward the gymnasium when he vaguely heard a female voice call his name. "Shay!" Shay continued running until he heard the voice call again. "Shay, wait a minute, Shay!"

Shay turned around; much to his surprise, it was Coach Denise.

The Crossover that Won the Game

"Hey, Coach Denise, what are you doing here?" he asked with a slightly disinterested tone, feeling as though she must not be early for him. *She doesn't like me very much*, Shay thought.

"We have a little while before camp starts, can we talk?"

"Sure, Coach! Something wrong?"

"Not anymore." She smiled. "I was wrong for not letting you start during freshman season. I was biased because of your size. Never let anyone crush your dreams! I came here to apologize and to tell you that you're starting point guard next season."

Shay's mouth hung open. "But, but..." he stammered.

"Let's just thank modern technology! Train hard, you've made a lot of growth during camp. How privileged am I to have had the opportunity to watch you grow. You have a great spirit and a lot of heart. A lot will be riding on you!"

Shay and Coach Denise walked into the gym to stretch, shoot around, and wait for the others to arrive.

♦ ♦ ♦

"Hey, John, I am going to need you to pick Shay up from summer camp. I have some important business to handle."

"Hey, hun, Jeremiah is picking him up today!"

"Awesome! Thank you!"

Ruby sat on the soft beige leather chair rereading some of her mother's letters, diary entries, and photographs. As she went through them, she smiled, laughed, and cried. Shortly after sitting down with the box of memories, she noticed a 3×5 photo in a letter she'd never read before. For some reason, she was compelled to open it. In the photo, to her surprise, was a Caucasian child. Looking at the photo longer and longer, she realized she'd seen the youth before. She opened the letter and read, glancing at the photo every so often. She tilted her head from side to side and even tried putting her reading glasses on. *Who is this young man?* she thought. The letter read simply:

> Dear Ruby,
>   I could never tell you this because I never wanted you to think badly of your dad, but it is time for you to know. This young Caucasian boy in the photo is your brother.
>
> Mom

Ruby dropped the diary and the photograph and just sat there. After the initial shock wore off, she reached for the photo and looked at the young boy with the basketball with a new perspective. "Oh my god!" she gasped and quickly covered her mouth.

"Coach Crossover!"

◆ ◆ ◆

Picking up her car keys off of the marble kitchen counter, she smiled and nearly chuckled. "I must be losing my mind," Ruby thought as she tossed the short letter and the photograph into her purse. She left the house, got into her white Toyota, and took a final look at the photo.

"Coach Crossover?" Ruby smiled and laughed as tears started to well up in her eyes. "The sooner I can address this, the sooner I can just

The Crossover that Won the Game

relax," she told herself as she began her journey to try and solve this new mystery.

◆ ◆ ◆

Coach Crossover sat up in bed, drinking the broth of his chicken noodle soup. Lately, he hadn't been able to hold anything down. *Maybe a good long walk will help,* he thought. Even though a walk for him right now was akin to taking a walk to the guillotine, he knew he needed to get some fresh air.

◆ ◆ ◆

Ruby pulled up to Coach Crossover's house like a deranged lunatic. Questions flooded her mind like a complex puzzle. Did he know? If he did, how long has he known? She ran up the front steps to knock on the door, but was interrupted by the man himself.

"Ruby!" he said in a surprised tone.

Coach Crossover stared in disbelief that Ruby was at his door. "Uhhh... what brings you by, my friend? Is it Shay?"

"No, Charlie, it's not about Shay! It's uhhh...ummm..."

"Ruby, would you like a glass of water or juice? You're sweating quite a bit and you look like you've seen a ghost!"

"Ahem! Ahem!" Ruby cleared the phlegm in her throat. "Yes, br...I mean a glass of water will be good."

"Did you just call me your...never mind!" Coach Crossover began walking into the kitchen.

"I don't think I can do this!" Ruby said as she quickly and inconspicuously wiped her forehead.

"Here you go, Ruby!"

"Thank you."

"So you never told me why you stopped over?"

"What is your father's name?"

"That's a rather peculiar question, Ruby! May I ask why you're asking?"

"Oh, please believe me, there is a method!"

"Okay then, I will oblige you and answer. I never spent much time getting to know my biological father, but his name was Darnell. He taught me how to do a crossover and came to a few of my games, but that was it!"

Ruby's mouth dropped and she began to tear up.

"What's wrong, Ruby?"

She remained quiet and slowly handed Charlie Crossover the 3×5 photograph and letter from her mom. Coach Crossover read intently and stared at the photo. He repeated this process several times.

"This kid is me…" Coach Crossover said confused. "It can't be! Could this really be poss…?"

"Charlie, you're my…"

"Oh my gosh! You're my sister!"

The two of them hugged and shared a few tears.

"I've always felt a natural connection to you, Charlie!" Ruby said while sniffling through tears.

Coach Crossover wiped his eyes. "And I to you! As you know, I've always felt like Shay was my own flesh and blood. Oh no, how will we tell Shay?"

"I am not sure. I know there has to be a way, but he has so much going on right now. I'm not sure we should—"

"Ruby, as the writer of Ecclesiastes notes, 'To everything there is a season and a time to every purpose.' The time will come for Shay to find out that I am his...um...his...uncle!"

"I've always wanted an older brother, but how would I have ever known I would have one? And it would be..."

"Me! Well, we're siblings, Ruby. We will find a way to tell the rest of the family. I'm all about relationships, so let's get together sometime...I'd like to share stories!" Coach Crossover said, coughing through his words.

"Well, I must go to prepare dinner for the family. You should stop by sometime...brother! I will get used to that," Ruby said while smiling through her tears.

The two embraced, and Coach Crossover walked Ruby to the door. "I would walk you outside, but I haven't been feeling so well. I will tell you more, but another time!" Coach Crossover said, barely getting his words out.

"Feel better. We'll talk again soon!" Ruby turned to walk away. They shared a final smile, then went their separate ways.

♦ ♦ ♦

On the other side of town, Jeremiah was picking Shay up from summer camp as promised!

"What's up, little bro?"

"Hey, Jeremiah! The campers loved my new Jumpmans."

"Weren't you afraid someone was going to steal them?"

"Ha! Ha! I had a plan," Shay said snidely. "I locked them in one of the lockers using my combination lock."

"Always thinking, huh, little bro?"

"You know it!" Shay said, laughing.

"Tell me about camp though!"

Jeremiah had never showed interest in Shay's camp activities and rarely his basketball experiences. Though it was the last day of camp, Shay was still glad Jeremiah began to show interest. "Camp was really good today. Coach Denise surprised me and told me I am going to start next season!"

"That is great, man!"

"I do not know why Coach Crossover wasn't there though." Shay quieted his voice.

"I am sure he has a good reason. He has always kept his word to you!"

The Crossover that Won the Game

"Yeah, I think you're ri—"

"Hey, it's about time you guys got here!" Shay was surprised to see James as they pulled into the driveway.

"Haven't seen you in a while!" Shay said.

"What's been up, bum?"

"James will never change, huh?" Shay asked himself.

"Let me guess, you still do not know how to defend others on the court or yourself off the court?"

"You know what—"

Shay was interrupted by a somewhat unlikely savior. "No more! Absolutely not!"

James was stunned by the voice heard from the front porch. At a loss for words he just stared.

"Had you come around more often, you would be aware of the new rules of the Ponder household. We speak words of life, words of affirmation, we encourage, not discourage, we speak positivity, not negativity!" Dad spoke in a very stern voice.

He's a totally different man! James thought. "O...oka...okay, Dad, I understand!"

Shay smiled and was comforted that Dad came to his rescue. He knew next school year and basketball season would be good. His dad was unaware of the pivotal impact his presence had on his life and development.

"Thanks, Dad!"

Vroom, Mom pulled slowly back into the driveway.

"Hey, guys!"

"Hey!" the family said in unison.

"How are you, honey?"

"I am better now that…oh, never mind!"

"We would all like to know what has been on your mind!" Dad responded.

"Yeah, Mom!" Shay said jokingly.

"None of you are ready to know, especially you, Shay!"

Silence christened the moment. "Here's a rain check! I am going to get dinner ready for you guys!"

"Let me take care of that tonight, Ruby! Take some time to relax!"

"You have no idea how much that means to me!"

Ruby sat in the same soft beige leather chair from earlier in the day. In her bedroom, away from the rest of the family, she tried to work through a way to break the news to the family, especially Shay.

"Hey, dinner is done, boys!" Dad yelled as he walked up the stairs to the master bedroom. "Ruby?"

"Yeah, John?"

"Dinner is done."

"Okay, I will be down in just a moment."

Dinner was full of laughter and smiles, though Mom continued to ponder her most recent dilemma. Dad could sense Mom's emotional distance but understood she had to work through whatever had her puzzled. Ruby and Charlie Crossover spent time together sporadically over the summer. The doctors continued to run tests. The medication they provided helped contain his illness. Crossover didn't get any worse or better. Ruby desired to know what was ailing Charlie, but he wasn't ready to share.

John continued to question Ruby as to why she had been spending so much time alone with Coach Crossover. John was flabbergasted when he read the letter and heard from both Ruby and Charlie that they were brother and sister. "We have to tell Shay!"

"In due time, John!" Ruby responded.

"Who should tell him?" Coach Crossover asked.

"We can set up a meeting and tell him altogether!" John answered. The three of them agreed.

The summer went by quickly. Shay spent a lot of time with Jeremiah and James came around more. Shay and his father continued to develop their relationship. Shay missed spending time with his pal Coach Crossover, but he knew that he had not been feeling well this summer. Shay harbored excitement for the start of the school year, but even more, the start of the basketball season.

Shay sat on the bleachers in the gymnasium after shooting 1000 jump shots on the eve of his first varsity game at Lion's Heart High School.

"I know that I can do whatever I set my mind to do. I do not know what the level of competition will be, but at the very least, I will bring the best of what I have to offer. I may get knocked down, but I will get right back up! I may get teased, but I will simply play harder. No matter what others say or do, no matter the results of tomorrow's game, I will be victorious!"

♦ ♦ ♦

"I'll be ready when you get back up!" the opponent stared up in disbelief.

Weight lifting proved beneficial. Coach Denise stressed defense during the camp and Shay learned to be a student of the game. As his opponent brought the ball down the court, Shay watched his body, not his eyes. The opponent taunted, but Shay remained silent while calculating the next move. Just as the opponent went to switch the ball to the other hand, Shay reached in and missed. The opponent smiled and went to cross the ball back to his right hand.

"Big mistake, my friend!" Shay reached with his other hand and stole the ball. As his opponent tried taking the ball back, Shay quickly put the ball behind his back. Faked left, then spun right. The rest was mere red carpet as Shay laid the ball into the basket.

Shay heard a familiar sound. One that he never came to truly appreciate. Coach Denise blew her whistle shortly before the buzzer sounded for substitution.

"Why'd you sub me out, Coach?"

"You're playing great, but I want to give other guys a chance to play as well. You'll go back in!"

Shay gave Coach Denise a high five, smiled, and took a seat.

The Crossover that Won the Game

The first quarter ended with Lion's Heart leading 18–13. The second quarter went relatively smoothly for Lion's Heart, but Blueberry Hill rallied back.

Shay scanned the audience and was pleased with the people that came to watch him play. Jeremiah was there, but this time, it was different. He cheered Shay on. He still yelled and pointed from the bleachers, but every word was in support of his little brother. Mom was there, showing her eloquent smile. Dad was there and that made Shay happy of course, but he was confused by how close Coach Crossover and his mother was. *Either Mom and Coach Crossover are dating or someone is keeping a secret*, Shay thought.

"Shay!" Shay continued scanning the audience.

"Hey there...Shay and Chris, you're in!" Chris hopped to his feet, but Shay did not.

"Let's go, Shay!" Chris poked Shay's arm. "Hey, man, you look as if you've seen your life flash before your eyes. What's on your mind?" Chris lowered his voice.

"Look at my mom and Coach Crossover!"

"What are you seeing? I'm not seeing anything too extraordinary."

"They're sitting a little too close, man!"

"You're tripping, Shay! They're on the bleachers! C'mon, we have a quarter to end."

Shay stepped onto the court with a fierce look in his eyes, yet simultaneously distracted look on his face. Shay crossed the ball into his right hand, then hopped right and faked left.

"There are only four seconds left on the clock, Shay!" Coach Denise yelled.

Shay voluntarily did something he rarely enjoyed. He diverted the onus of responsibility. He noticed Chris's hands waving from the left side of the court and passed the ball. With one second remaining, Chris released the ball. *Swish*, the ball snapped the net. Lion's Heart regained the lead at 31–30.

Halftime

"Hey, guys, I really like how you're playing. You've stayed right in this game in spite of your opponents' energy and brilliance. Make sure you bring more! I have faith in you, all of you. And your brilliance...yes, your brilliance is greater than theirs. Keep playing your game and I think we can take this," Coach Denise told the team. She quickly turned her head, surprised by the voice of reason coming from the back of the group.

"Hey! Hey! There's no thinking about it! We will take this victory with us!"

Whoa! This kid really has matured since freshman season! she thought. "I'm proud of you, Shay!"

"Thanks, Coach D, let's go show these guys how it's done!" Shay responded.

The team worked on shooting drills and layups. They ran over a few plays but didn't want to give their secrets away to the opposing team.

"Hey, your name is Shay, right?" Shay heard a voice from behind him. Shay slowly turned around. Much to his surprise, it was his opponent that guarded him in the first half.

"Let me guess, you read my jersey?" Shay said sarcastically.

The Crossover that Won the Game

The opponent, now face-to-face with Shay, so close their noses could touch, said, "You will get nothing this half! I got your number!"

"Ha! Read it off of my jersey! That's real original!" Shay said as he turned and walked away.

Third Quarter

Jerry, Shay's opponent from Brightest Day High School, brought the ball up the floor. Shay watched Jerry's waist close. Jerry lowered his shoulder and began running past Shay. Shay put his hands up and ran body to body. Jerry raised his elbow, hitting Shay in the face. Shay lay on the ground holding his nose and watching as the ball went through the net. Score BDHS 32–LHHS 31.

Shay walked back to the bench so the athletic director could make sure there were no broken bones. "Okay, Shay, you are all right, but be careful!"

"All right, Coach, I am ready to go back in!"

"Shay, have a seat. I'll be sure to get you back in the game, but I am going to give you a little rest. Save you for the fourth quarter, so rest up. You will need your A game for us to win!"

"C'mon, Coach Denise, I am ready!"

"Do you trust my..." Coach Denise turned her attention to the court. "Get back on defense, Chris!" Shay waited for Coach Denise to finish her sentence. "Trust my ability to coach this team. I will get you back on the floor!" Coach said in an animated voice as she lay her hand on Shay's back.

Shay sat for the rest of the third quarter. Lion's Heart High School played hard but Brightest Day High School kept the score close. Shay wanted to be out there competing, but he knew it was not his decision. He cheered his team on, yelled ideas from the sideline, and provided fellow teammates with Gatorade during timeouts.

"Shay, get back in here, bro! We need you."

"I want to, Chris, but I have to respect Coach Denise's decision. You guys can handle it. Aaron is a good player also!"

"Yeah, but he's no Sh—"

"Stop it, Chris! Believe in yourself and your teammates!" Shay responded.

"Shay, come here!" Coach Denise called as the players shuffled back onto the floor.

"Yes, Coach?"

"I overheard your conversation with Chris. That is the kind of leadership I am looking for. I really admire your humility, optimism, and faith in your teammates. And well, your acquired faith in me as well," Coach Denise said as she chuckled. "Get ready to go back in at the start of the fourth quarter."

"Thanks, Coach!" Shay said with excitement in his voice.

As the third quarter ended, Lion's Heart High School trailed by 6 points, 43–37.

Fourth Quarter

Shay brought the ball up the court. He scanned the court and recognized his teammates' difficulty finding optimum spots on the court. *I am going to have to take this shot pretty soon here!* Shay thought. He scanned Jerry's body, quickly drove left, and faked a pass. Jerry backed up and

The Crossover that Won the Game

Shay capitalized on the opportunity. *Swish*! Shay made the three-pointer. Lion's Heart High School only trail by 3, score 43–40.

Jerry brought the ball down the court. "Defense, Lion's Heart!" Coach Denise yelled.

Jerry turned his back to Shay. *Pit pat…pit pat*! The screams from fans and naysayers caused Jerry not to hear the approaching footsteps. *Smack*! Chris tapped the ball out of Jerry's hand and Shay bolted down the court. Chris passed the ball above Jerry's flailing hands and into the hands of Shay. Chris trailed behind as Jerry and Shay ran body to body. Jerry stood at 6'0" while Shay was only 5'7". Shay knew better than to fear anyone though. Sure, he respected the talents and abilities of others, but he'd learned to trust his skill set as well. Shay glanced back at Chris and smiled. Shay looked at the bigger Jerry running next to him. Approaching the foul line, Shay quickly spun right, faked the shot, and as Jerry jumped, Shay crossed the ball into his right hand and ran toward the basket. Shay made the layup and brought the score a little closer. LHHS 42–BDHS 43.

The two teams competed fiercely, at times, trading baskets while one team dominated at other times. In the final minute of the game, LHHS lead by 2. Coach Denise put the ball in Shay's hands and told him to run play 23 from the *Players Guide to Successful Performance Handbook*. Shay began calling the play while scanning the entire floor.

"Over there, Chris!" Shay yelled while looking at the right corner. Shay faked left and went to pass the ball right. Jerry was no fool, though. He didn't plan on letting Shay deceive him too many times. Jerry jumped as Shay began passing the ball. Jerry was very quick, but Shay was no quitter. Shay trailed Jerry and eventually got to the side of his body. One hand high, one hand by Jerry's waist, and footwork efficient, Shay felt pretty confident he could increase the level of difficulty of the shot or even better, he could take the basketball out of Jerry's hands.

"You got this, Shay!" Chris yelled from behind him.

"He can't shake you, Shay! Take that ball away!" Shay heard what he thought was Jeremiah's voice.

"It's all on you, Shay!" Coach Denise yelled as Shay ran past her.

Jerry, being as quick as he was, stopped instantaneously. Shay screeched his sneaker, trying to regain composure and positioning. Shay ran back to Jerry as quickly as he could. Shay had hands raised high, but to avoid fouling Jerry, all he could do was watch him ascend, release the ball, descend, and plant back onto the court. Shay and Jerry stood next to each other, blocking out the response from the crowd and focusing on that final shot. The ball flew through the air. Felt like forever, but the ball finally hit the rim. The rolled and rolled and rolled. Shay closed his eyes in sheer disbelief.

"How could I have let him create space like that?" Shay shook his head.

Smack! The ball hit the floor. Shay opened his eyes. Ironically, Jerry now had his eyes closed, shaking his hanging head. The ball rolled and rolled and rolled and then rolled some more until it eventually fell out of the rim. Jerry turned and walked away while Shay stood awestruck at the conclusion of the game.

"Never give up! You truly never know what can happen if you try!" Coach Denise had met Shay at the three-point line where this moment all began.

Pit pat! Pat pat pit! Pit pat pit! Coach Crossover stumbled a bit walking over to Shay.

"Ekhm...ekhm! She's right!" Coach Crossover said while speaking through his coughs.

"Hey, Coach Crossover!" Shay said in excitement.

The Crossover that Won the Game

"Great game, kid!"

"Thanks, Coach."

"Hey, Coach Crossover, are you sure you do not want a drink or to take a seat?"

"No, Coach Denise, I will be all right."

"What's wrong, Coach?" Shay asked.

"Oh, nothing, bud! I am all right. I am going to the doctor tomorrow though to make sure I am really fine."

"You must be worried, Coach, because..."

"Let's not talk about me right now. Let's celebrate your victory!" Coach Crossover said while placing his hand on Shay's back.

"Okay, well, let me know if anything is wrong!"

Shay's mother, father, and brother, Jeremiah, poured out the accolades on Shay for his performance.

"Guys, it's not like I did anything special! C'mon, I just chased some guy down the court."

"If you hadn't chased him, do you think he would have missed the shot?" Jeremiah asked.

"What about the other contributions you made?" Dad interjected before Shay could answer.

"Well, I guess..."

"You played a very good game so just stop it!" Chris punched Shay in the arm and the two laughed as they slapped hands.

"Hey, Charlie, we have to go now, but make sure you inform me of what the doctor says!"

"Okay, little si—I mean, Ruby, I will certainly let you know!" Coach Crossover responded.

The group traded several confused stares, finished small talk, and parted ways.

Summary of next 3 months

Coach Crossover was in and out of the hospital, but his prognosis gave him hope. The doctor ordered Crossover to take his medication as prescribed and get the necessary amount of rest. Another objective on Coach Crossover's action plan was that he would be required to attend dialysis every Monday, Wednesday, and Friday for the next two to three months while being closely monitored. The doctor informed Coach Crossover he may need a transplant, but that it was too early to tell.

Shay wondered why he hadn't been hearing from Coach Crossover or seeing him at any of his games. He had no idea that Crossover was faced with one of the toughest things he'd ever been forced to deal with. Every time Shay called, Coach Crossover seemed to be either sleeping or out of the house. *Man, I would really like to know if Coach Crossover is all right!* Shay thought to himself. Little did Shay know, his mother knew all that was going on with Coach Crossover!

Lion's Heart High School maintained a decent record. Shay continued to work hard and dreamed of playing in his first Section V Championship game. Shay and Chris practiced often outside of practicing with the school. They felt equip to perform at a high level in a variety of situations. Not many things in life are guaranteed, but Shay believed he and Chris would be friends forever. The two of them began having dinner at each other's house. And of course, there was talk about if they'd be going to prom and if so, with who.

Shay and Jeremiah's continued to improve. Jeremiah had kept his promise and no longer teased Shay. James still did occasionally, but Shay let the insults roll right off of his back. Dad continued to be a strong presence in Shay's life. Mom still had a way of making Shay feel loved, but he knew she was hiding something.

Shay's grades were amazing. He'd adopted the practice of obtaining extra help when necessary. Shay, fellow teammates, and Coach Denise was very excited about the team's progress and performance this season.

"I ask you to never stop dreaming! When reality stares you directly in the face, just know that you will always hold the power to create a different reality. Life is what you make of it! Live for the big moments, but make sure the smaller moments build character and endurance for the…well… not-so-small moments. We didn't get where we are today by laziness or allowing obstacles to divert us from dreaming and doing and being the best of who we are. Who are we? We are fighters! Why are we fighters? We are fighters because you either confront the challenge, rise to the occasion, or lose without question! We are here because your hearts are that of gold, of stone, of love, and of disdain. Hatred is never the answer, but what I am saying is that you boys, I'm sorry you men…ha…at Lion's Heart High School know what it means to be fierce and to get nitty gritty, down and dirty, altogether scrappy when the circumstance requires. You're loving and you may have hearts of gold. Yes, I may be…uh…well just a tad bit biased, but no one is going to take anything away from you without the fight of their lives. That's where the stone comes into the equation. You guys are rock solid, and remember this, an authentic rock of insurmountable stature will never be easily moved. Who are we? Why the silence boys, men…who are we?"

They stared at Coach Denise with a new fire in their eyes. "We...are... fighters!" Lion's Heart High School players yelled. It felt to some as if the walls shook and the floor rumbled beneath their feet. Like a pack of wolves or fleet of soldiers they ran, stomped, and shouted as would an unsilenced predator going to exterminate, further eliminate their prey.

"We...fight! We...conquer! We...fight! We...conq...!" And darkness covered the room!

Semifinals Game

Lights on! Time to play ball! *Swish!* Jerry drained his first shot of the game, a three-point field goal. Shay couldn't believe that he had to face Jerry and Brightest Day High School again.

These guys are so good! Shay thought to himself, as he brought the ball up the court. "Over there, Chris!" Shay motioned toward the left wing. Chris converted on the two-point field goal.

Jerry had a fierceness in his eyes that said, "I will not lose today!" But Shay was not one to quit. Shay timed Jerry's right hand crossover perfectly. Jerry crossed the ball while Shay strategically positioned his hand. Jerry was puzzled as the ball never arrived at its destination.

Shay ran up the court with Jerry right by his side. Shay crossed the ball between his legs from right to left. Jerry stepped over as Shay crossed the ball again between his legs. Ball now in his right hand, Shay neglected the layup and jumped for the three-pointer. Jerry, being slow to recover, could only watch as the ball burned the net.

Ha! That kid can shoot! Jerry thought to himself. "Well, we have 4 quarters of this mayhem!" Shay backpedaled down the court, holding his pinky, ring, and middle finger in the air.

… The Crossover that Won the Game

"That's 3, Jerry!"

The two teams battled hard in the first quarter. Shay's confidence continued to soar and he felt he'd figured out a method to contain Jerry. He knew Lion's Heart High School had a long game ahead. They were ready to fight to the finish though. Brightest Day High School led 14–13.

Second Quarter

"Look left!" Coach Denise yelled to Shay. Shay looked to his left and then ran right. As the double-team came, Shay quickly tossed an alley-oop to George, who promptly slam-dunked the ball.

"Good pass, Shay! Keep playing like that, kid," George stated.

"Hey! Turn around, Chris!" Shay yelled. Chris turned just in the nick of time. He stole the inbound pass, then quickly passed the ball to Michael, who dished the ball to Shay. *Snap!* The ball went through the net. Score LHHS 18–BDHS 14.

"We have got to stop this kid. Man, he's a nightmare!" Brightest Day High School's coach said.

Jerry slowly brought the ball down the court. Jerry faked the drive, pulled back, and nailed the three-pointer. Score LHHS 18–BDHS 17.

"Jerry! Great shot, but I do not need you to take the game into your own hands!" Coach Pratt said.

"Okay, Coach!" Jerry yelled as he stared Shay up and down.

Shay caught the inbound pass, but Jerry was right there waiting for him at the foul line. Before Shay could react, Jerry's teammate came from the blind side and stripped the ball.

"Where's my help?" Shay yelled as he lay on the floor, watching the ball fall through the net. Score LHHS 18–BDHS 19.

"C'mon, man, get up, there's still a lot of basketball to be played!" Michael said, as he held out his hand. Shay grabbed hold of Michael's hand, leveraging his weight to jump to his feet.

"You're no quitter, man!"

"You're right, Mike!"

Shay brought the ball up the court. Though determined, Shay still had to face the surging defense of his opponent.

"Right here, Michael!" Shay pointed downward toward the left side of Jerry's body.

Michael set the pick and Shay ran Jerry as close to Michael's body as possible. Larry, Jerry's teammate, stepped over to cover Shay. Shay quickly passed the ball to Michael and ran toward the basket. Michael passed the ball back to Shay who jumped, banged bodies with Larry, and suddenly made the behind-the-back pass to Chris. Chris leaped and released the floater.

I got this! he thought.

Smack! "Rejected!" Logan taunted.

Owen, the small forward, picked up the ball, dribbled four times, and passed the ball to Jerry. Jerry spun left and quickly passed the ball to Owen, who touch-passed the ball back to Jerry. Jerry crossed the ball and faked the shot. Shay didn't flinch, but shooting guard Brian was open for the shot. Score LHHS 18–BDHS 21.

"Time...out!"

"Okay, guys, what's going on out here? You guys look sluggish and sloppy. You can't stop pursuing. If they steal the ball, you must be the better team in transition. Defense is where it all begins! Offense is simply the reward to efficient defense! Go tweet that on your fancy smart phones, haha. Let's go out there and give them the best we have to offer!"

Lion's Heart High School played very well during the remainder of the second quarter. They remained confident and they refused to give up. Defense became their mantra. The score at the end of the second quarter: Lion's Heart High School was ahead 31 to 29.

Halftime

"Okay, guys, I will not say too much because we are playing a good game out there. I want you to continue fighting and giving your all out there. Shoot some shots, practice some layups, and let's go out there and give Brightest Day High School more than they can handle, guys!"

Lion's Heart High School geared up for the third quarter. Exhausted but ready was the message relayed on the faces of the team.

The third and fourth quarter yielded blood, sweat, and tears. The pain of flagrant fouls and excessive body banging was excruciating.

"Get up, Shay!" Chris helped Shay to his feet after his body thrashed the hardwood floor.

Shay shook his head and wiped his watery eyes with his jersey. "I'm ready!"

"I don't think so, bro!" *Beep*! The referee blew the whistle. "To the bench, Shay! You must take care of that." Shay looked down and jersey full of blood. He just shook his head. He had no other option but to watch his team struggle against Brightest Day High School. Shay's right eye no longer dripped blood. *I wish Coach would put me back in this game!* Shay thought.

"All right, Shay, you're back in. Time is short so there's no time to waste!" Coach Denise said as she patted Shay on the back.

Shay ignored the crowd that filled the room, and the sound that clouded engulfed his ears. Blood all dried up and eyes free from tears, Shay stepped onto the floor. Lion's Heart High School proved one thing: they were fighters! They rallied back from a ten-point deficit and now trailed only by one. Once again the most important moment would come down to the final second. Shay was accustomed to these situations, but they never became any easier. *Beep!*

"Timeout!" Coach Denise yelled. "Sit down, guys! Get a drink. Shay, I want you to take the final shot. Turn your eyes to the whiteboard, here is the play." Coach Denise designed the play that she wanted Lion's Heart High School to execute.

Jerry guarded face-to-face and body to body. Shay moved and moved but to no avail. Shay faked forward, then stepped back behind the three-point line. One hand in the air, basketball approaching. "I'm ready!" Shay said as he perspired from head to toe.

Sweat rolling down both of Shay's cheeks and incinerating the floor, it was time! *This moment would not return. I can leave nothing for tomorrow*, Shay thought. "What happens, happens right here, right now!"

Exhausted, with his chest heaving, his breath wheezing with every exhale, and his body aching from collisions and falls, Shay let the ball drop. Readjusting his limbs and repeating his pregame workup, he backed up.

The Crossover that Won the Game

Ball switching rapidly between both hands and his legs, Shay hopped left and reversed the ball behind his back to his right hand.

Jerry planted his feet. Shay threw the ball to his left, with his right foot to follow, ball moving back right, eluding the defense. Jerry stepped left, Shay moved right.

"This is my moment!" Defense shifting, offense rotating, Shay's clear path revealed itself.

On the road to victory, Shay seized the approaching moment. Feet alternating and steps getting lighter, his target inched closer.

Shay's vision was suddenly blurred by the obstacle meeting him at his destination. He faked left, with his opponent following suit, Shay continued right.

His target in sight. "It's time!"

Shay leaped. He rose higher and higher and released the ball. The ball floated up and up…

Boom, Shay's feet hit the floor. He stopped and stared, one eyebrow lifted, awestruck…

Book 8

Twelfth Grade

Fight to the Finish

Shay's eyes watched as the ball moved the opposite direction from the basket. Shay watched as the ball rolled down the floor. *Lion's Heart* players and fans lowered their heads in defeat. Shay had learned not hang his head. Failure would never again define him.

"How will I recover and do better next time?" Shay asked himself.

Shay looked at the coach and his teammates, but said nothing. The sad look on his face said it all. No words were needed. His facial expression spoke a thousand words!

"Good job," said a spectator.

"Stupid," another yelled.

"You blew the game!"

He had wondered who first came up with the adage, "Sticks and stones may break my bones, but words will never hurt me." Then he heard someone speak that took the pain away.

"Don't worry, you will do better next game! Look how many times great NBA players missed the final shot!" Jeremiah shouted. That statement, coming from his big brother, was the fuel he needed to carry on.

He heard so many negative remarks that cut like a blade through the heart with a goal of slicing will power. Shay simply shook his head as he listened to Brightest Day's fans and players celebrate.

"Hey!"

Shay turned to see who touched him. This voice was relatively unfamiliar. Much to his surprise, it was Jerry.

"Hey," Shay said with noticeable ambivalence. *What could Jerry possibly have to say?* Shay thought to himself.

"I just wanted to say—"

"What?" Shay interrupted. "I'm sorry, man. I am just a little frustrated."

"I really do understand, man!"

"How could you possibly understand? You get to walk around with a smile on your face and rejoice in your victory."

"We still have a tough road ahead though, man!"

"But at least you are still able to travel the road!" Shay said as he wiped the water from his right eyes, containing his emotions.

"Shay, you're right, but I really want to tell you something!"

"All right, man, I'm sorry. I'm all ears."

There was a sort of awkward silence that entered the conversation.

"What did you want to say?"

"I just wanted to say that you played a great game. You are a great player. I absolutely hated every second that I had to guard you. You literally are a headache!" Jerry laughed. Shay chuckled a bit.

He didn't know how to say it, but he was really happy that Jerry shared his thoughts with him.

"Thanks a lot, Jerry! The things you said means a lot to me. You are a good player also. I definitely wish it were Lion's Heart High School going to the championship, but I salute Brightest Day and I wish you guys the best in the championship game."

The two young men shook hands, embraced, and walked away to join their teams.

"Hey, Jerry!" Shay yelled.

"Yeah, Shay?"

"Maybe I will see you on the court next year!"

"Yeah, maybe you will!"

The two boys laughed and signaled their good-byes.

Shay walked over to the bench and sat down. Still in disbelief, he watched Brightest Day High School players and fans celebrate their victory.

"Team, bring it in!" The players hurried at the sound of Coach Denise's voice.

"Shay, that means you!" Coach Denise said.

Shay got up and slowly walked toward the huddle.

"Guys, do not hang your head. When we win, we win as a team. When we lose, we lose as a team. It doesn't feel good, but the hope is to learn from any defeat we encounter. You guys figuratively left it all on the floor, and no one, absolutely no one, can ask for anything more. And by anything, I mean nothing. We are called Lion's Heart for a reason. You guys were fearless out there. You have so much…"

"Heart! Coach, we know!" Chris interjected.

"Do you want to give this speech, Chris?" Coach Denise asked while giving Chris that stern grandma look.

Chris held his head down.

"Pick your head up, young man! Answer me with confidence. If you want to give the speech, I have no problem affording you this opportunity!"

Chris looked at Coach Denise. "No, I do not want to give the speech."

"All right, well then. Where was I?" Coach asked rhetorically. "Heart! That's it! You guys have so much heart. I need you guys to be clear about something: the outcome is not always indicative of effort. You guys pulled yourselves up by your boot straps, you dug your heels in, and you gave them the best that you had!"

"But we lost, Coach! We lost the semifinals game!"

"Shay, you should feel so proud of yourself. Your heart is so fierce. You had such a fire in your eyes and you were determined not to let anyone stop you."

"But they did!"

"Who's your favorite player, Shay?"

"MJ is my favorite player!"

"Did you know that he was cut from the varsity team during his sophomore year?"

"I may have heard that somewhere before."

"Okay, okay…here's another piece of trivia for you: did you know that MJ was most famous for his game-winning shot in his final season as a college basketball player? Do you know what I am trying to tell you?"

"No, Coach, I do not!" Shay said in a matter-of-fact tone of voice.

"I am saying that you weren't stopped. If anything, your big moment was simply delayed at worst."

"I never thought about it like that, Coach!" Shay said as he placed his hand on his head, followed by a smirk.

"I do not know if I would have even been as comfortable as you were taking that final shot."

"Really, Coach?"

"Yes, Shay! You gave your all. You didn't care that Jerry was a good defender or that his teammates were so much bigger than you. Like a wildcat against their prey, you went in for the kill when the moment presented itself. There is nothing that you could have done any differently in that moment. Certainly, throughout the game, players could have rotated better on offense and helped more on defense. But in the moments that mattered, everyone knew they had to face really good players. Though we are Lion's Heart High School, I saw the eye of the tiger out there. You guys put fear in the hearts of your opponents, and believe me, they know your names and will never forget. A majority of you guys are juniors and will have your opportunity at winning the championship next season. When you guys gallivant onto the court next season, all will remember you. Why? Because you gave the very best of what you had offer! Work hard this school year, continue practicing on your games, and preserve your sense of self-concept. I will see you all next season."

Shay began walking toward the door. He just wanted to get out of there. It was time to fall asleep. He'd secretly wanted to sleep the pain away. Perhaps the residual impact of losing wouldn't be so bad tomorrow.

"You feel like talking, son?"

"Thanks, Dad, but maybe tomorrow!"

Dad placed his hand on Shay's shoulder. "Anytime you're ready, son!"

"Thanks, Dad!"

Shay was overjoyed that his dad was concerned about how he was feeling. Not dismissive of his dad's concern, but admittedly, Shay was surprised that Coach Crossover wasn't at the game.

This game was pretty important, so I can only imagine that Coach Crossover must have a really good reason for not making it to the game tonight! Shay thought.

♦ ♦ ♦

Coach Crossover lay in bed, staring at the beautiful black and red ladybug climbing up the white string on the chandelier. He smiled! He chuckled! He then burst into laughter. "Ruby is my sister and I am half black!"

He laughed so hard that his kidney started aching again. He remembered all of the racist statements and jokes his coworkers used to make about the blacks. He did not like the statements or jokes, but he felt that they

The Crossover that Won the Game

were not talking about him. Now he knows that he was included in the group of people that they were talking about. Coach Crossover had to laugh to prevent himself from getting angry. There were times that his grandmother refused to let him play with the African-American neighbors because she said they were not him. Now, after all those years, he found that they were just alike. He had always believed that we all came from Adam and Eve, so we were all one race.

He was always smart, and his research showed that we all had Adam's DNA. "Oh my, I'm a black man for sure!" He laughed harder through his tears. All his life, he went through life not knowing who he was, but he wished he was black so he could fight against discrimination. He grabbed his stereo remote and played his favorite Michael Jackson song: "Even If I'm Black or White."

♦ ♦ ♦

Jeremiah walked into the backyard, intent on sneaking up on Shay. Shay appeared to be in deep thought. Shay breathed in and out as he flipped the ball high in the air, back to basket, three to four dribbles, and the ball swiveled through the air once more. This process repeated several times until his arms were no longer free.

Jeremiah wrapped his long arms around his little brother's shoulder and smiled. "Can a big brother spend time with his little brother?"

Shay was shocked at the affection coming from Jeremiah. "Sure, big brother, what's going on? I was just thinking back here."

"Do you care to talk about it?"

"Maybe a little later, man!" Shay said as he shook his head from left to right, right to left and back again. "Do you want to talk now?"

Jeremiah put his right arm on Shay's back. He chuckled and started to speak. "I never thought you'd ask. Last night, I had a dream that I had a son. Well, he came home crying, saying, 'Daddy, can I please not go to school anymore? All the kids pick on me and they take my lunch too.' He cried and cried so hard that even in my subconscious state, I really hurt."

Shay listened intently; listening has always been a strong suit of his.

"You know, in life we reap what we sow. I don't want what I used to do come back on my children," he said as his voice cracked. He found his voice again and continued, "You have something I didn't have and I admire you."

"Really?" Shay surprisingly asked.

"Really! In fact, I learned that I was jealous of you."

Shay arched an eyebrow. "You're joking, right?"

"No, Shay, I'm serious. Shay, you have drive and you have courage! You are the most determined kid I've ever met. You have no fear! Could you imagine what it takes for a person to attempt the game-winning shot?"

Shay looked at his brother. "No." He paused. "I love a challenge."

"Shay."

"Yes?"

"You are awesome," Jeremiah said with a smile. "That takes courage. At that moment, everything is riding on you. Your coach, your teammates, they're all depending on you. The opposing team is praying that you miss. Why do think players pass the ball in the last seconds of the game? That's because if they make the winning shot they're glorified. If they miss, everyone despises them, with the exception of the opponents, so they're afraid to take the shot. Not you!"

Shay stared and listened to his brother's logic.

"Yes, I used to be jealous of my baby brother. Now that I've matured, I idolize you."

For a moment, silence filled the air. "Wow, thanks, big bro!"

"No," Jeremiah replied and hugged his brother. "Thanks for being who you are. You are my hero." He backed up and looked Shay in the eye, "And here is something I never told you."

"What's that?"

"I love you, champ."

"Thanks, big bro. That means more to me than you could ever know. All I've ever wanted was to be loved, respected, listened to, and treated like I was valued. Dad's absence was hard to deal with, but I did my best. Big brother, your actions really compounded my stress, but—"

"Hold up, little brother!"

"What?" Shay laughed.

"Where did you learn that word?"

"I pay attention in school and I love to read!"

"I am proud of you. Reading is very important."

"Ha! Ha, thanks."

"You're welcome," Jeremiah responded. "What were you saying, Shay?"

"Well, your past actions compounded my stress. However, I must tell you something!" Shay became excited. Jeremiah's eyes lit up and then his countenance dropped as he revealed the puzzled nature of his thoughts.

"What does Shay have on his mind now?" Jeremiah asked himself. He ignored the nonverbal signs on Shay's face.

Shay continued to speak, "I am much happier now that you have made the changes you've made. It is so great to get along with you. It is nice to have normal conversations and not argue repeatedly. Your encouraging words mean a lot to me. Words fuel me, and to speak truthfully, negative words place a wall as complex and sturdy as the great pyramids of Egypt. Figuring out the formula for breaking them down and rebuilding with words that are life giving seems impossible."

"Oh, man, I am so sorry that I contributed to the construction of that pyramid in any way!"

"I forgave you long ago. The love of others has helped with the tearing down of the wall. Coach Crossover's involvement has taught me a lot. Dad's efforts have helped as well. However, if there is one thing that I have learned over the years, it is you truly do win from within. If you do not believe in yourself, then the only option is loss and losing. And separate from the love and encouragement I have been so blessed to receive, I know that simply because of me being me I am special. I have made a lot of growth, but it is not over yet," Shay said as he stepped toward Jeremiah.

Arms opened, the two embraced. Tears soiled their shoulders and a monumental moment was created.

Brightest Day High School went on to went win the championship for the local schools. However, they did lose in the state championship match-up

The Crossover that Won the Game

against Seaside High School. Despite Shay's wanting to win the local championship, he still preferred that a team from the local district would win the game.

Shay focused hard on his schoolwork. He sure loved basketball, but schoolwork comes first. His parents and Coach Crossover made certain he understood that his grades were just as important as basketball.

"Boy, I have told you so many times to put that basketball down and focus on your school. What's the point of being a great player if no colleges will look at you because your grades are no good?"

"Mom, you are right. I am putting the ball away right now and going to complete my homework!" Shay would say as he put his basketball on the shelf and sat down in the dining room to work on his homework.

Shay's hard work paid off. He finished his eleventh grade year with a 3.75 grade point average. When he got home, Shay was surprised at the amount of friends and family that awaited him in the home to celebrate his academic achievements. It felt great to shake hands, receive accolades, and spend quality time with those he loved most. Coach Crossover was there, but he didn't seem to be the typical happy Charlie.

"What's wrong, Coach?" Shay asked.

"Ah, it's nothing, buddy!" Coach Crossover brushed his pain away.

"I just watched you grab your side, Coach! I'd say that something is wrong."

"I have just been sick, neph..." Coach Crossover quickly covered his mouth, then began to cough.

"Ha! What did you almost call me, Coach?"

"Nothing! Nothing, Shay. I just…"

"Sorry for interrupting, Coach, but something doesn't feel right!"

"I understand, Shay. Believe me I do, and I promise that we will talk about it."

"All right, Coach. Well, I hope you feel better." Shay hugged Coach Crossover and skipped back into the crowd of people.

Coach Crossover hugged Shay back, but as soon as Shay released his grip, Coach Crossover stepped into the bathroom, sat down, and held his side. "Shay has no idea, but I am so worried that this may be more serious than I originally thought!" Coach Crossover shook his head and grabbed two sheets of Kleenex to wipe his watery eyes.

The Ponder family unit was cohesive and it surely made a world of difference in the lives of all immediate family members. James knew better than to tease Shay when he came to visit. Dad showed that he was a good leader and was able to be the man that the family needed him to be. He led the family in Bible studies, helped Shay with his homework, helped his wife around the house, and continued to facilitate growth of family relationships. Authentic love proved valuable for the family. Sacrifice became their motto. Dad would always say, "Authentic love demands genuine sacrifice!" The family spent a lot of time together during the summer. The family embraced both quality and quantity in regards to healthy relationships. Chris was included in many family activities. There was no Disney list, but the family invented the "Did We?" list.

Did We?

- Give each other hugs today?
- Say encouraging words to our loved ones?

- Thank God for life, health, and happiness?
- Talk to at least one family member about our day?
- Do at least one thing that we loved doing?
- Eat as a family?

Shay worked with Coach Denise to assure that he knew the plays like the back of his hand for his senior year. She was very impressed with Shay's persistence, confidence, and determination. She told Shay that she was confident he would have a good season.

"Off the record, Shay, I am pretty sure that you will get a full scholarship to a lucrative university."

"I really hope so!" Shay would respond. "I really love basketball and hope to have a success story that will one day touch the lives of others."

"I am very proud of your growth, Shay. I am looking forward to working with you next season. I hope your summer continues to go smoothly."

Shay prepared himself for next school year. "One more year of high school, then it's time to take on the world and make my dreams come true!"

Shay worked with a tutor over the summer to make sure he had clear understanding of his subjects for senior year. He was determined to graduate with honors. Shay had learned several things during his short life. One of the things he learned that ultimately the only person that can truly stop him was him.

"I just shut you down in the semifinals game last season!"

Shay turned around and looked at Jerry who walked up from behind as Shay was working on his jump shot at one of the local parks in the city. "Excuse me?"

"You heard me!" Jerry puffed his chest.

"Why don't you just get out of here?" Chris asked.

"I can handle this, Chris. No one stopped me except me. I could have found a pass to make, but you know what?"

"What?" Jerry responded.

"I had absolutely no fear and complete confidence in my ability to succeed."

"Wow, you never cease to amaze me!" Chris responded. "You have matured so much!"

"Thanks, man!"

Jerry stared in disbelief and anticipation. "What else you got for me, superstar?"

"Ha! You're so funny, but not really! I did the best I could. I put up a great shot and knew the possibility of it being blocked. The latter won the battle, but you forget that we are both seniors now."

"What does that have to do with anything?"

"The war is not over!"

Jerry stuck out his hand. Shay slowly put his hand in Jerry's. "No hard feelings, man. Like I said, you're a great player. I just wanted to give you a hard time real quick!"

"Ha! Ha! I am used to people like you so it doesn't bother me anymore!" Shay smirked and patted Jerry's back.

The Crossover that Won the Game

"Hey, you guys want to play a game of 21?" Chris asked.

"Sure, I'm game!" both young men said excitedly.

"Actually, guys, on second thought, I am going to sit this one out and just watch. You guys have this rivalry that I'm sure you want to add some fire to, but hey, I will be sitting right over there!"

"Game on, bro!" Shay said with a fire likely to produce fear.

"Well, Shay," Jerry said while spinning the ball on the tip of his finger, "this will tell if you are truly ready for the next level." He smiled, but truth be told, he was afraid.

For quite some time, he had known that Shay was one of the best players around, and this game would be, in many ways, an indicator of what Jerry could expect from Shay next season.

I'm ready! Jerry thought.

"Now check," he calmly said and passed the ball to Shay. "You take it out.

"You're giving me the ball first?"

"Yeah, it's your territory. I'm just intruding." Jerry laughed.

Shay smiled, but he knew this was time to really show what he was made of.

Shay put the ball on the ground. As soon as his opponent reached for the ball, Shay pulled up and sunk the three-pointer. At first, it did not bother Jerry until Shay just kept sinking the three. That is when he knew the king had arrived.

"4–0!" Shay said.

"Game up to 7!" Jerry said breathless.

Jerry passed the ball back to Shay. Shay faked right, put the ball behind his back, and went left. Jerry hopped in front of Shay only to be left in the wind as Shay spun right. Shay made the finger roll layup.

"That's 5–0 and the icing on the cake! Yeah, that's the gravy on grandma's garlic mashed potatoes!" Jerry couldn't help but laugh.

Jerry passed the ball back to Shay. Shay faked left, crossed right, stepped back, and shot the mid-range jump shot. Jerry grabbed the rebound off of a rare miss. Jerry stepped back behind the foul line. Jerry ran toward the basket and stopped short for the stop-and-pop jump shot.

"5–1! It's not game over yet." Jerry said.

Shay remained quiet because he was focused on Jerry's next move.

Jerry dribbled the ball quickly in front of Shay at the foul line. Shay didn't flinch. He watched Jerry's waist when suddenly, the ball left Jerry's hands and propelled toward the backboard. *Bang!* Shay could only observe as Jerry had passed the ball to himself off of the backboard.

"5–2! If you're not careful, I may make a comeback," Jerry taunted.

Jerry dribbled the ball in front of Shay. He faked left and crossed right. The ball met by Shay's right hand was stolen and left Jerry puzzled.

"What I've learned over the years is that not every word in your head needs to come out of your mouth. You know what the Bible says, right?"

The Crossover that Won the Game

"Nah, what does it say, Mr. Holy Man?"

"Basically, it says that a fool should keep his mouth shut instead of opening it and removing any doubt of whether he or she was indeed a fool."

"Ouch! That cut deep, man!"

"Are you ready for what I am about to do to you?"

"Bring it on!" Jerry said boldly.

"This is the finale!" Shay swiftly put the ball behind his back. Ball now back in front of him, put the ball behind his back knowing that Jerry would reach. Jerry did exactly what Shay thought, reached! Shay crossed the ball, causing Jerry to fall. Like a movie in slow motion, Shay watched Jerry become smaller and smaller, and the distance between them become larger as he took off for the basket and laid it in. Jerry could only smile and say, "I always knew you were great!" Jerry sat on his butt at the foul line, now silent and in awe.

Chris laughed and yelled, "You just got crossed over by Crossover Shay!"

"Hey, Chris!"

"What's up, Shay?"

"I've never liked being teased, so please do not tease others around me!" Shay said with a clear sense of seriousness.

"Wow, this kid certainly is amazing!" Jerry mumbled and failed to notice the figure standing in front of him.

Jerry looked up, puzzled at the hand reaching down to help him up. "Here, take my hand. Let me help you up, man." Shay and Jerry grabbed hands.

"Check ball!" Jerry said. "You have one more point to go!"

"Sometimes, it's not about whether you win or lose!" Shay dropped the ball in front of Jerry and walked off the court. Shay turned back. "I admire your heart, Jerry." Shay turned to walk toward the sideline.

No one noticed Jeremiah on the side line. He just stared in awe; truly, Shay was one of the best youngest players he had ever encountered.

"What's up, lil bro?"

"Nothing, man!" Shay said as he gasped for breath. "How long have you been here watching?"

"I have been here for most of the game actually."

"Oh, well, it's nice to see you. What's up?"

"Not too much at all. Going to go get some lunch in a few minutes. Do you guys want to join me?"

"Sure," all the teenagers said in unison and chuckled a bit!

"Jerry, this is not to take anything away from you. Or you, Chris, but, Shay, you truly are awesome. Not just at basketball, but what a phenomenal thing you did just now!"

"I didn't do anything special, big bro!"

"You just laid down your pride. You humbled yourself and sought to save your opponent from embarrassment. You have truly learned to maximize moments in your life." Jeremiah patted Shay on the back.

"When did these two get so close?" Chris asked himself.

The Crossover that Won the Game

The four of them began walking toward the parking lot, right of the basketball courts and playground.

Chris tugged on the back of Shay's shirt. "Hey, Shay, come here," Chris whispered.

"What's going on?"

"I thought Jeremiah was this mean older brother. When did he change? When did you guys get so close?"

"We first began talking things out. Sharing feelings, leaving nothing to the imagination. His apology went a long way toward amends making. We have taken things one day at a time and tried to spend quality time together. We started getting closer during last school year." Shay smiled.

"Oh, okay." The group got into the car and headed to the nearest diner to grab a bite to eat.

◆ ◆ ◆

"Ahh!" Coach Crossover yelled, in response to the grimacing pain he experienced when reaching for a can of chicken noodle soup on the top shelf of his cupboard. Coach Crossover stood in his kitchen, grabbed his side, and shook his head from side to side.

"It feels like the world heavyweight champ just punched me square in the chest," Coach Crossover muttered.

However, he was so resourceful and usually had a plan. He grabbed the broom and knocked down the can of soup to the floor. "There's my soup of the day!" Coach Crossover laughed, then coughed as the pain once again became too much to handle.

"Hey, there's Coach Crossover's house!" Shay told the guys as they rode past. "I haven't heard from him lately. I really should stop by and see him."

"I don't think he's doing well!" Jeremiah shook his head. "Why don't we stop by after lunch? We will not be too far from his house actually!"

"That's a good idea, Jeremiah!" Shay said as he turned his head and watched as they got farther and farther away from Coach Crossover's house.

They pulled into the diner. Hopped out of the car, grabbed their table, and got ready to enjoy a meal.

Coach Crossover bent over. He resituated! Bending over was just too much. Coach Crossover bent his knees and picked up the can of chicken noodle soup. He tried to get up and quickly fell on his butt. Coach Crossover felt nauseous.

"The pain is getting increasingly worse! I think I might vomit." Coach Crossover grabbed his cell phone out of his pocket. Still sitting on the floor, he dialed his primary care physician's office number.

"Hello!" Dr. Brown answered in a monotone voice.

"Hey, Dr. Brown, it's Charlie Crossover."

"I figured you may be calling sometime soon!"

"How did you figure that?"

"Well, your last prognosis wasn't very good, but what prompts your call today?"

The Crossover that Won the Game

"The pain is getting worse. I am beginning to feel even more handicapped!" Crossover said with a hint of sarcasm.

"How soon can you come see me, my friend?"

"I think I need to come as soon as possible!"

"I understand! I will fit you in. Try to drive yourself, and if you can't, then call back and I will send a medical transportation vehicle to bring you in."

"Thank you very much, Dr. Brown! I will see you soon." Crossover coughed as the phone went *click* and the dial tone was heard. "I really hope Doc can help me!"

Coach Crossover pulled himself to his feet.

Shay stood up at the table after finishing his lunch.

Coach Crossover slowly walked toward the rack where his keys were hanging.

Shay, full of scrumptious food, walked slowly toward the exit sign.

Coach Crossover grabbed his keys and walked slowly toward the door.

Shay pushed open the door, walked down a few stairs toward the car.

Coach Crossover opened the door, eventually made his way down several stairs, closed his front door, and headed toward the car.

The door of the diner slammed as Shay opened the car door.

Coach Crossover opened his car door. Door closed shut, he was ready to go.

Shay closed his car door. He was now ready to go.

Coach Crossover pulled away to head to his destination.

Shay rode in the front seat of Jeremiah's car as they headed to their destination.

Coach Crossover arrived at his doctor's office.

Shay arrived at Coach Crossover's house.

Coach Crossover eased himself out of the car and walked toward the front door.

Shay hopped out of the car and walked toward the front door.

Bang! Bang! Coach Crossover's physician's assistant knocked on Dr. Brown's door.

"Your 3 o'clock is here."

Bang! Bang! Shay knocked on Coach Crossover's door. "He's not here!"

Coach Crossover stepped into Dr. Brown's office and took a seat.

Shay stepped into the car and took a seat.

Dr. Brown began to speak.

The Crossover that Won the Game

The car drove away.

◆ ◆ ◆

"So why don't we start by having you tell me how you've been feeling lately, Charlie!"

"Well, Dr. Brown, the pain has been getting worse."

"Where are you having this pain?"

"The pain has been on my right side and my chest. Now that I am thinking a little more clearly, I believe my feet have been a little swollen on occasion."

"On a scale of 1 to 10, with 10 being 'this pain is unbearable,' and 1 being 'there's hardly any pain at all,' how would you rate the pain you have been experiencing?"

"Well, Doc, today, I'd say the pain was approximately a 6."

"Mr. Crossover, I do not like to make haste decisions as a doctor so I am going to schedule a kidney biopsy to see if you may be experiencing kidney failure, and if so, how far along you are. Whatever is going on, don't you worry, we will catch it!"

"Are you going to admit me?"

"I would like to keep you overnight. Monitor you and then conduct the biopsy tomorrow morning."

"Okay, can I make a phone call?"

"Sure you can!"

Coach Crossover's jaw dropped as his eyes followed the stretcher that came for his delivery to the laboratory. "I just can't believe this is happening to me!" Coach Crossover shook his head just enough to avoid the resurfacing of excruciating pain. He lay in the hospital bed, flabbergasted, but knew he had to get to the bottom of whatever was ailing his body.

"I better call Ruby!" he said to himself.

♦ ♦ ♦

"Hello!" Ruby sounded surprised as she answered the strange number on her caller ID. Her fear was now validated. It was indeed the number from the hospital, and it was in fact Charlie on the phone.

"Hey, sis!" Coach Crossover struggled to speak fluidly.

"Hey, brother! How are things?"

"Well, you've probably figured out that I am in the hospital. With that being said, I am not sure I can truthfully answer your question until tomorrow morning or early afternoon."

"Why is that, Charlie?"

"Well, Dr. Brown will be monitoring me overnight and will conduct a kidney biopsy in the later part of the morning."

"Oh no, I am very sorry, Charlie. I really hope everything is all right. I had no idea it was this bad!"

"Well, I will wait for the test results." Charlie tried to be positive.

The Crossover that Won the Game

"I will pray for you. Do you want me to tell Shay or anyone else?"

"Thank you so much, sis! No, I do not want anyone to have to worry about me. I may need a ride home from the hospital though, I am not sure of that yet."

"Well, anything I can do to help, you just let me know!" Ruby reassured her brother of her support.

"Thank you!"

"You're welcome! That's what family and friends are for."

The said their good-byes and ended the conversation.

♦ ♦ ♦

Just as the phone hung up, Mom heard Shay and Jeremiah walk into the house.

"I can't believe Coach Crossover wasn't home!" Shay said to his mother.

"Well, son, I'm sure he has a good reason."

"How would you know, Mom?" Shay questioned.

Just as she was about to speak, Dad stormed into the house and asked to speak to his wife as soon as possible.

Conversation between Mom and Dad

"I do not like to argue, but, Ruby, we really have to talk!" John began his journey to figure out the truth.

Ruby had an idea of what John wanted to talk about, but decided to ask anyway.

"I hear a sense of urgency in your voice. What do you want to talk about, John?"

"Would you like to go somewhere a little more private?"

"Yes, John, that would be a great idea."

Jeremiah and Shay watched as their parents walked up the stairs toward the sitting room. The door shut and the rest of the conversation, for some time, would remain a mystery.

"John, you look rather disturbed! What's on your mind?"

"We are a house of honesty, correct?"

"Yes, John, we are!"

"Then I will just ask the question that's weighing on my mind."

"What is it?" Ruby asked.

"Are you having an extramarital affair?"

Ruby laughed. "John, definitely not!"

John's facial expression became a little less intense.

"Is that a smile I see beginning to form?"

John laughed a little and then put on a slightly more serious face. "Well then… why…uhhh! This is very hard for me to ask!" John said out of frustration.

The Crossover that Won the Game

"John, you can ask me anything! And I do mean anything!" Ruby's animated tone of voice reassured John of safe nature embodying this conversation.

"Okay, let me try this one more time..."

For what felt like a minute or two, silence became the loudest voice heard. John finally mustered the strength to ask a direct question.

"Why have you been spending so much time with Coach Crossover?"

"How did you know?"

"I was coming home from work a few times and I saw your car parked outside of his house."

"John, I can explain!"

John waited patiently. Ruby took a deep breath and began to speak.

"How can I begin to say this?" Ruby lowered her eyes and began to shake her head from left to right.

John's patience ran low. "Ruby!" he spoke in a stern tone.

Ruby lifted her eyes and stopped shaking her head. "John, Coach Crossover is my older brother."

"Oh my! I thought we were a house of honesty!"

"John, we certainly are!"

"Then tell...me...the...truth!"

"John...he's my brother."

"Ruby, why would I believe that? Coach Crossover is Caucasian!"

"He's actually not Caucasian. He's half-Caucasian and half–African-American."

"Then why does he look 100 percent Caucasian?"

Ruby paused for a moment. "Charlie is albino!"

"This is absolute nonsense, Ruby! Nonsense!"

"I have the answer to all your uncertainty."

John looked as if he had seen a ghost. He waited to hear what his wife would say next.

"Follow me!" She led her husband into the attic. "Take a seat, John."

John sat down and, in great anticipation, waited for what was to come next. Ruby shuffled through papers until she found what she was looking for. She pulled out a piece of paper and handed it to John.

"Read this, John, and this will all make sense."

Ruby sat down next to John, placed her right hand on his back, and patiently waited.

John's eyes blazed the page of almost unfathomable writing.

The Crossover that Won the Game

Dear Ruby,
   I could never tell you this because I never wanted you to think badly of your dad, but it is time for you to know. This young Caucasian boy in the photo is your brother.

Mom

John looked at Ruby, covered his mouth, and cocked his head to the left.

"I just can't bel—" John stopped. He read the letter audibly this time.

Dear Ruby,
   I could never tell you this because I never wanted you to think badly of your dad, but it is time for you to know. This young Caucasian boy in the photo is your brother.

Mom

"Is this a joke?"

Exasperated, Ruby spoke, "No, John, it is not."

"How long have you known?"

"I have known for about a year." Ruby said, bearing a look of embarrassment on her face.

"One full year, Ruby? Have you told anyone about this?" John stomped his foot.

"Only myself and Coach Crossover know that we are brother and sister."

"I am utterly confused...why keep this news a secret? Shay admires Coach Crossover. They've been very close for almost ten years now. It is neither your nor Coach Crossover's fault that you only recently learned that you were biologically related."

"John, I am not sure why we decided to keep it a secret. I guess, in some odd sense, we were worried about hurting Shay...oh, and since we are embellishing secrets, I have a bit of unfortunate news!"

"What is it?" John replied.

"Coach Crossover may be experiencing...uhhh...I just think he's really sick, John. The doctors are monitoring him tonight and running tests in the morning. I should know more tomorrow."

"I am really sorry to hear that. A condition such as kidney failure can be life threatening. Oh, I have to tell Shay..." John began running down the stairs.

"Wait!" Ruby yelled.

"What, honey?"

"I don't think that now is a good time due to Charlie's condition."

"Maybe you're right." John walked slowly back up the attic stairs.

"Perhaps we should let Coach Crossover tell Shay himself," Ruby suggested.

"We will figure out an agreed-upon plan."

There was as sort of awkward silence for a moment, then John continued to speak, "But what if Coach Crossover doesn't make—" John's statement was interrupted by Ruby's thoughts of her older brother, Charlie Crossover.

Beep! Beep! Beep! The alert sounded off and doctors rushed to Charlie's bedside.

First Basketball Game of Senior Year

Beep! Shay swished the three-pointer as the first quarter came to an end.

"Get your hands off me. You're too slow!" Shay laughed as he taunted his opponent from Brightest Day High School.

"You talk a lot of junk, Shay," Jerry said.

Shay smiled; he was so good at getting into his opponent's heads. He turned around, put the ball on the floor, and dribbled from left to right. "You're still there?" he asked his opponent.

"Yeah, I'm not going anywhere. And neither are you!" he bragged.

Then, as though his opponent was invisible, Shay backed up and took the three-pointer, leaving his opponent, teammates, and even Coach Denise shocked as the ball soared through the air and through the rim.

"You believe me now?" Shay asked his opponent as he jogged back down the court.

"Great shot, Shay!" Coach Denise yelled. "The kid has heart," she said to a teammate.

Shay gave Coach Denise a thumbs-up. "She hasn't seen anything yet, I haven't even warmed up!"

Jerry brought the ball up the court. He looked left to right, but Shay was quick as lightning. He lunged in, tapped the ball away, dribbled quickly behind his back, sending Jerry the other way. Now at the three-point line, Shay released the shot. The whipping of the net was met by the sound of the buzzer.

The first half ended, and Shay shone brighter than anyone else in the building.

Third Quarter

Brightest Day High School came out with a different game plan. They were determined to not allow Shay to torch them for an entire game.

Double-teams came, but Shay went through most of them.

"What's the matter, Jerry? You can't guard me one on one?"

"Shut up!"

"Oh, you'll pay for that, my friend!"

Shay crossed the ball between Jerry's legs and stepped into a double-team. Shay stepped back and released the three-pointer. The coach from Brightest Day High School couldn't believe Shay's heroics.

Brightest Day High School players executed very well, in spite of Shay's quality play. The third quarter ended with exhausted players and banged-up bodies.

"We never give up!" Shay yelled in the huddle.

"Game 1, guys. Let's go show these guys what we are made of!" Coach Denise told Lion's Heart High School players.

Fourth Quarter

The double- and triple-teams continued to come. Shay wasn't complaining, though. He was prepared for whatever challenge would come his way. Two players on him only meant that someone on his team was open, and he knew he would find the person.

Shay dribbled and waited for the double-team. He faked the drive, then reversed the ball to Chris. Chris sunk the three.

The two teams battled fiercely, but it came down to one final play.

Jerry brought the ball up the floor. Luke's pick was fierce on Shay's back. He fell down but got right back up. Defending Jerry like his final breath depended on it, Luke rolled to the basket.

"Michael, look up!" Shay yelled.

The ball flew through the air and Luke leaped to catch it. Shay sprinted and leaped. *I do not want to lose to these guys again*! Shay thought.

Hand extended for the block, Luke, soaring like a star, continued onward toward the rim. The loud sound of the hand against the backboard was heard across the entire gymnasium. However, the sound of the ball hitting the floor resounded into Shay's heart, reflected on his face, and would be his motivation for bigger moments to come.

"We'll be back!" Shay said as he walked off of the court and out of the gymnasium with Jeremiah.

Shay hopped into the car to head home. "I wonder where Mom, Dad, and Coach Crossover were at for my first game. Man, I just can't believe they all missed the game!"

"Hey, little bro, it is okay, I am sure they will come to some of your other games this season," Jeremiah said as they drove home.

Conversation between Mom, Dad, and Coach Crossover
Knock! Knock!

"Hey, little bro, come on in!"

"Hey, sis! How are you?"

"I am doing pretty good…how are you holding up?"

"I am doing better. The medicine that Dr. Brown prescribed has been working really well!"

"Hey, do you want to sit down for a drink of warm tea?"

"Why, of course! I wondered what you were waiting for!" Charlie and Ruby chuckled.

The two of them walked into kitchen and sat down at the nook Ruby so dearly loved.

Charlie sat at the breakfast nook, which Ruby used as a kitchen table. He laughed hysterically with his newfound sister.

"Wow," he chuckled, "All of these years I never knew I was a black man!"

"Hey, that's why you are able to teach all those kids how to do a devastating crossover. Only a black man could do that!" Ruby laughed.

"Well, I…"

The Crossover that Won the Game

"Wait a minute, big brother—" Ruby interrupted

"What's wrong?"

"I know I am not supposed to interrupt, but I almost forgot something!"

"What'd you forget, little sis?"

"You are only half black so maybe a half-white man can teach African-American kids how to do a destructive crossover!" The two of them laughed and laughed until they cried.

"I think I am a little more black than white."

"Why would you say such a thing, Charlie?"

"Because I have always loved black-eyed peas and cornbread!" Charlie leaned in with a smile.

Ruby laughed. "But…but what about fried chicken?" Ruby asked as she leaned back in her chair in laughter.

"Um…well…I…uh…"

"Ah, never mind…you want to know something?"

"Anything you want to tell me, little sister!" Neither Ruby nor Charlie heard the front door open and close.

"I love you, big brother!" she said as she placed her arms around his neck and gave him a kiss on the cheek.

"I love y—" Ruby's eyes widened as if she had just seen the grim reaper.

"Ruby, is everything o—"

"What the heck is going on in my home?" John said as he lunged toward the unfamiliar man sitting across from his wife.

"John, what are you doing? It's only—"

Smack! It was too late! John had already slammed Charlie to the floor.

"Oh my goodness! I am so sorry, Charlie!"

"Geez, John, I didn't know I had to tell you when my own brother would be coming over!"

John lowered his head. "I hate to admit this, but I have been a little jealous lately, because you've been spending more time with your 'newfound brother' than your own family!" John ended his statement cynically.

"Sorry, Mr. Ponder, I can leave now if you'd li—" Charlie began to speak.

"No, Charlie, you're going to stay here and we are going to talk as a family!" Ruby turned and stared John square in the eyes. "Because that's what families do! And Charlie is my…no, he is our family!"

"You guys want to talk?" John asked as he took a seat across from Ruby. "Let's talk then!"

"As a matter of fact, John, I would love to talk!" Ruby said.

"It's certainly beyond time to get to the bottom of this mystery!" John replied.

"Well, guys, I don't…" Charlie stopped and quickly turned as he heard a familiar voice.

The Crossover that Won the Game

"No one! Really? So no one came to my...?"

Shay stopped as he looked at the strange scene in the kitchen. Coach Crossover looked as if he had just seen a ghost. Ruby covered her mouth in disappointment, and well, John just shook his head in disbelief that everyone forgot about Shay's game today, as they were engulfed in their own drama.

"Hey, Shay, let me—" Coach Crossover and John stopped and stared at each other, speaking in unison.

Shay interrupted, "My first game of senior year. Ahh, no big deal. You guys clearly had bigger games to play, and I guess I understand!"

"Shay, we are very sorry. We have been talking about some really important matters though," Mom replied.

Coach Crossover stared at the "once child, now young adult" whom he's loved for so many years. He should have known, but would never have guessed that he was his own flesh and blood. The bigger question now was, how does he and the parents tell Shay?

"Shay, there is something I must tell you!" Coach Crossover said in a sharp tone.

"You can tell me anything!" Shay replied.

"Shay, I am yo—"

"Really sorry that I have not been able to make it to your games!" Ruby interrupted.

"Is that what you wanted to say Coach Crossover?" Shay focused attention on Coach Crossover.

"Well, Shay, it was a little bit dee—"

"Son, your beloved Coach Crossover has been really sick lately. He has been in and out of the hospital and that is why he has not been able to come to your games."

Momentarily, Shay forgot all about what Coach Crossover had previously began saying. "Oh no...Coach Crossover...is this true?" Shay asked as he put his right hand on Coach Crossover's shoulder.

"Yes, it is true. I have good news though. My doctor, Dr. Brown, doesn't believe it is anything too serious. He gave me some medication and says I should be back to 100 percent health in approximately three months!" Coach Crossover said with excitement in his voice.

"Well, you know I'd do whatever necessary to make sure you were all right, Coach?"

Charlie smiled. "I know, neph...uh...buddy!"

Shay smiled. Jeremiah looked at Shay in a way he'd never done before.

Ruby looked at Charlie and Charlie back at her. There was something different about their smile. John could only accept Ruby's closeness to her brother, Charlie Crossover. Shay and Jeremiah were no longer convinced that everything was truly still the same.

"Well, it was very nice to see you again, Coach! I look forward to seeing you at some of my games. Most importantly, the championship game because I just have a feeling that Lion's Heart High School will be there."

Coach Crossover smiled and nodded. "My frie...uh...Shay, it's time you start calling me Charlie!"

The Crossover that Won the Game

Shay smiled and gave Charlie a manly hug. "All right, guys, I really have to go do my homework. I do not want the time to slip away from me."

Jeremiah followed Shay upstairs.

"Ruby, why wouldn't you let me tell Shay that I am his uncle?"

"I do not think it's time yet."

"Hun, well then, when would the right time be?" John asked.

"I don't mean to overwhelm you, Ruby, but Shay and I have been so close for many years. No offense, John, we were so close that he's felt like a son to me. We have never kept secrets from each other! I mean he's my nephew and that's a good…no, it's great thing!"

Ruby shook her head. "Guys, I'm sorry. Tell him when you're ready, Charlie."

The three of them got caught in the moment of rejoicing about Charlie's positive prognosis from Dr. Brown.

"Okay, something was really weird in that kitchen!" Shay told Jeremiah.

"Yeah, bro, Coach Crossover…I'm sorry, Charlie was definitely trying to tell you something!"

"I really want to know what it was!"

Shay heard the front door open and shut as Charlie left for the night.

"Whatever he had to say, I am positive I would love him anyway!" Shay and Jeremiah stared at each other, chatted a bit more, and the night slipped away.

The Next Three Months

Lion's Heart High School was having an amazing season. They stood a great chance of going to the championship this year. Their only loss was to Brightest Day High School, their first game of the season.

Shay's relationships with Jeremiah and Chris continued to be a consistent source of joy and meaning for Shay. Shay was happy to have Coach Crossover present more often than in recent times.

Charlie spent much more time with his newfound family over the next three months. Ruby and Charlie continued to build a strong relationship. The two families found time to spend with each other. Ruby met Charlie's uncle, his two older brothers, and other younger sister. They managed to keep the news that Charlie was his uncle away from Shay. Shay felt an abnormal sense of closeness to Charlie.

"So why can't I call you Coach Crossover anymore? You've always been Coach Crossover!" Shay said as he chuckled a little.

"Well—"

"Well...what?" Shay interrupted.

"Still interrupting people, huh?"

"I'm just saying. It's not rocket science, it's not a surgical procedure... uh...Coach!" Shay teased a bit.

Charlie became silent, his face changed a bit, and Shay had no idea what his beloved coach had already been through. Charlie felt great, but he knew that an illness like his could return.

"One day, it will all make sense, Shay. We have been close for so long. I just need you to be patient, buddy."

The Crossover that Won the Game

"You know, Coach, you always did know just the right things to say in order to help me feel at peace with whatever situation was happening!"

"Well, being involved in your life has always warmed my heart!"

"Thanks, Coach!"

"Shay, I'd really like you to call me Charlie."

"Okay, I will, but only because I have so much respect for you."

"Shay, I want to tell you something!"

"Anything, Coa...I mean, Charlie!"

Charlie laughed. "I've been taking a lot of time to truly understand what it is like to be African-American."

"I'm confused!"

"I hate to say this again, but one day, it will all make sense. Let me tell you some of what I've been learning!" Charlie said with excitement in his voice.

The two of them talked about different black history facts that was on Charlie's laptop from the research he'd been doing.

"Thurgood Marshall was the first African-American ever appointed to the United States Supreme Court. Mr. Marshall was appointed by President Lyndon B. Johnson and served on the Supreme Court from 1967 to 1991."

"A judge? Really?" Shay asked.

"Yes, a judge and listen to this..."

"What?" Shay leaned forward, communicating his attentiveness and interest.

"Africans were kings and queens prior to being forced to come to America as slaves," Charlie responded.

"I never knew there was such a rich legacy left by my ancestors," Shay interjected.

"Yes, Shay, there was! Listen to this. In 1969, Shirley Chisholm became the first black congresswoman. It was then that she began the first of seven terms. After initially being assigned to the House Forestry Committee, she shocked many when she demanded reassignment. She was placed on the Veterans' Affairs Committee, eventually graduating to the Education and Labor Committee. She became one of the founding members of the Congressional Black Caucus in 1969."

"Ha! Ha! How awesome? An African-American in Congress?"

"Yes, Shay!"

"I guess I shouldn't be too surprised."

"Why not? If you do not mind me asking!"

"Well, we have African-Americans in Congress today, and well, we do have a black president!"

"Things were different then!"

"How so?" Shay asked.

"To put it mildly, African-Americans were a lot less equal to Caucasians in 1969."

"I guess I didn't think about that!"

"You talk about us having a black president, but listen to this next Black History fact: Shirley Chisholm became the first African-American woman to make a bid to be president of the United States when she ran for the Democratic nomination in 1972. A champion of minority education and employment opportunities throughout her tenure in Congress, Chisholm was also a vocal opponent of the draft. After leaving Congress in 1983, she taught at Mount Holyoke College and was popular on the lecture circuit."

"I guess a lot has happened that I do not know about!"

"There is always time to learn. Knowing where you came from is important in order to know how to get where you're going!"

"You always did have a way with words and teaching of memorable life lessons!" Shay replied.

"Thank you, pal. Hey, can I tell you about the Underground Railroad?"

"I think I have heard about that, but I am interested in hearing what you have to say, Coach."

"Shay, it's okay…you really can call me Charlie."

"I know, but right now, you are my coach. You're just teaching something different than basketball!"

Coach Crossover laughed. "All right, I suppose you are right."

"So tell me about the Underground Railroad, Coach!"

"Gladly! So the Underground Railroad was the term used to describe a network of persons who helped escaped slaves on their way to freedom in the northern states or Canada. Northern free blacks, who had little or no support from white abolitionists, were the most active of the railroad workers. The most famous 'conductor' was an escaped slave named Harriet Tubman. Some sources say that Harriet Tubman made nineteen return trips to the South and helped some three hundred slaves escape. A number of individual whites also aided runaways, as did 'vigilance committees,' often biracial in character, in northern cities.

"Estimates of the number of slaves assisted vary widely, but only a minuscule fraction of those held in bondage ever escaped. Few, particularly from the lower South, even attempted the laborious journey North. However, the idea of organized 'outsiders' undermining the institution of slavery angered white Southerners, leading to their demands in the 1840s that the Fugitive Slave Laws be strengthened.

"As you see, Shay, there were several African-American women that were also pertinent to how far we...um...African-Americans have come."

"What did you just say, Coach?"

"I will explain later."

"I thought we didn't keep secrets!" Shay challenged Charlie.

"Shay, we do not, but there is a time and place for everything."

"So we are keeping secrets now?"

"I simply do not have the words to tell you what I so desperately need to tell you, Shay!"

"I understand, Charlie. I will be waiting though!" Shay laughed.

The Crossover that Won the Game

After the silence persisted long enough, Shay's curiosity got the better of him.

"All right, what other facts do you have for me?"

"Well, here's another one: Frederick Douglass who lived from 1818 to 1895 was a prominent American abolitionist, author, and orator. He was born a slave, but Douglass escaped at age twenty and went on to become a world-renowned anti-slavery activist. His three autobiographies are considered important works of the slave narrative tradition as well as classics of American autobiography. Douglass's work as a reformer ranged from his abolitionist activities in the early 1840s to his attacks on Jim Crow and lynching in the 1890s. For sixteen years, he edited an influential black newspaper and achieved international fame as an inspiring and persuasive speaker and writer. In thousands of speeches and editorials, he levied a powerful indictment against slavery and racism, provided an indomitable voice of hope for his people, embraced antislavery politics, and preached his own brand of American ideals."

"Wow!" Shay was at a loss for words.

"Those are just a few facts, Shay. I want to play a song for you, but let me share some other important information I think you should know."

"I am truly amazed. Thank you so much for sharing that information with me."

"Hey, what's going on here, guys?" Dad said with a hint of sarcasm. Dad walked in and joined the conversation. He was very excited to have an opportunity to educate his son about their history.

"What do want to add, Mr. Ponder?"

"Please call me John! You know, I want to tell you about a man named Marcus Garvey. First of all, he said that a 'hungry man has no respect for law, authority, or human life,' but he's said much more than that. Here's some more information about him: social activist Marcus Mosiah Garvey Jr. was born on August 17, 1887, in St. Ann's Bay, Jamaica. Self-educated, Garvey founded the Universal Negro Improvement Association, dedicated to promoting African-Americans and resettlement in Africa. In the United States, he launched several businesses to promote a separate black nation. After he was convicted of mail fraud and deported back to Jamaica, he continued his work for black repatriation to Africa."

"It sounds like he really did a lot, but I thought we were supposed to go to school in order to become educated?"

"Son, while this is true, you must understand that in the nineteenth century and years following, often African-Americans or blacks were not allowed to go to school to receive a 'formal' or 'public' education."

"Oh!"

"Let me tell you more about Mr. Garvey!"

"Okay, Dad, I'm listening."

"Okay, so Mr. Marcus Mosiah Garvey was the last of eleven children born to Marcus Garvey Sr. and Sarah Jane Richards. His father was a stone mason and his mother a domestic worker and farmer. Garvey Sr. was a great influence on Marcus, who once described him as 'severe, firm, determined, bold, and strong, refusing to yield, even to superior forces if he believed he was right.' His father was known to have a large library where young Garvey learned to read."

"We have a few things in common!" Shay sounded surprised.

"What's that?" Charlie and John said in unison.

"Well, we have almost the same number of siblings!" Shay laughed. Charlie and John laughed also.

"Is that really it?" Charlie asked.

"No way, that's not it. I am just being silly. Bringing out my inner comedian!" Shay winked at them.

Laughing a little, John asked, "So what is it, son?"

"Well, over the years, I have learned to be determined and bold. I am strong, and I have come to realize that I am a strong-willed and do not yield just because someone may be bigger, stronger, or feel that they are superior to me!"

"That is really great insight, son!" John said as he smiled at Shay.

"I am going to have to agree!" Charlie said as he laid his hand on Shay's back.

"You're seventeen, son. Correct?"

"Yes, Dad, you know how old I am!"

"Well then, listen to this…"

"Okay, I am sure it will be good. This Marcus Garvey was a real social activist, huh?

"Oh, he surely was, Shay!" Charlie interjected.

"Charlie is right, and so are you, son. Get this, at age fourteen—"

"Sorry to interrupt, Dad, but did you say fourteen?"

"Yes, son, at the age of fourteen, Marcus became a printer's apprentice. In 1903, he traveled to Kingston, Jamaica, and soon became involved in union activities. In 1907, he took part in an unsuccessful printer's strike and the experience kindled in him a passion for political activism. Three years later, he traveled throughout Central America working as a newspaper editor and writing about the exploitation of migrant workers in the plantations. He later traveled to London where he attended Birkbeck College (University of London) and worked for the *African Times and Orient Review*, which advocated Pan-African nationalism."

"Wow, I wish I'd learned all of this sooner. I can't believe Mr. Garvey was only fourteen! I feel like all I do is play basketball."

"Shay, I think it is great that you love basketball, but never forget where you came from. Never forget what others endured to pave the way for you. My son, last but not least, if I could give one piece of advice, it would be this: Live a life of value, be sure to do something of meaning, and at the end of the bigger moments in your life, sacrifice for the good of others!"

Shay sat in awe of all that transpired before he stepped foot on the earth. How happy he was that his dad and Charlie decided to educate him in a manner school had not. "I believe I will be forever changed by the newfound appreciation for what my ancestors endured. My courage doesn't even compare to theirs!"

"Hey, my son, sometimes, you do not know how courageous you are until challenged!"

"Your dad is right, but don't hold your breath, you may have a chance to prove just how courageous you are!"

There was a sort of unexplainable silence as Shay mulled over Charlie's last words.

"Hey, guys, I want to play a song for you!" Dad began playing "Lift Every Voice" by James Weldon Johnson.

Championship Game of Senior Year

Shay stood with eyes lowered and hands behind his back as he listened to the words of the "Star-Spangled Banner." Another song emasculated the elegant sounds of the national anthem. It was the victorious sounds of the well-known song, "Lift Every Voice"!

"Sing a song full of faith that the dark past has taught us!" Shay hummed internally. "I know faith will carry me. My past hasn't been roses and chocolate, but it sure has taught me much!" Shay thought. "Allow my past to transform my present in a positive way!"

"A song full of hope that the present has brought us!"

"Stony the road we trod. Bitter the chastening rod, felt in the day that hope unborn had died."

I have not gone through what they did, but all the martyred as well as those that both endured and survived have paved the path of persistence and determination for me! Shay thought.

"Hmm, I really like that," Shay thought. "Hope contained is fear restrained!" Shay thought aloud.

"Hey, man, shhh!" Chris lightly elbowed Shay and laughed. Shay stood a little straighter and gave a look of apology.

"Chris really messed me up. What was that next part? I cannot remember, but I'm sure that more of the song will come to me!"

"Yet with a steady beat, have not our feet come to…"

What's next? Shay thought.

"We have come over a way that with tears has been watered. We have come, treading our path through the blood of the slaughtered. Out from the gloomy past, till now we stand at last…"

Well, certainly my experiences doesn't compare to that of my African ancestors, but I've cried a few…no, a little more than a few tears. Despite how many times I fell, here I am…standing! And I know those that came before me were fighters, both physically and intellectually. I may be young, but I know names like Nat Turner, Malcolm X, Martin Luther King Jr., Marcus Garvey, and many more, Shay thought.

"Thou who has by thy might, led us into the light. Keep us forever in the path, we pray lest our feet stray from the places, our God, where we met thee."

"God, let me never forget to give you thanks for the skills and opportunities you have blessed me with!" Shay prayed quietly.

As a person in rebellion, Shay stared at the lights in the ceiling. "Facing the rising sun of our new day begun, let us march on till victory is won."

"I am the rising sun, and on this day, we will be victorious!"

The Crossover that Won the Game

First Quarter

Ball between legs, then quickly behind back, Shay leaped, scooping the ball underneath the opponent's arms and into the rim. Shay smiled. Oh, how happy he was to have an opportunity to defend his school's honor against Brightest Day High School!

The next time Shay brought the ball up the court, his opponents had constructed a different plan. Shay crossed the ball in front of Jerry's face, faked left, then quickly went right. As he stepped right, Shay met the body of the six-foot-six power forward. Shay stumbled back!

Jerry lunged in! Jerry took the ball coast to coast and converted on the layup. Shay watched and wondered, "What will I do next?"

Shay felt a hand lightly hit his back. "Hey, bro, just try again next time!"

Shay stared Chris right in the eyes. "Try is a…"

"Let's go, guys. Simply talking about it doesn't win games, defense does!"

The rest of the quarter entailed much body banging, floor thrashing, and sweat soaking the hardwood floor.

Second Quarter

Shay crouched over with his hands on his knees. Focused on the primary goal, Shay ran toward the inbound player and then quickly changed directions, leaving Jerry behind. Ball in hand, Shay spun around the shooting guard, stopped on the drop of a dime, and swished the three-pointer.

Jerry brought the ball up the court. After a flurry of passes, Brightest Day players found a hole in the defense. Lion's Heart High School players stood and watched as the small forward, Luke, reverse dunked the ball.

He pointed at Lion's Heart players and delivered his message, "No one on your team can guard or stop me!"

I appreciate and admire his confidence, but I believe in myself first and foremost! Shay thought.

Shay passed the ball to Chris, who touch-passed the ball to Michael. Jerry stripped the ball. *It's all about timing!* Jerry thought.

Jerry shot the alley-oop to Luke.

Shay remembered Luke as the player that blocked his shot in the semifinal game last season.

Luke rose! His intention to slam dunk yet again, he spread out like the assumed new National Basketball Association logo.

"Sometimes, revenge is sweeter than necessary!" Shay told himself.

Shay took flight! Luke continued to rise. Luke approached from the right side of the rim and Shay from the left. Luke looked as if he was en route to claim his next victim. Shay looked like an Egyptian warrior staging the attack against Sparta. Sparta fell, and so did Luke. The Spartans laid on their back, as did Luke. He looked up amazed at what had just happened.

"Shot blocked by a…" Luke began saying.

"Payback is a…" Shay stopped and smiled. Waited awhile. "Don't ever take me for a quitter!" Shay brought the ball up the court.

In a game-time situation, he knew all too well the time was ticking toward zero. Shay hopped left and then passed the ball to Chris. Shay cut toward the basket as the ball reached Michael's hands. Ball tossed high, Shay jumped to catch the alley-oop. Shay caught the ball and rose higher and higher. Shay put ball and hand on rim. Shay landed and shook his head as the ball hit the floor and time expired in the second quarter. "I just can't believe I missed that dunk!"

Halftime

"I need motivation! I need discomfort! Why, you might ask...because discomfort must be present before change can take place. We are right in this game, and if I had to guess, I'd say we will be champions in the next twenty-four to thirty minutes."

Shay never looked up. Breathing a little slower, relaxing a bit more, Shay placed his hands on his legs. "I'm ready!" Shay told himself.

The third quarter was challenging for Lion's Heart High School. They proved that if they one thing, it was heart. There was no lying down and taking whatever was handed to them. Shay thought of a line from his new favorite song: "Let us march on til victory is won." Shay hummed a bit. "Guys, we're not going to stop. Like African warlords marching, we will keep on moving until we get the victory we came here for!"

"Yeah!" Lion's Heart High School players yelled as the buzzer sounded for the final segment of their journey: the fourth quarter.

The two teams battled.

"Leave it all out on that hardwood floor, guys!" Shay encouraged the team.

"Yeah, whatever we do...we do now! We do not have tomorrow!" Chris chimed in.

Rallying back from a 17-point halftime deficit, Lion's Heart High School players put them themselves in a position to win. Chris tied the game with a long range, twenty-seven-foot three-pointer. Jerry brought the ball up the court. Brightest Day High School designed an almost unstoppable play. Shay remembered how they lost their last game.

This play looks strikingly similar to the strategy they used last year to beat us! Shay thought.

Jerry began his series of movements. He passed the ball, but Shay intercepted and history now lay at his fingertips. Glory was within his grasp.

The final moments approached. The sweat smashing the gym floor sounded like rain hitting the armor of warriors. Fear began to seep into Shay's blood and run rampant through the very core of who he was. Shay's mind became a whirlwind of all that he'd heard over the years.

"Shay you have drive and you have courage! You are the most determined kid I've ever met. You have no fear! Could you imagine what it takes for a person to attempt the game-winning shot?" He remembered Jeremiah's words of encouragement.

Shay wiped the sweat from his face. Jerry stared at him like a hungry lion. Feeling cowardice, Shay closed his eyes and savored the moment.

Big moments often come around only once. I am afraid, but fear is simply another opponent to be defeated! Shay thought.

"Never give up. If you work hard enough, you will—" Jerry's movement interrupted Shay's reminiscing about Coach Crossover's words to him as a sixth grader. Shay crossed the ball between his legs, then faked left. Jerry tapped the ball out of Shay's hand.

The Crossover that Won the Game

Running toward the loose ball, Shay remembered what Dad said to him: "Hey, my son, sometimes, you do not know how courageous you are until challenged!"

Back on the floor. Jerry hovering over him. Shay lay on his back, continuing to dribble the ball with one hand. Shay remembered his prior moments of fame and learning.

◆ ◆ ◆

Swish! That was the sound the ball made as it fell through the net.

"Yes!" the crowd roared as little Shay sunk the three-pointer with two seconds left in the fourth quarter.

"Shay, Shay, he's our man. If he can't make it, no one can!" the cheerleaders chanted.

9…ball switched from right to left.

8…Shay faked as if he was going to drive the past his opponent. His opponent flinched.

7…"Where you going?" Shay laughed as he asked the question.

6…ball dribbled twice quickly between both of Shay's legs.

5…ball switched from left to right hand.

His opponent made the biggest mistake of his career, he reached.

"CS now. CS now," Coach Crossover yelled.

4…Shay flinched. His opponent reached.

3…Shay flinched again. His opponent reached. Now crossing the ball over to his left hand, his opponent reached and fell.

♦ ♦ ♦

"Coach Crossover taught me that," Shay said with a smirk as his reached into to steal the ball. After crossing the quickly to his left hand, Shay stepped back behind the three-point line. With his opponent a far enough distance away, feet squared beneath his shoulders Shay pulled up for the three.

"Are you ready for what I am about to do to you?"

"Bring it on!" Jerry said boldly.

"This is the finale!" Shay swiftly put the ball behind his back. Ball now back in front of him, he put the ball behind his back knowing that Jerry would reach. Jerry did exactly what Shay thought, reached! Shay crossed the ball, causing Jerry to fall. Like a movie in slow motion Shay watched Jerry become smaller and smaller, and the distance between them become larger as he took off for the basket and laid it in. Jerry could only smile and say, "I always knew you were great!" Jerry sat on his butt at the foul line, now silent and in awe.

♦ ♦ ♦

"Whether you win or lose, you decide the amount of effort you put into your performance. Do I have faith in you? Yes, I do have faith in you…in all of you! But! Yes there is usually a 'but' whether we like it or not. So I will ask again…do I have faith in you? You already know that the answer is yes. But what good is it if I have faith in you, if you do not have faith in yourself?"

"It is no good, Coach Scott," Shay yelled out.

"Correct, Shay! The most important thing is that you have faith in yourself. Faith fuels fire. The fire necessary to burn through any circumstance, challenge, and conflict, and anything that tries to stop you from reaching your end goals in life. The end goal is not always winning. Any positive outcome is a winning result. Never give up. If you give up, you will never know what the result would have been. If you continue to pursue your goals, no matter how many times you lose eventually…you win. I've heard that it's not about whether you win or lose, but how you play the game. Just as you are going to play a basketball game, life is akin to a game. In neither is there ever a draw. You will either win or lose. Enjoy small victories and know that you may lose some battles, but the war is usually far from over. You are under my supervision to learn new perspectives that carries you not only through basketball games but through all of life's greatest and toughest moments. With that being said, leave your all on the floor out there tonight, guys. Bring your hands in here, guys. Faith, Confidence, Determination on 3."

"One…two…three, Faith! Confidence! Determination!"

♦ ♦ ♦

Shay hopped to his feet, crossed left, then right. Shay began remembering the way in which Jerry and Brightest Day High School defeated Lion's Heart High School in the semifinal game last season. Feeling a little discouraged, Shay reminisced about key words from Coach Scott.

♦ ♦ ♦

"First, Shay, let me address something else. I noticed that when I used the word 'fail,' you lowered your eyes and began looking discouraged. By no means are you a failure, but everyone has moments of success and failure. What is important is that you figure out what needs to be done differently in order to be successful whether it takes you one, two, or fifty tries!"

◆ ◆ ◆

Shay smiled, moved left, then spun right. Jerry now in Shay's past, victory his future.

"I am the rising sun!" Shay said as he leaped. As Shay rose, so did Luke. Shay flew through the air like the newest rising star, and Luke defied gravity like the great Neil Armstrong. Eyes to eyes, one arm defending the ball, the other seeking to destroy, both had met their fate.

Bodies banged, one teen on their butt looking up, the other falling from the rim staring down his most recent victim.

Book 9

His name to be forever in the record books and his courage to forever remain in the hearts of that fans that came to love him dearly.

The opponent looked up in disbelief. "I can't believe that this is how my high school career will end."

Staring down at his opponent, reveling in his glory simultaneously embracing humility, he extended his hand.

"Thanks for the hand up!"

The two hugged. "You truly are great and the whole world will know!"

Shay looked around, puzzled! His high school career had reached its final moment. Shay walked away and stood on the sideline. The fans and antagonists roared at increasingly high volumes. Shay took a deep breath.

"Thank you, God, for giving me strength! Thanks for courage and thanks for always being by my side!" Shay said a short prayer.

Shay thought collectively about his experiences. "I'm here and as I told myself...I am, no, we are champions. No one will ever stop me, accept me!"

Shay broke free from all of the attention to land in the arms of Coach Denise. "Shay, you're a hero. You're fearless and the world of sports will be seeing more of you!"

"Thank you, Coach Denise. I appreciate how much you've invested in me. I will never forget about all those who have impacted me…"

"Well, that's—"

"Hold up, Coach! Wait just one minute!" Shay laughed. "Just one more interruption for the road…I meant to say that I would never forget those impacted me both positive…" Shay paused. "And negatively!" Shay finished.

Coach Denise put her hand on Shay's back. "Your journey is not over. In fact, I have a surprise for you!"

"What is it?" Shay asked inquisitively.

"Patience, my friend!" Coach Denise laughed. "I will bring it to your house!"

The celebrations continued and eventually ended. Shay could not think of a better ending to a tumultuous and challenging road. He stepped off of the court and he knew one thing to be true:

> "No matter what happens from this point forward, I will be remembered as a winner!"

Shay walked slowly, wanting to soak in the last moments of his glory, he spoke his final words on the hardwood floor he'd made his throne.

"Even more than being remembered as a winner, I'd like to be remembered as the one who never quit!"

Deep inside, Shay knew this was only the beginning, and greater was to come!

◆ ◆ ◆

The Crossover that Won the Game

"Oh my gosh, I can't believe this! A scout from Georgetown University is in my living room telling me that I've earned a full-ride scholarship. A scholarship to one of the best colleges in the world!"

"Yes," Mr. Freedom said. "My job was to come here and convince you that you should come play for our school."

The rain had finally ceased and the reddish sun was beginning to make its beautiful presence known. Then, something colorful outside of the window caught Shay's eye. He turned and stared out of the huge living room window toward the mountains in the distance. Atop the tallest one sat the most beautiful rainbow he'd ever seen. Tears built up in his eyes and began to fall.

"Are those tears of joy or sadness? Because you will deny us the chance to have you play for us?"

Shay turned and faced the man. Ruby and John sat staring at their baby son. None of the adults in the room had a clue what was going on, so they all waited patiently for Shay to speak. "Well, I asked for a sign, then I looked out the window, and bam! There is His promise to me. All of my young life, I've been put down, told I'd never amount to anything, that college basketball was just a dream. Those negative words hurt me so badly, but I kept believing against so many odds. A rainbow told me all that I needed to know. I'll glad…"

The loud knocking on the door caused everyone to turn. Shay ran to the door and snatched it open. Shocked, Coach Scott and Coach Denise stood at the door, smiling, but where was Coach Crossover?

♦ ♦ ♦

"I have to get out of this bed and get to the hospital," Coach Crossover said to his black lab while coughing hysterically.

"Woof, woof," Blackie responded.

"Yeah, Blackie," he said, while his coughing continued uncontrollably. "I have to see who can tend to you because something tells me that they want to admit me when I go this time."

"Woof," Blackie barked as she tilted her head to the side and stared at her master.

The rain had finally ceased to cover the streets of Rochester after what seemed like an eternity. At last, the colorful sun filtered in through the Venetian blinds, and he smiled, knowing what a great day Shay would have. He knew the scout would visit today, but he knew he could barely get out of bed, let alone drive. He decided to ask Coach Scott and Denise to be present in his absence. When he was questioned as to why he wouldn't be there, he lied and said that Blackie had a vet appointment. He looked at his painting on the wall, which read "Knowing How to Fight Is a Near Must."

"I know how to fight back, but how do you fight an invisible opponent?" he asked himself.

"Roof, roof," Blackie responded as though she was reading his thoughts.

He was proud of Shay, the young kid he's mentored has grown into a decent young man and was now college bound. He smiled as he stared at all the gifts with labels that read "Georgetown University" that he had bought for Shay.

"Maybe, just maybe, I can conjure up enough strength to go by Shay's to drop off the gifts. Then I'll head to the hospital." He grabbed the side of the bed and tried to stand. At first, he felt like he was in a calm sea, but then it seemed as though the sea became turbulent. It was now dark and the room began to spin. He reached for something, anything, to hold on

The Crossover that Won the Game

to so he can brace himself, but found nothing. He felt as though he was falling into an abyss. His head smashed against the side of the dresser, and he didn't feel the crimson blood that flowed near his left eye.

Blackie barked frantically, running from room to room. She stopped at the front door, and then the back door, trying desperately to find help. She whined and whined, finally deciding to go to the phone. With her mouth, Blackie grabbed the receiver and dropped it on the floor. With her nose, she pressed the red button that her owner taught her to hit.

"911, what's your emergency?" a voice said.

"Woof, woof, woof!" Blackie barked and ran to her master's side. She licked his face, whined, and laid her head on his chest.

◆ ◆ ◆

Shay stood watching as airplanes flew over the terminal. Shay smiled at Mom, Dad, Chris, and Jeremiah, but missed his friend and confidant Coach Crossover.

"How could he miss so many of my big moments?" Shay readjusted his shoulders, then felt his dad's hand on his back.

"Son, there's a reason for everything!"

"For what reason does your best friend…well, one of," Shay paused and looked at Chris. "Your best friends fail to take part in the big moments of your life?"

"Only time will tell, Shay."

◆ ◆ ◆

Shay folded his arms. Mom unfolded and embraced her beloved son. "We all love you very much and so does, Charlie! One day, it'll all make sense."

"I hope so," Shay said as he shook his head, took a deep breath, and turned to Chris. "You better call me, man! And we have to hang out on my breaks." Shay laughed.

"You know I will!"

"Cool!" Shay said as the boys high-fived.

"I know you'll light it up down there."

"I'm not so sure, it's a different level of play now!" Shay said.

"Hey, little bro, stop doubting yourself. Courage and confidence have carried you this far, and only you can make sure they continue doing just that!"

"Thanks, Jeremiah."

"And no one can talk more nonsense to you than I have!" Jeremiah said, as the two boys shared a laugh.

"Yeah, you've prepared me for a time like this," Shay lightly punched Jeremiah in his right arm.

"All passengers for United Airlines Flight 1270 may now board at Terminal 18," the representative spoke over the intercom.

◆ ◆ ◆

On the other side of the city, Charlie was on a hospital stretcher coming in and out of consciousness. During a moment of lucidity, he spoke of

The Crossover that Won the Game

his newfound nephew. "I have to get to the airpo..." Charlie slipped into unconsciousness before being able to finish his sentence.

♦ ♦ ♦

After saying good-bye, Shay boarded Flight 1270. He threw his carry-on bag in the overhead bin and plopped into his seat. Donning his headphones, he began playing "Eye of the Tiger" by Survivor.

"I'm so happy I can use my electronics on planes now!" Shay settled in and started quietly singing some of the lyrics.

> Rising up, back on the street
> Did my time, took my chances
> Went the distance, now I'm back on my feet
> Just a man and his will to survive
>
> So many times it happens too fast
> You change your passion for glory
> Don't lose your grip on the dreams of the past
> You must fight just to keep them alive
>
> It's the eye of the tiger
> It's the thrill of the fight
> Rising up to the challenge of our rival
> And the last known survivor...

Shay fell asleep listening to one of his favorite songs.

A few hours later, the plane shook and began its descent. Shay was so nervous, but likewise ready. If there was one thing he'd learned over the year, it was that fear is merely an obstacle to overcome, not an invisible enemy to succumb to. Shay stepped off the plane.

"I'm fearful, but courageous! I'm afraid, but I'm...yeah, I'm ready!"

First College Game

Basketball socks pulled high, laces to my Jordan's tied, and once I step onto that court, I know this where I was meant to be. Yeah, this is just where I belong! Shay thought to himself as he waited for the referee to throw the ball into the air.

Shay caught the ball and began his journey toward victory. Just like his high school days, he found himself on his butt looking up.

"I'll never give up though! If they want this game, they will have to take it from me," Shay told himself.

These players were much quicker and bigger than he'd ever imagined. Shay never imagined being blocked as many times as he had been in this game.

Shay expected better of himself, but college basketball certainly was an adjustment. Ten minutes left in the first half, and Shay found himself on the bench watching the action happen in front of his eyes. Shay couldn't believe that his coach kept him on the bench until the five-minute mark in the second half.

Shay was used to taking the final shot, but he was the "new kid on the block" at Georgetown University.

Time ticked away and the center called for the ball. Shay saw the hand and began dribbling around his defender. Shay lobbed the ball, but the defender was too quick. Shay stepped into the lane, but the opponent put the ball behind his back and sealed the fate of Georgetown University in their first game of the season.

"You better make a better pass next time...freshman!"

The Crossover that Won the Game

Shay knew that none of his prior moments of success meant anything to any of these college players. Shay just stared at his teammate and walked away.

Postgame

"Shay? Hold up, Shay!" the female reporter called. Shay reluctantly turned around.

"Shay, is that the sort of game you expected to have?" the unfamiliar reporter asked.

"Of course not, ma'am! You have to expect great things of yourself. Doing them is, and always will be, the challenge."

"But, Shay, unarguably you failed out there today. Four points, one steal, no rebounds, and no blocks, though your own shot was blocked three... yes, three times, Shay!"

Shay raised an eyebrow and took a deep breath. "I can accept failure, but it will never stop me. The thing I cannot accept is not trying just one more time!"

"What makes you so sure that you will succeed next time? This isn't high school basketball anymore!"

Shay laughed and laughed and then laughed a little while longer. "I've failed and failed and failed countless times, and that is the reason I succeed. I'm not afraid to fail. I will never give up until I've given out, given the very best of what I have to offer!!" Shay turned quickly away from the microphone and headed down the long busy hallway leading to the locker room.

Shay didn't know exactly what he had to do yet, but he knew he needed to progress in order to compete at this higher level. Shay never forgot the value of having a mentor. He talked to the coach and spent extra time with the athletic trainer.

Shay changed his diet and workout regimen. He slowly but surely got quicker and his jump shot got better. He did layup drills against tall obstacles and became efficient on his passes.

Shay's play improved and the coach began playing him for more minutes. Georgetown University won enough games to get them to the final four and eventually into the championship game.

Championship Game

Shay looked up into the stands. "I think that's an NBA scout up there!" Shay hopped around and listened to his motivational song.

> Face to face, out in the heat
> Hangin' tough, stayin' hungry
> They stack the odds till' we take to the street
> For we kill with the skill to survive
>
> Risin' up straight to the top
> Had the guts, got the glory
> Went the distance, now I'm not gonna stop
> Just a man and his will to survive
>
> It's the Eye of the Tiger
> It's the thrill of the fight
> Rising up to the challenge of our rival"

"I've put in the time!" Shay said as he hopped up and down in his warm-up suit.

The Crossover that Won the Game

Running through all kinds of weather! Sweating through every condition imaginable. I'm built not only to survive, but to thrive! Shay thought as he slapped the hand of his teammate.

"I've been in many games and situations. What I've learned is that I must always rise to the challenge of my rival!"

Shay sat down on the bench, stretched, and bounced his head to the music.

♦ ♦ ♦

"There is no fear here! Fear is a figment of your imagination!" Shay told his opponent.

"Me, taking the final shot for a Division 1 college?" Shay smiled.

"This is my moment, and I am ready!"

Shay ran toward his opponent, stepped back, and crossed the ball between his legs. His opponent was right there and Shay began to perspire a little.

Shay faked right, bringing the ball back to the left side of his body. "Just enough space!" Shay told himself.

The ball flew through the air. Shay watched and thought, *My level of success will often be a direct correlation to what I expect of myself!*

Eyes glared and watched with unchallenged anticipation. Limbo met the present moment. Some faces snarled while others smiled.

Arms encircled Shay. The hugs produced a memorable smile. Shay watched with great joy as the ball took its final bounces after snapping the net.

Pitter-patter! Pitter-patter! Shay heard footsteps hurrying over to him.

"Oh my goodness! No really...oh my goodness! I am a believer, Shay!"

Shay remembered the reporter from the first game.

"Do you have any words for those around the world that just witnessed history? Even better, they are looking at a star, the wave of the future!"

Shay broke free from all of the hugs and other forms of celebrations. "I've listened to negativity for so many years, but perhaps it's my fault that they failed to see that failure produced strength, and my pain became my inspiration!"

The Ambulance Ride

"Give me the defibrillator, we're losing him!" Jim and Diane were the EMTs on duty that night. As it hit the patient's chest, he heaved with the shock.

"We lost him!" Diane exclaimed. "Okay, now we have a weak pulse, but at least we have a pulse at all!"

Coach Crossover lay on the gurney, oblivious to his surroundings.

Ruby held her chest to the sound of the sirens screaming by the house, something bothered her about this sound more so than normal.

"Are you well?" her husband John asked.

"Yes, I'm fine," she lied. Her woman's intuition told her to speak up. "Who are they whisking away?" she said out loud. But she knew who it was.

The Crossover that Won the Game

The call came in around 1:00 a.m. Ruby picked up the phone and heard the voice on the other line say, "Ruby?"

"Yes, speaking," she answered.

The voice continued, "This Dr. Edwards with Strong Memorial Hospital. I've called to speak with you regarding your brother's condition and to ask you to please come to hospital because you are listed as next of kin on our patient's paperwork."

Ruby dropped the phone and cried. She knew it had to be bad if the hospital was calling her.

"No, no, no!" she pleaded.

John, on the other hand, snored the night away without a care.

"How is my brother, Mr. Edwards?" She had rushed all the way to the hospital.

"Your brother experienced serious kidney failure and we have a kidney that matches his blood type available for transplant immediately. He needs to be kept under constant observation for a while. We are doing everything we can for him, but you need to take care of yourself as well, so please go home and get some rest."

Ruby squeezed her brother's hand as he lay there in a coma. As she leaned over to kiss his forehead, a tear fell on his face and she lost it.

Two weeks later, Crossover slept with a low beeping sound in a cold white unfamiliar room. He couldn't tell where the beeping was coming from, but he could always hear it. He could tell this room wasn't a part of his home. He tried to move, but his body would not respond to his commands. He attempted to call out for help, but couldn't make a sound. Finally, he realized where he was, a hospital. He knew things were serious when he felt the oxygen mask on his face and knew he couldn't breathe on his own. He wondered how long he had been in the hospital.

Ruby sat at his bedside and held his hand the whole time except for when she played solitaire. Every day, she spoke to her brother and prayed he could hear her. Then one day, she felt something squeeze her hand and she jumped as Crossover sat up in bed and blankly stared as he scanned the room. "Thank you, God! You're awake!" she said as she pressed the emergency button for the room.

The Call

Shay heard the words, but couldn't fully grasp what they meant to him. The commissioner's voice came through the phone, "Your plane ticket is waiting. All you need to do is pick it up. Welcome to the Los Angeles Lakers, we look forward to having you!"

"Mom, Dad, come here hurry!" he shouted as he hung up the phone.

"Yea son?" John said.

"I've been drafted by the LA Lakers!" he said with pure enthusiasm. As he hugged his dad, the phone rang again and his mother answered it. He watched as the tears began to stream down her face as she listened.

"The kidney we had lined up is no longer available and your brother might not make it."

Ruby looked at Shay. He was the only one with the same blood type as Coach Crossover.

The Crossover that Won the Game

"What's wrong, Mom?" he asked as he hugged her. "Son, Coach Crossover is dying and he needs a kidney immediately."

"No!" Shay yelled, then tears began to well in his eyes. "You have no idea how desperately I wish I could help!" Shay said.

"Shay, you're the only one with a matching blood type that can help him, you realize that, right?"

He backed up. "How could that be?"

"There is something that we have to tell you. There is no better time than now!" Ruby said as she lowered her head.

"Okay," Shay said with ambivalence.

"Coach Crossover is your..." Mom paused, she held her chest and sat down on the couch.

"Come on, Mom...tell me! It can't be worse than hearing that Coach Crossover is dying!"

"I found out about a year ago that Coach Crossover is my older brother!"

"What?" Shay yelled.

Mom and Dad looked stunned.

"So he is my uncle!"

"Yes, Shay," Mom said, "we were waiting for the right moment to tell you, Coach Crossover is your uncle."

All of a sudden, the room started to spin and became very hot. It felt like Shay was on a turbulent sea. Then, he slipped in and out of consciousness.

Now darkness overtook the room until Shay opened his eyes to face his new reality.

He heard three beeps, then a steady high-pitched sound that revealed his greatest fear.

Mom held the phone as this sound persisted.

"Mrs. Ponder, I am sorry, but your brother is dead!" Ruby dropped the phone, then crashed to the floor.

The sound of Mom falling or the cell phone shattering did not faze Shay. It took him 14.7 seconds for Shay to replay eighteen years of his life. Most of those memories centered on the beloved Coach Crossover. Shay's face changed and anger encircled his emotions.

"I have loved this man for such a long time…" Shay paused. "And now I am losing him at what should have been one of the happiest moments of my life." Shay shook his head and dropped a few tears. "I cannot believe I am just learning that he is so much more than a friend."

Shay began to shake and tears began to forever stain his skin…

"Are you all right?"

Dad stared at Shay, dazed and at a loss.

"Can I get you anything?" Mom tried to be strong once she rose back to her feet.

The Crossover that Won the Game

Dad was finally ready to admit that he had come to genuinely love Coach Crossover. He'd heard that real men do not cry. Now he understood the truth. The reality is that everyone cries and it does take a real man to shed tears when life beckons them.

Dad knew he had to be strong. He knew that his greatest strength and necessary act was to hold his family at the time they needed him most. Dad shed a few tears, but mostly, he wiped the tears of others.

Shay jumped to his feet.

"Let's go! Let's go right now!" Shay demanded. "I must see him one last time...outside of a casket!" Shay wiped his tears.

Dad held Shay close. "It's okay, my son. Cry if that's what you're feeling. It's better to let it out than to hold all of your emotions inside."

The family walked slowly out to their vehicle. The car moved faster than any car Shay had ever been in. Shay remained in a foggy state of darkness. Mom had become near inconsolable.

Shay had never walked a walk as long and painful as the one down the long white hospital hallway with windows all along the way.

"Maybe jumping would be ideal at such a time as this!" Shay contemplated, then overcame once he remembered what Coach Crossover said to him. "Never give up!" Shay remembered that no matter what he was experiencing Coach Crossover always told him not to give up.

Shay paused. "Even in your demise, you save me..."

This would forever be known as the silent walk to their final good-bye.

They finally reached the hospital room where Coach Crossover lay. Ruby fell to her knees, grief-stricken. "God, please don't take my beloved brother!" she wailed.

Shay rushed to Coach Crossover's bedside. He quickly grabbed his hand and was truly happy that God allowed Coach Crossover to stay alive long enough for him to have a proper good-bye. Shay held Coach Crossover's hand as he dropped tears on his chest. Shay placed his chest on the chest one of the best friends he'd ever had. The tears flowed, as did the thoughts.

◆ ◆ ◆

"Never give up, Shay. If you work hard enough, you will learn how to do a crossover very well," Coach Crossover would always say. Shay remembered the hand of Coach Crossover lying on his back as he encouraged him to never give up.

"Shay, it's okay. You played a great game. I think you got a little arrogant, but in life, there are always lessons to learn. Never get overconfident, but likewise, never stop believing in yourself. Now wipe those tears from your eyes and cheeks and walk with me to the locker room. This is only the first game. We have a long road ahead of us," Coach Crossover said with a huge smile.

◆ ◆ ◆

"I am going to miss you so much, Uncle Charlie!" Shay cried and cried.

Baffled, Little Shay opened the door and stared into the watery eyes of Coach Crossover, who placed his arms around Shay's neck and declared, "I will always be a part of your life." His tears soaked Shay's back.

"Will you really be in my life forever?" Shay asked in anger. "Because right now, it seems a lot like you're leaving me…" Shay paused. I never thought you would leave me, and definitely not like this!" The memories continued coming.

◆ ◆ ◆

The phone was abruptly snatched away from his hand, "Don't you ever speak to your dad like that again. Whether he is good, bad, or indifferent, he's still your biological father and you will respect him as…"

"He is not my dad!" Shay spat, "he is just the one who donated…"

"Enough!" Coach Crossover said before speaking into the phone. "Sir, please give us thirty minutes and your son will call you back with a different attitude."

John, Shay's father, did not know what to say or think. Here was a coach, a white coach at that, having the type of relationship with his son that he wished the two of them could have.

"Wow!" he said audibly, "If I could turn back the hands of time, yet time awaits no man. That time is gone forever. Like vapor, it's gone."

"Listen," as though he heard neither of their statements. "Yesterday is the past, and today is the present, and that's why they call it a gift. Let us work on this gift. You and Shay have to work on the present and let the past remain the past. I will not always be around, my days are numbered," Coach Crossover said, revealing no emotions whatsoever.

"What?" John said through the phone.

"What?" Shay echoed.

Coach acted as though he didn't hear them. "Give me some time to speak with Shay and he will call you later with a different attitude," he said before hanging up the phone, leaving John feeling as guilty as a child who had just gotten caught with his hand in the cookie jar.

"Coach, I…"

"No, you have already spoken earlier. I think it's fair that you allow me to speak now. If you remember nothing else I've shared with you, please remember this old adage: be quick to listen and slow to speak."

"What's an adage?" he questioned.

"It's just an old saying that society uses, Shay."

"Yes, Coach."

"Although your dad has not been there and assumed the role as Dad, he's still your father. Each day, he is a day older. One day, he will fail to exist. The last thing you want is for your dad to pass away and you guys never had the chance to make amends. Or you never had the chance to tell him, 'Dad, I forgive you for your absence and I love you.'"

"But, Coach, how could I love him when I do not even know him? I don't love him."

"Hahaha," Coach Crossover laughed.

♦ ♦ ♦

Shay looked at his dad and replayed Uncle Charlie's past words, "One day he will fail to exist…yesterday is the past, and today is the present, and that's why they call it a gift. Let us work on this gift. You and Shay have to work on the present and let the past remain the past. I will not always be around, my days are numbered."

Shay burst into tears. *Give a man their flowers while they are still with us!* Shay thought.

"You mean more to me than you know. You've done more for me than you could ever imagine! Losing you is the worse pain I could ever envision experiencing at this stage of my life," Shay paused.

"Well, the NBA wants me. Um…the Los Angeles Lakers to be exact. Ha! Ha!" Shay chuckled almost uncontrollably until the laughter turned to tears.

"They're your favorite team, Coach!" Shay got close to Coach Crossover's face and grinned. "I know you're my uncle." Shay whispered and smiled a smile his parents would never forget.

"I cannot believe we didn't tell him sooner!" John said, out of frustration, while looking at his wife.

"I wish I had known sooner!" Shay's tears increased. "I wasn't ready to lose you, Uncle Charlie!" Shay became almost inconsolable, but gathered himself once more.

"I was ready more than ever to get to know you."

Chris walked into the room. "Not…Coach Crossover!" The two young men embraced and shared tears, along with memories.

◆ ◆ ◆

Coach continued on. "Now imagine him telling you, 'I will always love you and you will always be a special part of my life. I will give you the world. If you need a liver, I will gladly give it to you. If you need my heart in order to live, and that meant I had to die, I will give my life for you and not even give it a second thought. I love you just that much.'"

"All righty, children, as you all know I am Coach Crossover and I coach the fifth and sixth graders. I coach at Confidence Elementary for so many great reasons," the coach said with pride in his voice and a sparkle in his eyes.

"Sir, why is this school called Confidence Elementary? And did your parents name you Crossover or did you give yourself that name?"

♦ ♦ ♦

"You always did ask so many questions, Shay!" Chris attempted to laugh, then choked on his tears.

Shay turned and smiled a bit.

"Hey, Coach, are you going to answer me?"

"I really think you interrupted Coach's daydream or something, Shay!"

"Yeah, bro, I think you're right! You know what though?"

"What?"

"He has always been there for me, no matter the situation!"

The boys began thinking of other special moments with Coach Crossover.

♦ ♦ ♦

"You miss a hundred percent of the shots you do not take." Coach Crossover surprised Shay. Shay had no idea that Coach Crossover had come to support him.

The Crossover that Won the Game

Shay just looked and waited for Coach Crossover to say more. "Coach Crossover, I'm sorry that I let you down! I am such a disappointment!" Shay said as he choked on his words a little.

Coach Crossover cleared his throat. "Shay, do you know what I really liked about the last shot that you took?"

"What did you like about that last shot, Coach Crossover?" Shay asked sarcastically. "I missed and we lost the game because of me!" Shay said using a harsh tone of voice. Coach Scott overheard Shay's frustration while he was talking to parents and the other coach.

Coach Crossover touched Shay's upper arm. "You believed in yourself and that will never be a disappointment."

"I agree!" A voice was heard from behind Shay. It was Coach Scott. Coach Scott and Coach Crossover shook hands and greeted each other.

"Hello, Coach Crossover."

"Hello, Coach Scott," Coach Crossover replied.

"Thanks for coming out to support us," Coach Scott said.

"It was my pleasure! And I plan to be a positive role model for my buddy Shay here for as long as I can," Coach Crossover said with a smile.

♦ ♦ ♦

Shay took a deep breath and ceased to reminisce.

"I'd ask you not to leave, Uncle Charlie, but God and God alone controls how many days we live on this earth. You certainly have maximized your moments though, Uncle Charlie. It's people like you that the world needs, so why are you leaving?"

Shay looked at Chris, and Chris at Shay. They had no words to say, but their faces and the silence told it all.

"If God is so gracious as to spare your life, there is so much I have to tell..." Shay stopped speaking and slowed the pace of his breathing. *Let me not get my hopes up*! Shay thought.

Shay looked at his beloved Coach Crossover, whom he now knew was his Uncle Charlie. Shay's eyes widened..

Surprised at the ringing of his phone at the worst possible time, Shay ignored the phone. This ringing persisted. There was the ringing phone, then...

Beeeeeeeeeeeep!

Uncle Charlie was gone, presumably a thing of the past.

"Gone but not forgotten!" Shay said as he wrote the phrase on Uncle Charlie's pillow in permanent marker.

It was then and only then that Shay understood that Coach Crossover/Uncle Charlie was inclusively his past, his present, and his future. His impact in Shay's life would live on in Shay's memories and heart forever.

Shay opened his ringing phone, closed his weary eyes, with his hand on Uncle Charlie's forehead.

"Good-bye!"

Book 10

When Opportunity Knocks!

"No!" Shay yelled as his tears poured out at an increasing rate. "I can't lose my…!"

Beeeeeeeeep! The heart monitor flat-lined as Coach Crossover lay lifeless on the hospital bed.

Spirit now gone from his body, Ruby screamed hysterically, "God, don't take my brother!"

John held his wife. "Honey, he's gone. Everyone must leave this world at some point in time, and I am so sorry that now is your brother's time to go." John held his head low and wiped his eyes. He knew he had to be strong for the family. "How will Shay handle this?" Dad asked himself.

"You were not supposed to die. I gave away my kidney as well as my chance at playing in the NBA."

It was too late. Coach Crossover, now known as Shay's beloved Uncle Charlie and the older brother Ruby always wanted, was now deceased.

♦ ♦ ♦

The lightning flashed! The thunder roared, and still Ruby's wailing was heard.

The preacher approached the podium. "He was a good man. He gave his all to benefit everyone else around him, but our Lord has called him back from whence he came," he said as the first layer of dirt was poured on Charlie Crossover's casket.

"I would give anything to have you back, Coach!" Shay said.

The viewers watched in disbelief as more and more dirt was poured on the casket that now sat six feet in the ground.

"We will get through this together!" Chris said as he placed his left arm around Shay's shoulder.

Shay looked at Chris, then back at the casket. He was speechless. Every hit of the shovel against the dirt caused Shay to cringe.

The tombstone read, "A man sent by God to change the world around him, and change the world he did. Now may the remnants of Mr. Charlie Crossover live on in our hearts forever and ever and ever, Amen!"

"No, Uncle Charlie, I can't lose you ye." Shay's words were interrupted as he fell on his back. Shay continued to scream as the sweat once again poured down his forehead. Shay sat up on his butt, back supported by his hands as…

"Shay! Shay!" his mom called. "Wake up! Wake up, son! It's only a dream…"

Beeeeeeeeeeeeeeeeep! Shay's alarm clock malfunctioned and continued to sound. To the sound of his mother's voice, Shay opened his eyes in what was temporary heaven amid present-day hell. Shay sat up and looked down at his pillow. It was soaked from the sweat and tears that persisted through the night. Shay thought of Uncle Charlie and the biggest decision of his life.

The Crossover that Won the Game

"I know what I must do!" Shay said confidently.

Shay opened his phone and began to dial.

With each ring came a little more doubt, fear, and frustration. "Hello!"

"Hello, Mr. Brown!"

"Hello, Mr. Ponder!" Mr. Brown said with such enthusiasm that Shay was taken aback.

"Well…um!"

"Whatever it is, you can say it, my friend…"

Shay remained silent, and when he did speak, it was broken English, at best.

"Well, since you do not know what to say, I will speak. The Los Angeles Lakers are very much looking forward to seeing you at training camp next month!"

"That's why I was calling, Mr. Brown…"

"Okay!"

"I may be facing breaking contractual agreements!" Shay said quietly.

"Uh…did…did I hear you correctly?"

"What do you think you heard?"

"You may have to break your contractual agreement"

"Yes, sir! You are correct!"

"Okay, it's not April Fools' day in Shay Ponders's world, is it?"

"No, Mr. Brown, it is not!" Shay laughed a little.

"Okay, well, how about you explain, Mr. Ponder!"

"Do you want the long version or the short version?" Shay asked, trying to soften the impact of what he was about to say.

There was silence that defined the severity of the situation.

"Shay, are you still there?"

"Yes, sir, I am still here!"

"Is this a joke?"

"This is not a joke!" Shay changed his tone. "Mr. Brown, I have to give my kidney to the man I'd previously known as my best friend. I now know that he's my uncle!"

"Wow, I do not know what to say? This is not the call that I expected to receive!"

"What are my options, sir? What are the potential consequences?"

"Well, the short answer is that the NBA can cancel your contract. They can also require you to tryout all over again once you recover and are medically cleared to play again."

Shay took a deep breath. He then began counting from 10 to 1 while holding his breath.

"Shay!"

"I am sorry, Mr. Brown! I just got caught in my own thoughts. Can you explain my situation to the league?"

"Sure I can!"

"It would be at least three to six months recovery just for me to be at full strength again. I would then need approximately two to three months to hone my skills again." Shay shook his head and unfortunately welcomed silence. *I cannot believe my dilemma!* Shay thought.

"Yes, Mr. Ponder, I will!"

"Thank you!" Shay listened to the dial tone for what felt like forever. "What have I just done?" Shay asked himself.

Shay put the phone down and prepared to call Chris.

♦ ♦ ♦

Ring! Ring! Ring!

"Hey, what's up, bro?" Chris said as he answered the phone.

"Hey, man, I have to go, it's my agent…"

"Hello!" Shay said when he answered the phone.

"Hello, Shay!"

"Hey, Mr. Brown! Do you have any news for me?"

"Yes, Shay, I'll be brief."

Shay remained silent as he waited for Mr. Brown to continue.

"Well, the Lakers will cancel your contract if you are not able to participate in the first day of training camp!"

"That's what I was afraid of!" Shay buried his head in his hands.

"Can I give this some thought and call you back?"

"Yes, Mr. Ponder, you can!"

The phone conversation ended, but Shay's thoughts did not.

"All I've wanted to do for as far back as I can remember was play basketball and positively impact the lives of other people...especially those struggling with low self-esteem issues like I did." Shay paused, then closed the door to his bedroom. Shay plopped down on his bean bag. "Sometimes, the best thing and the hardest thing are the same!" Shay said as he stood to his feet.

Shay paced back and forth. He placed his right hand on his forehead. Shay sweated as he did during big game time moments he'd experienced prior to his present moment. The present moment was clearly the biggest moment of Shay's life. Shay was noticeably flustered as he sometimes was when having to make other important decisions. Unfortunately, this time, the decision involved much more than simply shooting a basketball or passing to the right player at the right time.

"I guess that all of life is about the legacy you leave!"

Ring! Ring! Ring! "The hospital is calling," Shay said.

Ring! Ring! Shay ignored the call. "I will let the voice mail pick it up!"

"Hi, this call is for Mr. Shay Ponder. Hello, Mr. Ponder, my name is Aleah and I am calling you from Peers Memorial Hospital. This call is regarding a Mr...uhh... Mr. Charlie Crossover. It is essential that you call us back at your earliest convenience. He doesn't have much time left. The surgery must begin by tomorrow. Please call us back at your earliest convenience. The number is 998-881-7765."

Shay listened to the message.

"God, you know my heart! You know my passions and my desires. It's not an easy decision to sacrifice my dreams for the benefit of another. But I really do understand that it is the right thing to do. I know what the best decision is, but I need strength!"

Shay packed an overnight bag and walked downstairs.

"Shay, you look as if you've seen your life flash before your eyes. You look pale, and overall, just not well!" Mom said.

"Mom, I am going to do it!"

"I know this is a hard decision, but it means the world to so many people!"

"Thank you, Mom! Is Dad here?"

"No, son, he went out to get dinner for tonight."

"Okay, well, I will talk to you guys later!"

"Okay, son!"

They embraced and Shay walked out of the door. He wondered if he had made the right decision. Shay wondered if he would ever regret this moment. What he was sure of is that in his life, so far, this was his greatest sacrifice.

"But without genuine sacrifice, there is no authentic love!" Shay reasoned within himself.

Shay slammed the car door and prepared to commute to the hospital.

"Love demands sacrifice!" Shay furthered rationalized his decision.

During his drive to the hospital, Shay continued repeating these statements.

Shay finally arrived. He slammed the car door and could not help but wonder if he had just slammed the door on a dream.

"I am here for surgery!"

"Okay, what's your name, sir?" the hospital personnel asked.

"My name is Shay Ponder!"

"Oh my goodness! I knew you looked familiar!" The medical secretary smiled.

Shay smiled, then frowned immediately after.

"What's wrong, superstar?"

"Well, today, I learned what it finally means to be a star!"

"What do you mean, Mr. Superstar?"

"Please call me by my name."

"I'm sorry, Mr. Ponder!"

"It's okay. Here is what I meant, real superstars sacrifice for the benefit of others!"

"I guess you're more super than I could have ever imagined!"

"Thank you." Shay half-smiled.

"You're welcome! The surgeon will be here soon to take you to your room."

"Thank you, ma'am! You have been very helpful!" Shay smiled as he walked away from the desk.

Shay rolled to the room, and for once in his life, he knew he would wake up a winner.

"Tomorrow, I will certainly be someone's champion, and no one will ever be able to take that away from me!"

Shay closed his eyes. He lay and awaited the arrival of his life-changing moment. It was a countdown like never before, and when the clock struck zero, all would be different.

♦ ♦ ♦

Coach Crossover lay in bed, incognito, and unaware of what was going on. Little did he know that the kid he once helped would now help him! He had no idea that he'd helped create a winner that would now be the star of the biggest game of his life. More than any other day, more than any other game, he needed Shay to follow directions and...make the shot!

The most important game winner! Shay thought as they stuck the needle into his side. Shortly thereafter, Shay fell into a state of unconsciousness.

The surgical knife cut deep into Shay's body and the blood poured out at a steady pace.

In the next room, the physician's assistant began preparing Charlie Crossover for the biggest moment of his life. Even they knew he needed a superstar to rise to the occasion.

♦ ♦ ♦

The blood poured out of Shay like water into a kitchen sink. It rolled away while a majority soiled the operating table under him. Shay squealed through the oxygen mask over his mouth and nose. In the midst of dead silence and a REM-like slumber, Shay cried and displayed an expression of anguish. His face twisted; the discomfort he had was obvious. While relatively oblivious, the smile that shone bright before surgery was no longer present.

Shay would soon realize that this pain would be worse than any he'd ever experienced. The scalpel incision alone would hurt much more than any of the times his body had smacked the hardwood floors he'd both won and lost on.

The white glove slipped on and a foreign hand entered Shay's right side. The discomfort would be greater than any of the times he'd been hit on the court. The doctors cut artfully, slowly removing the kidney from its anatomical location. The kidney moved, blood slowly leaking from sliced veins; meanwhile, two tears made a popping sound as they hit the floor.

♦ ♦ ♦

Charlie Crossover's body was moved as the doctors and nurses gently pushed, pulled, and positioned his body for surgery. The entire time, Charlie remained in a comatose state.

"I believe this one is going to make it!" a nurse said through a smile.

Charlie Crossover whimpered lightly as the scalpel slowly cut along his right side. The blood slowly gushed; it needed cleansing desperately, and help was on the way.

♦ ♦ ♦

Charlie saw his life flash before his eyes. Though comatose, he still had his feelings, thoughts, and emotions. Most of his family had passed on. He didn't know his dad very well, but perhaps he was still alive. The man he'd always known as his father was already deceased.

Charlie always dreamed of being close to his family. This saddened him, but he knew he had newfound loved ones that he had to get to know. Shay did not know just how happy he was that they were... family.

He was Shay's uncle, and that would forever be a sense of joy. They had so many experiences together.

It was like a magnetic force drew them together. God knew the purpose of their timely meeting and continued relationship. No matter their moments of separation, they always found themselves back together.

"I can't wait to open my eyes. A new man in a new day."

♦ ♦ ♦

Mom, Dad, Chris, and Jeremiah sat in the waiting area. The family waited and hoped for the best. Their prayers were sent to heaven's door, as Shay and Uncle Charlie were in surgery.

"I really hope they both make it out all right!" Chris said with a sense of desperation in his voice. Sweat dripped from his forehead.

"Oh, well listen to me, Chris! I do not know my Uncle Charlie very well, but I do know my brother quite well. And let me tell you, he is really a trooper…"

"Hey, do not talk about my brother and your uncle like that!" Ruby said.

"I am not talking badly about him, Mom. I am just speaking positively about Shay. Mom, he is so strong, so courageous, and I know he will be all right!" Jeremiah said as a tear formed in his left eye.

Mom stared at Jeremiah and patted him on the back.

"Where do you think Shay got his strength from?" Mom asked.

"Well, he was always…" Jeremiah began to say.

"Okay, okay, okay, guys, let's all just relax. Both of them will do great in surgery and will be fine afterward!" John calmed the tension and eased the moment.

It would be a short while longer that the two of them would be in surgery. Shay made the hardest decision of his life, but the law of the harvest was on Charlie Crossover's good side. Fate brought them together, and fate has since reunited, healed, and saved a life.

"The good book says, 'There is no greater love than for a man to lay down his life for his friends!'"

Shay didn't exactly lay down his life, but he did give something of value. Shay's gift was love personified. Now he had forever solidified his legacy. The expression of self-sacrifice and love was greater than most would have ever done.

Coach Crossover (now also known as Uncle Charlie) gave his time, his effort, his sincerity, and knowledge. He gave Shay a chance at new life and perspective. In return, Shay gave Uncle Charlie life and new perspective on love.

Uncle Charlie and Shay would be forever indebted to one another. The purity of both hearts would compel neither of them to never ask the debt to be repaid.

A chance at life and a chance to live would forever define their relationship's existence. At the very core of both Uncle Charlie and Shay's heart was pure, unadulterated love. Truth be told, that love carried them through some of their toughest of moments, and amazingly, love had now aligned their lives at no better time than this.

Today marked the day new life would begin. A new dimension and new chapter had now been activated. Neither of them knew the magnitude of what awaited them.

◆ ◆ ◆

Uncle Charlie opened his eyes, baffled by his new reality. He noticed the female surgeon, male physician's assistant, male nurse, and the female nurse's aide by his side. "Did I just have a really bad dream with a wonderful ending?"

The nurse's aide stared at him in a very nonchalant-like manner.

"What happened?" Charlie Crossover demanded to know.

"You passed out, and eventually, your kidney completely failed," the surgeon responded.

"Then why am I here? Why am I alive?" Charlie Crossover said with a tear in his eyes and a confused look on his face.

After a brief silence, the nurse's aide spoke up, "Because God sent you an angel!"

"An angel?"

"Yes, an angel!" She smiled.

"Wow!" Charlie Crossover shook his head lightly.

"Oh yes, this person gave up so much to assure your well-being and preservation of the God has blessed you with! They gave more than just an organ, Mr. Crossover!" She smiled at the gratuitous nature of Charlie Crossover. Further, she smiled because another life had been saved by the benevolent deed of another.

"Who would do such a thing for me?"

"Someone that I am sure you will meet sometime!" she said with a smirk on her face as her coworkers continued concluding the final details of the surgical procedure.

"Well...well...when can I meet him?"

"Turn your head and look to the right, Mr. Crossover!"

"Please call me Charlie, Regina!" he said as he read the name tag and slowly began to turn his head.

Charlie Crossover squinted and looked closely at the figure being rolled toward him.

"Who is that?" he asked.

"It's your superstar!" Regina said as she smiled.

Charlie Crossover leaned a little more in the direction of the person coming toward his bed. He watched with immeasurable anticipation. He struggled to raise his left hand to his eyes. With a little assistance from Regina, he finally wiped the remaining water from his right eye. Now seeing clearly, he was undoubtedly awestruck.

"Oh my!" Charlie Crossover shook his head, then wiped the remaining water from his right eye.

The wheelchair moved a little closer. Charlie Crossover was at a loss for words.

"Um…is that…uh…"

Charlie Crossover's eyes were now dry. The next thing he saw was a face of one whom he loved dearly. His jaw dropped.

The next thing he heard was "Uncle Charlie!"

His eyes began to tear up. Shay's eyes began to tear up. Their tears met and soiled the sheets.

"I can't…um…I can't…belie…!"

"Yes, Uncle!" Shay said as he sniffled and motioned for a Kleenex.

They hugged, they laughed, and they cried, then reminisced. Then they hugged some more, laughed a little more, more tears fell, then the two reminisced further.

♦ ♦ ♦

Ring! Ring! "What? Why is Mr. Brown calling me?"

"Shay?"

"Hello, Mr. Brown! How are you?"

"I am doing well. How are you doing, Shay?"

"I am doing all right."

The Crossover that Won the Game

"What have you been up to these days?

"Well, Mr. Brown, I have just been recovering from the surgery!"

"Well, I hope it has been going as good as could be expected!"

"No complaints, sir."

"Great! So I have been thinking…"

"Uh oh…what have you been thinking?" Shay chuckled a bit.

"You know, Shay…we had a good thing going for us and I do not think you should give up on your dream to play in the National Basketball Association!"

"They have already canceled my contract!"

"I am sure I can get you press conferences, speaking engagements, and even a tryout with an NBA team once you are ready!"

"You can really do that?"

"Do you know what my name is?"

"Of course I do!"

"Okay, so do you know what my job title is?"

"Okay, those things are common knowledge, Mr. Brown!"

"Well, if you know those two things, then you know I can get you a tryout with an NBA team!"

"That's great, Mr. Brown. Thank you for calling and I will keep you posted about how my recovery is going!"

The two hung up the phone.

"I am going to call Chris and Uncle Charlie…"

◆ ◆ ◆

The phones began to ring as Shay conference-called Chris and Uncle Charlie.

"Hey, guys, you have to hear this!" Shay said to Mom, Dad, Jeremiah, and James while sitting at the kitchen table.

"Hello!" Chris and Uncle Charlie answered the phone almost in sync.

"Hey, how are two of my favorite people doing?"

"Pretty good!" they spoke in unison.

"That was a little weird!" Shay chuckled.

"So why are you disturbing us on this Sunday evening?" Uncle Charlie said.

"Never a distraction, buddy!"

"Ha! I almost forgot how close you guys were."

"Well, guys, I have some good news!"

"Well, what are you waiting for, nephew?"

The Crossover that Won the Game

"For you guys to stop talking! Ha!" The three of them shared a laugh. The family that was present just shook their heads at how funny Shay could be sometimes.

"He's really grown up to be quite a young man, huh?" Ruby asked John.

"Yes, darling!" John replied as he lightly rubbed his wife's back.

"I got a call from—"

"From who?"

"All right, Chris, no more interruptions. I am convinced that some things may never change!" Charlie spoke as though he was back at Confidence Elementary coaching the boys.

"Mr. Brown called and said that he can get me press conferences as well as a tryout with an NBA team once I recover and I am ready for such a rigorous workout!"

"That is really amazing, Shay!" Dad said.

"My boy Shay is about to tear it up!" Chris accentuated the word *up*.

"I always knew you were a star!" Uncle Charlie said.

Jeremiah laid his hand on Shay's right shoulder. "Me too!"

"Okay, little bro, I always knew that you had some game, and I knew that you would be way better than I ever was!"

This comment more than any other surprised Shay. "Wow, thank you very much, James!"

After a brief silence, Shay thanked everyone. There was one person that hadn't spoken yet.

"You may be a star, but you're still not bouncing that basketball in my house!" Mom reiterated the rules of the house.

"Oh, I know, Mom!" Shay laughed.

"Hey, Uncle and Chris, I will talk to you guys later!" Shay attempted to hang up the phone.

"Wait a minute. Can I have the phone, Shay?"

"Sure you can, Mom!"

"Guys, you are invited over for dinner tomorrow!"

"Thank you, Mrs. Ponder," Chris responded.

"You're welcome anytime, Chris!"

"And of course, I am looking forward to seeing my older brother!" Ruby said as she smiled.

"I am looking forward to seeing all of you, but I will need a ride!"

"Oh, that's right, you're still not cleared to drive! I will pick you up."

"Good-bye, guys, see you soon!" Ruby hung up the phone.

♦ ♦ ♦

The phone began to ring again. Shay was clearly puzzled.

"Why is Mr. Brown calling me back?"

"Hey, Shay!"

"Hey, Mr. Brown!"

"I will not take up too much of your time, Shay. I scheduled a speaking engagement for you in two days."

"Where will this speaking engagement be?"

"You will be speaking at Confidence Elementary!"

"Wow, that is literally where it all began!" Shay said as smirked.

"I will pick you up at 4:00 p.m. This will be open to the public, Shay!"

"Don't worry, Mr. Brown. I will be ready!"

♦ ♦ ♦

Shay awoke bright and early the next day. He was looking forward to dinner with some of his favorite people tonight. Shay made sure to read, and before he knew it, dinnertime had come.

"What's up, Shay?" Chris said as he flung the door open.

"My main man, Chris, I am good. How are you, my friend?"

"I am doing well. I am looking forward to some of your mother's scrumptious cooking."

"Ha! Yeah, bro, Mom is an awesome cook."

"You're wrong, Shay!"

"What?"

"Your mom is a great cook. She needs to work in a restaurant, maybe you should buy her a building to open up her own when you start making those millions!"

"I don't know about ever making those millions, man. I do not know if I will have another chance to play in training camp. I may have lost that opportunity, but it was worth it because I saved the life of one of the most important people in my life." Shay stared at the floor.

Shay felt a hand on his back. "Everything happens for a reason, Shay! There was clearly a deeper reason that God brought us together. Not only has there been reunification, a life was saved. The law of the harvest forgets no one. As no bad deed goes unpunished, no good deed unrewarded."

Shay looked up, once again in awe of wisdom embedded in the words of his lifetime coach.

"I cannot even begin to express how grateful I am for your existence. In every sense of the word, you saved my life, but for several years prior, I was beyond blessed to have the opportunity to positively pour into your life."

"Uncle Charlie, my life has been forever changed because of you. I cannot think of a better way to say thank you for being the man that you are, at the times I needed you most!" Shay said as he and Uncle Charlie embraced.

Mom finished up the last steps of her preparation for dinner. The other family members walked into the house ready for dinner. Shay, Chris, and Uncle Charlie exited the living room and made their way to the kitchen.

"Hey, Mom, do you need help setting the table?" Shay asked.

"Take a seat and relax, Shay. You're still in recovery!"

"I am not helpless, Mom!" Shay laughed. "I can carry the silverware."

"Fine." Mom shook her head and smiled at Shay's eagerness to help.

The family and Chris, who was like family, sat down to share in Mom's tasty food. The conversation was rich and food was plentiful. The family shared memories.

James talked about the time he stood in the window of the house, watching Shay play basketball at the park. "Man, I never knew how talented you were until that day, and yet I still teased you because I wanted to break you. You know what though?"

"What, big bro?"

"Your spirit was too strong! I knew your will would eventually withstand any wind that blew against it."

"Being confident didn't come easy, but the effort to reach such a state was definitely worth it!" Shay smiled and winked at James.

"Shay, once again we are very sorry for our contribution to your lack of confidence!"

"We definitely are, Shay," Jeremiah readily agreed.

"I am pleased with all of the warmth going around the table," Dad interjected with a smile.

"Well, I am just happy to have my family together, and it is nice to see Shay and Chris maintain their friendship so well," Mom joined the conversation.

Chris smiled and Shay lightly elbowed him in the side, communicating his joy about the preservation of their friendship. Chris flinched at Shay as if to punch Shay in the head. Shay stood up. "You don't want any of this?" Shay chuckled as him and Chris stood face-to-face.

"Sit down, boys. Act like men!" Uncle Charlie said as he disguised his voice to be deeper than usual.

The family laughed and laughed and then Dad interrupted, "Okay, pass the mashed potatoes and meatloaf!" Dad mumbled through his laughter.

"Oh no! We must thank God for the food first." Mom intercepted the dishes.

Dad blessed the food, then the family proceeded to take part in the food that Mom prepared. Shay had always wanted to sit down as a family and eat dinner. He was older now, but there was still something very special about this moment.

Shay looked around and smiled at all of the loving faces he saw. His favorite people were sitting right here at his dining room table. He could not think of a better way to be spending his time.

The family finished dinner, and their conversations and eventually their time together came to an end. Shay got ready for bed so he could

The Crossover that Won the Game

be well rested for his speaking engagement tomorrow at Confidence Elementary.

◆ ◆ ◆

Honk! Honk! The horn blew.

"I have to go, Mom! Are you and Dad coming?"

"Of course, we will be there, Shay!"

"Okay, Mom!" Shay said as he gave her a hug and a kiss. Shay was very surprised as he opened the door.

Mr. Brown was standing at the door, getting ready to knock.

"Whoa!" Shay laughed. "You surprised me!"

"Well, here I am, and there is my car, superstar, so let's hit the road!"

"Okay, I'm ready!"

"Wait a minute!" Mom hurried toward the door.

"Yes, Mrs. Ponder?"

"How tall are you?"

"Ma'am, I am six foot six!"

"Have you ever owned a black Lamborghini convertible?"

"Yes, Mrs. Ponder, I have."

"And have you ever been in our neighborhood prior to meeting us at the house for the first time?"

Mr. Brown remained silent.

"Okay, you got me! I have been scouting Shay for many years and it was my honor to finally meet him," Mr. Brown said as he looked at Shay.

"Why didn't you just come to the door?"

"I hadn't received clearance from the proper channels or persons, so I could only watch. I knew this kid was something and someone special with a bright future!"

"Well, thank you for sustaining your belief in my son. Well, I will see you guys soon at Confidence Elementary. You will do well, son, I know it. I am going to pick up Uncle Charlie and Chris also."

"Thank you, Mom, I cannot wait to see your faces out there!" Shay stepped out of the door and then into the car.

♦ ♦ ♦

The car ride finally came to an end, and now Shay stood in the place where in so many ways, it all began! He looked around and remembered being a young boy in need of confidence and belief in himself. He was about to attempt to do something that he once needed himself. He never forgot what his beloved Coach Crossover did for him so many years ago. He now knows that Coach Crossover is his uncle, but for as long as Shay has breath in his lungs, he will forever see that man as the coach who never let him settle for less than his best.

The Crossover that Won the Game

One day, he hoped to impact children's lives the way his life was impacted by people who went the extra mile, spent the extra minute, and did a little more than was required of them.

Guests filed in and eventually filled the gym room.

"I never knew I was loved this much!"

There was standing room only, and Shay was sincerely amazed.

"For me?" Shay asked himself as he leaned on his crutch.

He had no idea how much he was truly loved. He looked at all who showed up to hear him speak. Fear was completely eradicated. Now, Shay lived for big moments. Shay slowly stepped onto the stage.

"Over here!"

Shay looked around. "Hey! Over here, Shay!" one little kid yelled.

He reminds me of myself at his age, Shay thought.

Shay reminisced about his first day of practice at Confidence Elementary. He remembered how intrigued he was by Coach Crossover's last name. He didn't care what Coach Crossover was thinking about at the moment. He just wanted his questions answered.

Before Shay could acknowledge the little kid, he and Uncle Charlie looked right in each other's eyes. So much had happened and been revealed since they met at the first day of practice. It all began with the decision to face his fear and tryout for the team.

"Did your parents give you the name Shay? Or did you make it up?" the kid yelled.

Shay could not believe it. "My parents gave me my name!" Shay noticed Uncle Charlie's laugh at the irony of what just happened.

"Dreams aren't reality. Why even waste time dreaming?" This kid looked to be between thirteen and fourteen years old.

"You're right, sir! Dreams may not be reality, but often, they are directly correlated with changing one's reality."

"So then why do you dream?" one of the parents asked.

"I dream because it is possible for them to come true. For everyone out there listening, fulfilling dreams are usually a result of hard work, determination, and persistence!"

The sound of hands clapping drowned out the next statement Shay was trying to make.

"There's a special dream inside of each and every one of you! Never stop believing in yourselves! A coach once told me that it's no good for him to believe in me if I do not believe in myself!"

"But what if I fail?" another kid yelled.

"Then you try again. Always have the strength to try just one more time. Learn what you need to do in order to succeed, and never let failure cause you to give up."

"What if people tease me?"

"Ha! Ha! Find the person or people that believes in you, and anyway, what others think of you is far less important than what you think of yourself."

"You were teased, Shay!" another parent interjected.

"And I didn't let them win. I learned to hold my head high and acknowledge that even in failure, I did the best that I could!"

"Why did you keep trying, Mr. Ponder?"

"It was courage, persistence, determination, and confidence in myself and those around me. I learned to believe in myself and trust those closest to me."

The oos and ahs rang out all over the room. Shay was a star in a way that he hadn't imagined happening so soon. There was reason to be proud and reason to smile and that's what Shay did. He smiled as the sounds of hands clapping faded and cheers disappeared. The room was now quiet.

"I used to despise being challenged, but I have learned something about our challenges: they will make you stronger, they will push you to try harder, success will be more highly appreciated, challenges will hone your character and inevitably provide the strength you need to be brave, challenges create an environment of hope within you. Appreciate those small victories, because when challenges arise and you are successful, your courage and belief in yourself will definitely increase."

The crowd was clearly captivated.

"Any last words for our guests, Mr. Ponder?" the master of ceremony asked.

Shay paused and pondered his next response.

"You never know how far you can go, or which dreams can become reality if you only believe in yourself!"

Shay slowly hobbled off the stage.

♦ ♦ ♦

"Great job, Shay!" Mr. Brown said.

"Thank you, sir!"

"Spoken like a true star!" Uncle Charlie interjected.

"I learned a lot of it from you!" Shay laughed.

"But you have taken what others have taught you and used to your benefit and…well…clearly to the benefit of others!"

"Man, I am so glad that you are my uncle!" Shay said as he hugged Uncle Charlie.

"It has been nothing short of amazing and life changing to have been a part of your life for all of these years!" Uncle Charlie said as he held Shay's left shoulder with his right hand and Shay's right shoulder with the left.

"Hey, Shay, I will definitely be arranging other speaking engagements for you so stay close to home!"

"Thanks, Mr. Brown. Hey, I am riding home with my family! We will talk soon though."

The Crossover that Won the Game

"Sounds good, superstar! I will talk to you soon." Mr. Brown began walking away.

Mom and Dad walked over. "Great job, son!" Mom said.

"Yes, son, your mom is right. You have really grown so much, and we are so proud of you."

"Thank you, guys! It really does mean a lot to me!"

"Well, guys, why don't we hit the road?" John asked.

"Please!" Shay begged sarcastically. "I just want to take a seat and relax!"

The family left the gymnasium where, in so many ways, it all began. There was no better ending to the beginning.

♦ ♦ ♦

Several days passed by and Shay had not heard much from Mr. Brown, until one day, while shooting foul shots with Chris, he heard his phone ring.

"Hello!"

"Hey, Shay!"

"How are you, Mr. Brown?"

"I am doing very well. Are you free tomorrow at 5:00 p.m.?"

"I can certainly make myself available for the right reason."

"Well, you will want to make yourself free!"

"Why? What's so important?"

"Grace Better from News Channel 13 wants to do a press conference with you in an open forum!"

"That would be nice. I remember meeting her when I was in seventh grade at New Perspectives Junior High School. She asked me something like how I learned to shoot a three-pointer."

"Well, tomorrow, she will be asking you much more than that!"

"I will be there. I will ride with my family this time."

"Okay, that is fine. Don't be late!"

"I will not, sir."

"See you tomorrow at 5:00 p.m., Shay, at Lion's Heart High School."

"See you tomorrow!"

♦ ♦ ♦

"You know guys I am very fortunate to have all of you in my life," Shay said as they filed into Daddy's sport utility vehicle (SUV).

Dad, Uncle Charlie, Chris, Mom, and Jeremiah, all at different times, told Shay how glad they were to be in his life and to have him in theirs.

"All of my success means nothing without being able to share it with people you love and who loves you!"

"You have found great success, little brother, but your passion for achieving your goals has been unexpectedly high."

The Crossover that Won the Game

"I cannot believe we have known each other since we were twelve years old, man!" Chris said.

"And we have been close ever since. Ha!" Shay said while laughing a bit.

There was silence for a brief moment, then...

"Wow! Do you remember that rap from seventh grade, bro?" Shay asked Chris.

"Oh my goodness. Do not remind me of those lyrics. Ha!"

"Wait a minute, I think I remember some of them!" Shay said.

"Let's see if I can get these words right!"

"Oh no," Chris said in the background as Shay began to rap his words:

> "Hey there, Shay, you're the man. If you can't do it, no one can."

Chris shook his head in disbelief. "I cannot believe you remember that!"

"Hold up! There's more."

"You have the perfect jumper like the great MJ, but then there's more... you have his fade away."

"That sounds so bad, bro. You should definitely stop now!"

"No, Chris, we like it!" the other people in the car said almost simultaneously.

"You guys want me to keep going?"

Everyone said yes, except Chris, of course.

"Okay, I think I remember the last part..."

Everyone else waited patiently while Chris secretly prayed that Shay would not be able to regurgitate those words from way back in seventh grade.

"Never let anyone get in the way. You're the best on the team, you're Crossover Shay."

Chris shook his head some more. Shay was finally finished.

"I'm sorry, friend, but I had to do it!"

"It's okay, I'll forgive you after I..."

"After you what?" Shay challenged Chris.

"Knock you out!" Chris flinched at Shay.

"Geez, not only can you rap...you're a comedian!" The car exploded in laughter.

The car ride came to an end, and Shay was ready to deliver his speech. Shay stepped out of the car and there was Grace Better.

"Wow, he has gotten so much bigger. I remember interviewing that kid when he was in the seventh grade. I cannot believe how much time has passed!" Grace said to herself as Shay walked toward the door.

Shay stepped into the double glass door and looked around at the facility. Shay didn't even feel like he belonged there because of how pristine and prestigious the National News Channel facility was.

The Crossover that Won the Game

"Ouch!" Shay said as he felt a poke in his side.

"Believe in yourself, Shay!" Uncle Charlie said.

Dad smiled. "You're phenomenal, son. Never forget that!"

"Shay, you have more heart than anyone I have ever met!" Chris said as he tried to ease Shay's nerves.

"You're my hero, Shay. I do not know how many times I have told you that, but there seems to be no better time than right now," Jeremiah said.

"Son, I love you. You're awesome, and deep down inside, you know you can do whatever you tell yourself you can. If you walk onto that platform thinking you will fail, then I know this is tough love, but, my beloved son, you will!"

"Thanks, guys!"

"Hey! Hey! Wait just a minute, Shay!" Mr. Brown ran to catch up with the bunch. Breathing heavily, Mr. Brown asked, "Are you ready, champ?"

"I am literally more ready than I could ever be!" Shay stared at his family, including Chris, and smiled, then winked.

Shay walked with just the amount of confidence he needed. What Shay understood is that success was inevitably in his control.

Grace Better stood there waiting patiently as Shay walked toward the platform and podium. She quickly reviewed her list of questions that she prepared for Shay to answer and the world to hear. She always knew he was a star, and she couldn't wait to tell the world.

"Over here, Mr. Ponder!" another reporter yelled as Shay hobbled onto the platform.

"Yes, sir! What is your question?"

"Do you ever think you will play professionally?"

"The honest answer is I am not sure, but let me tell you what I am sure of: There will be obstacles in life and I can accept that, but it is my duty, and mine alone to conquer that obstacle. I will never turn my back and give up. I will find a way to climb over, go through it, or work around the obstacle before me!"

Silence overtook the room until all finally heard, "Next question?"

Shay caught eye contact with an unexpected member of the audience. He inched closer and closer to Shay through the large crowd of people in the room. He held an envelope in his well-manicured hand.

Shay could not believe the voice from which the words were emanating. His jaw dropped and his eyes glistened as he focused intently on this well-known individual. Shay was even more in awe at the words he spoke.

"The NBA would love to have you back!" He smiled as he handed the envelope to Shay.

Shay was at a loss for words.

"Would you consider being present at the first day of training camp for the Lakers?"

"Well!" Shay said as the room erupted in applause. Shay scanned the audience, smiled, and looked the commissioner in the eyes. Hand now

The Crossover that Won the Game

firmly shaking the commissioner's, Shay leaned in, pushed the microphone aside, and began to whisper...

For the audience, mystery remained the greatest hope!

www.ingramcontent.com/pod-product-compliance
Lightning Source LLC
Chambersburg PA
CBHW051034160426
43193CB00010B/944